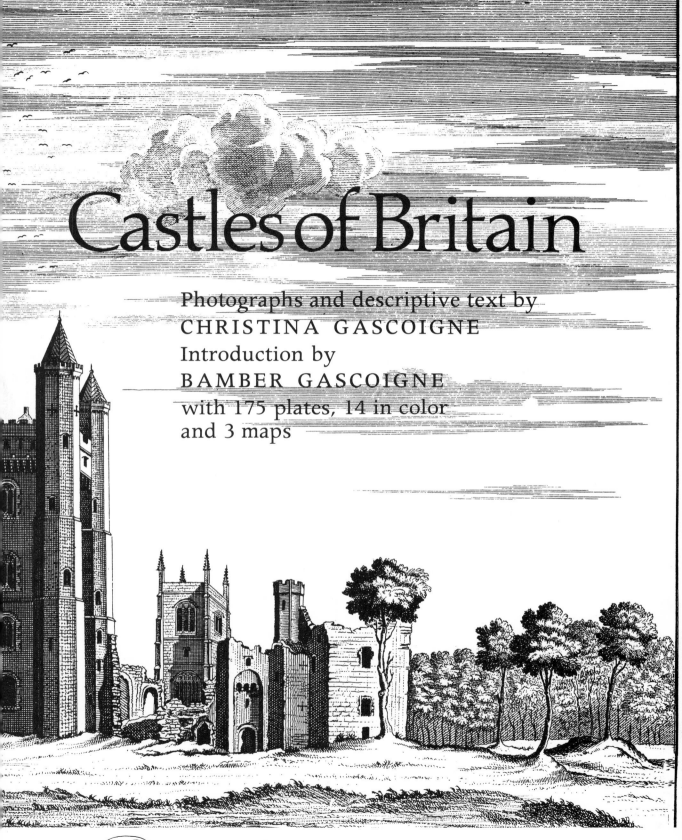

Castles of Britain

Photographs and descriptive text by
CHRISTINA GASCOIGNE
Introduction by
BAMBER GASCOIGNE
with 175 plates, 14 in color
and 3 maps

THAMES AND HUDSON

Frontispiece
Castle Rising, near King's Lynn, Norfolk.
Staircase in the mid 12th-century keep of the
Albini earls of Sussex

Title page
Tattershall Castle, Lincolnshire. Engraving
dated 1727

page 7
Linlithgow Palace, West Lothian. Engraving
from John Slezer's *Theatrum Scotiae*, 1693

Acknowledgments
Maps drawn by T. D. Odle
Aerial photographs supplied by Aero Films,
Ltd, pp. 19, 21, 31, 55, 82, 106, 107, 125, 128,
136, 141, 153, 158; also photograph on p. 52
Detail of Bayeux tapestry on p. 14 supplied by
the Phaidon Press, Ltd
Engraving of Coxton Tower on p. 32
reproduced by permission of Aberdeen
University Library
Engraving of Balmoral Castle on p. 172
reproduced by gracious permission of Her
Majesty the Queen

First published in the USA in 1975 by G. P. Putnam's Sons
Published in 1980 by Thames and Hudson, Inc.,
500 Fifth Avenue, New York, New York 10110

Library of Congress Catalog Card Number 80-50807

Phototypeset by Tradespools Ltd, Frome, Somerset
Printed and bound in Japan

Contents

List of Castles

ENGLAND

ACTON BURNELL CASTLE *Salop*
ALNWICK CASTLE *Northumberland*
ARUNDEL CASTLE *West Sussex*
BAMBURGH CASTLE *Northumberland*
BERKELEY CASTLE *Gloucestershire*
BERRY POMEROY CASTLE *Devonshire*
BODIAM CASTLE *East Sussex*
CARISBROOKE CASTLE *Isle of Wight*
CLIFFORD'S TOWER *North Yorkshire*
COLCHESTER CASTLE *Essex*
CONISBROUGH CASTLE *South Yorkshire*
CORFE CASTLE *Dorset*
DONNINGTON CASTLE *Berkshire*
DOVER CASTLE *Kent*
DUNSTER CASTLE *Somerset*
DURHAM CASTLE *County Durham*
EASTNOR CASTLE *Hereford and Worcester*
FRAMLINGHAM CASTLE *Suffolk*
HELMSLEY CASTLE *North Yorkshire*
HERSTMONCEUX CASTLE *East Sussex*
HEVER CASTLE *Kent*
KENILWORTH CASTLE *Warwickshire*
KIRBY MUXLOE CASTLE *Leicestershire*
LAUNCESTON CASTLE *Cornwall*
LEWES CASTLE *East Sussex*
LINDISFARNE CASTLE *Northumberland*
LUDLOW CASTLE *Salop*
NEWARK CASTLE *Nottinghamshire*
NUNNEY CASTLE *Somerset*
OLD WARDOUR CASTLE *Wiltshire*
ORFORD CASTLE *Suffolk*
RABY CASTLE *County Durham*
RESTORMEL CASTLE *Cornwall*
RICHMOND CASTLE *North Yorkshire*
ROCHESTER CASTLE *Kent*
ROCKINGHAM CASTLE *Northamptonshire*
ST MAWES CASTLE *Cornwall*
SCARBOROUGH CASTLE *North Yorkshire*
SKIPTON CASTLE *North Yorkshire*
STOKESAY CASTLE *Salop*
TAMWORTH CASTLE *Staffordshire*
TATTERSHALL CASTLE *Lincolnshire*
TINTAGEL CASTLE *Cornwall*
TOWER OF LONDON *Greater London*
WARKWORTH CASTLE *Northumberland*
WARWICK CASTLE *Warwickshire*
WINDSOR CASTLE *Berkshire*

WALES

BEAUMARIS CASTLE *Anglesey*
CAERNARVON CASTLE *Gwynedd*
CAERPHILLY CASTLE *Mid Glamorgan*
CAREW CASTLE *Dyfed*
CASTELL COCH *Mid Glamorgan*
CHEPSTOW CASTLE *Gwent*
CHIRK CASTLE *Clwyd*
CONWAY CASTLE *Gwynedd*
HARLECH CASTLE *Gwynedd*
KIDWELLY CASTLE *Dyfed*
PEMBROKE CASTLE *Dyfed*

SCOTLAND

BALMORAL CASTLE *Aberdeenshire*
BLACKNESS CASTLE *West Lothian*
BLAIR CASTLE *Perthshire*
BRAEMAR CASTLE *Aberdeenshire*
BRODICK CASTLE *Isle of Arran*
CAERLAVEROCK CASTLE *Dumfriesshire*
CASTLE CAMPBELL *Clackmannanshire*
CORGARFF CASTLE *Aberdeenshire*
CRAIGIEVAR CASTLE *Aberdeenshire*
CRATHES CASTLE *Kincardineshire*
CRICHTON CASTLE *Midlothian*
CULZEAN CASTLE *Ayrshire*
DOUNE CASTLE *Perthshire*
DUART CASTLE *Isle of Mull*
DUNNOTTAR CASTLE *Kincardineshire*
DUNVEGAN CASTLE *Isle of Skye*
EDINBURGH CASTLE *Midlothian*
EDZELL CASTLE *Angus*
EILEAN DONAN CASTLE *Ross and Cromarty*
GLAMIS CASTLE *Angus*
HERMITAGE CASTLE *Roxburghshire*
HUNTLY CASTLE *Aberdeenshire*
INVERARAY CASTLE *Argyllshire*
KISIMUL CASTLE *Barra, Hebrides*
LINLITHGOW PALACE *West Lothian*
ROTHESAY CASTLE *Bute*
STIRLING CASTLE *Stirlingshire*
TANTALLON CASTLE *East Lothian*
THREAVE CASTLE *Kirkcudbrightshire*

Preface

THIS BOOK contains a personal selection of some eighty-seven castles, chosen from the many in England, Scotland and Wales which are open to the public. We have deliberately excluded those, however striking, which are not open on some regular basis. Frustration of the visitor, irritation of the owner—these are the predictable results of mingling a handful of castles where the drawbridge is still up with the many where strangers are welcome.

Of the several hundred castles open to the public, a majority—immaculately looked after by the Department of the Environment—are primarily of interest to the specialist. A few jagged walls rising from neat turf can tell much to the expert in barbican and bailey, but for a book such as this there are more than enough surviving castles, from all periods, which will seem immediately attractive to any visitor. Of these we have included all the most important and famous ones. Outside this five-star category we have been guided by our own preferences, but these range all the way from the sturdiest of Norman strongholds to the dottier extravagances of nineteenth-century medievalists.

Christina and Bamber Gascoigne

I Tower of London

Probably the most important military building in Britain, begun by William I, added to by almost every one of his successors to promote its dual purpose of royal residence and state prison, and finally restored in 1875 by Salvin. Seen here from the south across the River Thames, from which access was obtained through the once much used water-gate or Traitors' Gate. *See* p. 122.

II Bamburgh, Northumberland

6th-century fortress, held successively by Saxons, Vikings and Normans, abandoned as a ruin in the 17th century, it was restored in the 18th and 19th centuries. *See* p. 46.

III Kenilworth, Warwickshire

Begun in the early 12th century, Kenilworth was extended and embellished by John of Gaunt, Roger Mortimer and Robert Dudley, Earl of Leicester. Seen here from the south across the meadows which once were covered by a large artificial lake of over 100 acres, known as the Great Mere. *See* p. 88.

Introduction

SIR WALTER SCOTT clings, as tenaciously as the ivy, to our conventional image of the castle. In the dungeon Isaac the Jew was being tortured for his money-bags. His beautiful daughter Rebecca 'awaited her fate in a distant and sequestered turret' which gave on to 'an isolated bartizan, or balcony, secured, as usual, by a parapet, with embrasures'. The fate in store for the lovely Jewess was indeed to be that variety worse than death, but the bartizan proved her salvation:

'Remain where thou art, proud Templar, or at thy choice advance!—one foot nearer, and I plunge myself from the precipice; my body shall be crushed out of the very form of humanity upon the stones of that courtyard ere it become the victim of thy brutality!'

'The Templar hesitated'—which proved sufficient. And all the while the wounded Ivanhoe lay hidden in a horse-litter in another distant apartment of this hoary and ancient castle of Torquilstone, with its 'grey and moss-grown battlements, glimmering in the morning sun above the wood by which they were surrounded'.

It was a fortress of no great size, consisting of a donjon, or large and high square tower, surrounded by buildings of inferior height, which were encircled by an inner courtyard. Around the exterior wall was a deep moat, supplied with water from a neighbouring rivulet. Front-de-Boeuf, whose character placed him often at feud with his enemies, had made considerable additions to the strength of his castle, by building towers upon the outward wall, so as to flank it at every angle. The access, as usual in castles of the period, lay through an arched barbican, or outwork, which was terminated and defended by a small turret at each corner.

This is Scott in his informative vein, and, apart from the surrounding woods (no place to site a castle) and the peculiar cast given to events by his neo-Gothic filter, he provides in architectural terms a reasonably accurate image. But only of the later castles of the Middle Ages, or those that survive for us as ruins. The earlier reality was rather different.

*   *   *

One reads with something of a shock that William the Conqueror, between landing at Pevensey on September 28 and fighting his battle at Hastings on October 14, built himself a castle. But the Bayeux tapestry gives the clue, saying that William ordered a castle to be dug, and supporting the information with a delightful sketch which shows labourers digging earth and picking stones while others pat the mound firmly into place with their shovels.

Detail from the Bayeux tapestry

Map showing all the *mottes* in England redrawn from D. F. Renn, *Norman Castles in Britain*, John Baker, 2nd ed, 1973

What they are erecting is a *motte* and when they have added to it a bailey, by enclosing with wooden palisades an adjacent patch of land, they will have the basic 'motte and bailey' castle. This is a phrase which is often used in academic discussions of castles, but it is an unnecessarily confusing one. The only recorded use of 'motte' in the English language is as an obsolete variant of 'moat', a feature highly relevant in the study of castles but almost the precise opposite of a *motte*. In French, and therefore Norman, *motte* is quite simply the word for a mound (*motte de taupe*, mole-hill). A mound is what William's men dug for him at Hastings, and mound-and-bailey is a more useful name for this particular type of castle.

The great advantage of a mound, as a rapidly constructed unit of defence, is that it can only be made by digging something almost equally useful against an enemy—a circular ditch, all the earth from which is thrown into the centre. A flattened area at the top of the steep mound is a natural next step, with a tower at its centre and a protective palisade round the edge. But there is not sufficient room up there, except in an extreme emergency, so it is also necessary to enclose with a ditch and palisade an adjacent area where livestock can be kept against marauders and where the garrison can live until, in a crisis, they are perhaps forced back into the ultimate refuge of the mound and tower.

It is no accident that the castle which a child builds on the beach is a mound with a ditch around it, for the technique is the most obvious one. The Norman castle is a sand-castle writ large, and so elementary is the mound as a unit of defence that a map of all the *mottes* in England and Wales (not necessarily all of Norman origin) looks more than anything like an advanced case of measles.

To construct such a castle in a hurry, the Conqueror required only timber and a large but almost wholly unskilled labour force. If the first can be found, as in England it usually could, there was little difficulty for an invading army in coercing the second. And the speed of that first castle at Hastings seems hardly to have been an exception. William's efforts at York suggest something similar. He built one castle there in 1068, and added a second in 1069. Both were destroyed by the English and the Danes in 1069. Both were rebuilt by William in 1070. They must have been rather attractive features in the landscape, these hasty fortresses, gay and almost toy-like in appearance (though not, perhaps, to the eyes of the English), for it is thought that the woodwork was painted in bright colours and that the tower often stood on stilts on top of its mound. An Anglo-Norman chronicle of the following century suggests that on occasion a prefabricated castle was even used, which could be erected within the day:

The carpenters had great axes dangling from their necks, planes and adzes draped at their sides. They brought timber from the ships and dragged it to the spot, already bored and smoothed off. They brought, in large casks, the joining pegs completely dressed. Before it was evening, they had constructed a wooden castle. They made a ditch around it.*

Castles had been a familiar part of the landscape in feudal Normandy. The earliest examples in western Europe had been built by the Franks in the ninth century, to protect themselves against the encroaching Normans, and the Normans had themselves soon adopted this type of personal fortress. The concept of the castle seems to have been borrowed from the Byzantine empire, where it had survived in an unbroken line from Roman traditions of fortification. Indeed the word *castellum* is itself a diminutive of *castrum*, a fortress, so familiar to every old-fashioned schoolboy in its plural form as the word for a military camp (the wooden palisade on top of the Hastings mound is labelled *ceastra* in the Bayeux tapestry). The Anglo-Saxons had used *burh*, ancestor of the word borough, for any such walled and fortified place, and the contrast between these civilian and military connotations seems to reflect a genuine difference. The fortified places of the Anglo-Saxons were villages and towns, while those of the Normans were in effect garrisons and rather more reliable. Ordericus Vitalis, an Anglo-Norman chronicler born within ten years of the Conquest, gave as one of the main reasons for the defeat of the English that there were almost no fortresses such as the French call *castella* in the land, wherefore the English, though warlike and courageous, proved too weak to withstand their enemies.'

The castle was an essential element in the feudal system of the Normans, under which a baron held land from his king and in return had to provide a body of knights, led by himself, to fight for the king when required. Seen from a purely military point of view, the baron and his household knights were a detachment of the army, living off a certain area of land and controlling it on behalf of the king. Naturally their residence had to be something in the nature of a castle, when a hostile country was being held in subjection by a small number of foreigners.

The Conqueror founded his castles with clear strategic aims in mind. In 1068 he marched in a vast circuit through southern and central England as if beating the bounds of his new parish, and during his progress he established a castle at Exeter (which, sheltering behind its Roman walls, was the only town to risk a siege and held out against

---

* Wace, *Roman de Rou*, III, verses 6533–49, quoted Urban T. Holmes, *Daily Living in the Twelfth Century*, University of Wisconsin Press, Madison, Wisc., 1952, p. 153.

him for as long as eighteen days), to be followed by others at Warwick, Nottingham, York, Lincoln, Huntingdon and Cambridge. In each of these castles one of William's companions would be installed as the king's vassal and the lord of that district—or, in non-feudal terms, as the military commander of the region. In the more dangerous border districts the baron was allowed a solidly grouped portion of land as his fief, which was known—in another word new to the English—as a *castellaria*, or area of land specifically intended for the support of a particular castle. Only in this way would the marcher lord be powerful enough to hold the district, and the strong earldoms of Hereford and Chester are cases in point. In the less threatened centre of the kingdom a nobleman was more likely to be given land scattered in small portions through several counties. Many Saxon estates had been of this widely dispersed kind, and it was easy for the Conqueror to hand a friend the entire possessions of an enemy. There was the added advantage, from the monarch's point of view, that it was much more difficult for a baron with such fragmented holdings to build up an independent regional following.

At some strategic place on his estates an important nobleman would be given permission to build a castle—by a river, or on a bluff commanding a valley—from which the surrounding district could be controlled. Thirty-three castles are known to have been founded in the first five years of the Norman conquest, and another fifty-one in the subsequent fifteen years, and there must have been many others of which no records remain. The possession of a castle was almost a *sine qua non* of baronial status.

It is an indication of how fully this was a military occupation by a foreign power that there were in 1086 only two Englishmen, in the entire area covered by the Domesday Book, who held baronial estates directly of the king—while in the almost equally important field of ecclesiastical tenure the only English see still to have an English bishop was Gloucester. The process by which England had been divided up among the Normans and their followers from Brittany or Flanders can be seen in miniature in what the Conqueror did for his cook, a certain William Escudet. He asked the Bishop of Winchester to give the cook some land, which was not quite such a favour on the part of the good prelate as it might sound. When the see of Winchester had been given to a Norman, he became automatically the feudal overlord of all the land held by that cathedral and its various abbeys. Much of this land was already granted to feudal sub-tenants, for whom the change of their lord need imply no intrinsic upheaval. It was the land of one of these vassals (who had either died or gone out of favour) which the bishop now granted to the cook. In future Master Escudet would enjoy the produce of this land, collected for him by a bailiff while he was away cooking for the king, and in return he would provide the bishop with either money or armed men which the bishop would include in his own contribution to the king. Everyone, until either the bishop or the cook grew more ambitious, was happy.

*　　　*　　　*

Serious castles, as opposed to the castellated residences of more recent times, were built in England and Wales for about 400 years after the arrival of the Normans, and in Scotland for another century or two beyond that. Thus a few castles in England date from as late as the fifteenth century, and some of the most fascinating in Scotland were built in the seventeenth. Nevertheless it is true to say that the practical development of the castle as a military unit, from the simplest mound-and-bailey to its final flowering as the most sophisticated of fortresses, was complete as early as the end of the thirteenth century, little more than 200 years after the death of William the Conqueror, when Edward I was building his chain of magnificent castles in Wales.

It is possible, with considerable difficulty, to trace a gradual development in castle design over these two centuries, but at the price of so many important exceptions that the exercise is hardly worth while. There are certain obvious changes—from wood to stone, for example, as the material for tower and walls—but even in something as simple as this there are awkward chronological bumps. It is true to say that the majority of castles in the eleventh century were built of wood, and in the twelfth of stone. Yet the Tower of London, on which work began in the very year of the Conquest, was constructed of stone from the start, as were other major castles of that first reign, such as Colchester and Pevensey. Even at Windsor, founded by William but long thought to have been in those early days a wooden castle on a man-made mound, it has recently been discovered that the foundations of the outer shell of the Round Tower rest on a bed of natural chalk, which suggests that this great castle too was probably of stone from the beginning. And there were exceptions in the other direction. Barons running up unauthorized castles in the troubled times of Stephen, around the middle of the twelfth century, reverted in their haste to timber fortifications. The truth was that any fool could recognize from the start that a stone castle was superior to a wooden one. Where there was time, money and a natural mound strong enough to support stone walls, castles were of stone. By the twelfth century the Normans had more time, more money and more scope in siting their castles than had been available in the first hectic years after the Conquest. So in the twelfth century there were more castles of stone.

The only true constant that runs through the development of the castle is the ingenuity with which men made the most of their opportunities. It is the possibilities of the particular site, rather than the latest fashion in fortification, which has the greatest influence on the shape of each castle. The early arrangement of mound and bailey provided the basic and most logical pattern by which a castle could be built rapidly in a flat area, and it was the ingredients of this elementary kit—tower, mound, ditch and encircling walls—which castle-builders on more promising natural sites would continue to deploy in appropriate ways. Thus at Durham, where there is a promontory high above the river rising to a narrow peak, the peak was naturally used for the tower or keep and a single bailey was enclosed in a triangular shape down the hillside below it. At Windsor, by contrast, a chalk mound sits in the middle of a flattish ridge above the river; as a result the Round Tower is at the centre of the castle and there are two baileys, one on each side of the mound, which between them occupy the hill top. At Exeter the Conqueror found sturdy Roman walls still standing (the very walls that had resisted him for eighteen days). He chose the strongest corner of them for his castle and the inevitable result, making use of the two sections of Roman wall, was a rectangular keep. At Caerlaverock in south-western Scotland there is a triangular rock in low-lying coastal land, so Caerlaverock, delightfully, is a triangular castle and around its walls there is a moat.

Even the separate architectural elements of the mound-and-bailey castle—the tower at its highest point, with one palisade round the top of the mound and another round the bailey—were capable of quite different development at the same period. The tower, strengthened until it can stand on its own, becomes in the very earliest years of the Conquest the solid rectangular keep of such castles as the Tower of London or Colchester. At the same time the palisade at the top of the mound became elsewhere, as at Windsor, so magnified that it replaced the very tower which it had been intended to enclose; the Round Tower, an early example of the so-called shell keep, is not a tower in the normal sense but merely a high wall enclosing a circular courtyard, in which low buildings leant against the inner circumference. In other places the outer wall of the bailey might be so strongly built that by itself it seemed to constitute a castle, and frequently the different elements become so intertwined that to identify their precise derivation is almost meaningless. There is, for example, a massive and early circular shell keep at Restormel in Cornwall. With fairly low walls and an internal diameter of nearly forty yards, it has the appearance as much of a small bailey as of a large keep. Is it therefore a case of the wall round the top of the mound becoming enlarged, which would make it a keep, or of the wall round the bailey having shrunk, in which case we should call it an inner bailey or ward? (See page 106.)

The question is one which can be asked more and more frequently about the central walled areas of later castles, but it is, in every known sense of the word, academic. All that matters is whether the wall, one of the main items in the castle-builder's repertoire, has been used to best effect on that particular site. Very often it is the non-architectural features of the basic equipment—mound and ditch, rather than tower and walls—which predominate. Nature can provide such magnificent mounds, as at Edinburgh or Stirling, and such spectacular ditches for almost any seaside castle, that tower and wall become no more than the finishing touches. At Tantallon, on the Firth of Forth, the Douglas family owned a promontory which plunged, on three sides, down steep cliffs to the sea. All that they needed to fortify it was a strong wall across the fourth side, and access to this was made more difficult by two dry ditches cutting across from cliff to cliff and crossed by drawbridges. With few of the conventional ingredients, and almost nothing of the traditional pattern, they had a castle which was well nigh impregnable.

Only in the smaller details of castle architecture was there a clear progression over the years. Refinements were introduced in one district and soon heard of in another; once thought of they seemed obvious and so gradually became general. It was not enough, for example, that the wall of the bailey should merely grow in size and strength—for however thick and high it might become, an enemy who had once reached its base was out of sight and reasonably safe unless those on top leant over and offered an easy target. One solution was a projecting area along the top of the wall or tower, with gaps in its floor through which missiles or oil could be sent vertically downwards; such projections, visible now in many castle ruins, became known as machicolations. Another was to build out towers at intervals, which would give the defenders a view and a field of fire back along the wall. In the early years such towers were often square, for square towers are easier to build. But they are also easier to demolish, since anyone undermining them can pick away at any one of the corners and will stand a good chance of bringing down two of the walls. Moreover a square tower still has one blind side, at its outer edge. So the round wall-tower soon became the norm.

The weakest part of any castle is its entrance, and it did not take long to discover that flanking towers could protect it just as they could a stretch of wall. At the gate itself a portcullis, through which one can shoot, has obvious advantages over a wooden door if someone is trying to batter their way in. An arrangement of walls, leading out from the gatehouse, will force an enemy to approach from an angle convenient to the defenders, and such outworks—under the name of a barbican— soon became a standard feature, directing the invaders across open spaces where their flank would be exposed to fire from the castle walls, and then leading them through passages lined with arrow slits or under arches from which unspeakable horrors might rain down on them from 'murder-holes' in the roof. Such were the refinements with which the later architects of castles were able to use their natural sites ever more effectively, but the essential ingredients of their craft—mound, tower, wall and ditch—remained as they always had been.

Aerial view of
Tantallon, East Lothian

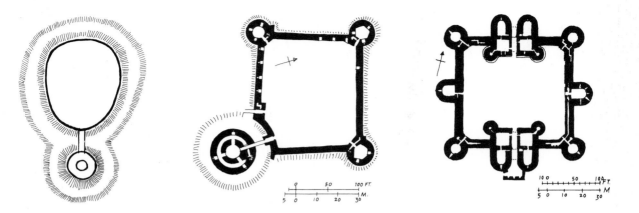

The way in which it had been possible to move from simplicity to sophistication within one unaltered pattern can be seen by comparing the ground-plan of a typical mound-and-bailey castle with that of Flint, built by Edward I between 1277 and 1280 in the very heyday of castle architecture in Britain.

The basic mound-and-bailey castle has the rough shape of a figure of eight, one part of which—the mound—is much smaller than the other. The ditch round the mound separates it from the bailey, and a steep wooden bridge crosses this gap between the two parts of the castle, rising sharply and having a drawbridge somewhere in its length so that the mound, in an emergency, can be defended on its own. Several such bridges up to the mound can be seen in the castles of the Bayeux tapestry.

The ground-plan of Flint shows precisely the same pattern, but with certain sophistications of a later century to make it more effective. A drawbridge crosses a moat which separates the larger bailey from the keep, just as before, but flanking towers have been added to protect the walls of the bailey; moreover the entrance to the bailey is now immediately beside the keep, instead of being at the greatest distance away from it. Thus the great circular keep at Flint fulfils both the new function of a tower flanking the gatehouse and also the ancient one of providing a place of last resort.

To draw a mound-and-bailey castle as a simple and evenly spaced figure of eight is to present an abstraction. But an abstraction is also an ideal design, undistorted by the requirements of a particular site. In the landscape only an entirely flat terrain provides the *tabula rasa* on which an architect will put into effect such a plan, and since a flat plain is far from the best place for siting a new castle the ideal contemporary design has rarely been achieved. But there is one example which was built as a unified conception in a featureless landscape during the greatest period of the British castle. By comparing its ground plan with that of a mound and bailey it is possible to identify in their final form the improvements of two centuries. The castle is Beaumaris, the last of Edward I's great chain of castles in Wales.

Beaumaris was started in 1295 on a flat coastal site on the island of Anglesey. Under the now experienced control of its architect, Master

Far left, typical mound-and-bailey castle

Flint Castle, *left centre*, and inner bailey of Beaumaris Castle, *left*. Plans redrawn from Sidney Toy, *Castles of Great Britain*, Heinemann, 1954

Right, aerial view of Beaumaris Castle, Anglesey

James of Saint George (Flint had been his first effort in Britain, eighteen years before), Beaumaris was designed to incorporate the very latest ideas. Its square inner bailey is flanked by several rounded towers, four of which serve also as gatehouses protecting the two entrances on opposite sides of the bailey. The keep—the ultimate refuge in earlier castles, and the descendant of the tower on those first mounds—has been entirely dispensed with. Each of the gatehouses is now massive enough to contain quite comfortable rooms for the lord of the castle, and each on its own can fulfil the other function of a keep—that of being a separate defensible unit. Even if attackers fight their way through the treacherous passage and archway under the gatehouse, they will only emerge on the other side into the bailey with the gatehouse itself still intact behind and above them. Then those extra flanking towers on the inner side of the gatehouse will come into their own, protecting it against its own courtyard (as also on that other possible occasion, when the garrison itself gives trouble to its commander).

At first sight the ground plan of this inner bailey at Beaumaris appears to have nothing in common with the mound-and-bailey pattern, but seems instead remarkably close to the square design with corner towers at Flint. Yet I was able to suggest above that Flint itself showed a clear and logical development from the mound-and-bailey castle. The reason is that Flint (admittedly something of an architectural oddity in its own day) can be seen in two ways. With the mound-and-bailey plan in mind, the large tower with its moat and drawbridge seems to play exactly the same role as the old mound and tower, and therefore earns the name of keep. But seen with hindsight from Beaumaris one might just as well say that Flint consists of a square bailey flanked by four corner towers, one of which has become greatly enlarged—like the huge right claw of certain lobsters—because it has the added function of guarding the entrance beside it. Interpreted along these lines, the later decision to have two opposite entrances into the bailey leads almost inevitably to the rearrangement of the towers which can be seen at Beaumaris. Clearly the castle is something of a chameleon in its architectural development, always the same and yet always different—and rightly so, since like the chameleon its task is to adapt itself to its surroundings and survive.

21

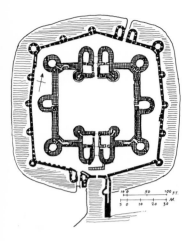

Beaumaris Castle,
complete ground plan
redrawn from Toy,
op. cit.

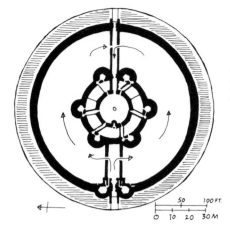

Queenborough Castle,
plan redrawn from Toy,
op. cit.

If one adds to the ground plan of Beaumaris the outer bailey with its wall and moat, a new principle becomes apparent which was undoubtedly the most important single departure from the old mound-and-bailey pattern. For Beaumaris is what is known as a concentric castle. In the earlier form of castle, the tower or keep was the last unit to fall. The defenders might lose the entire bailey to the enemy and then retreat to this ultimate cramped refuge. The disadvantage was that the keep was of comparatively little use in defending the bailey, so the bailey, once lost, could be occupied by the enemy for their final assault on the keep. But in the twelfth and thirteenth centuries the crusaders had seen a more sophisticated concentric arrangement in the castles of the Byzantine empire. They had adopted it first for their own great eastern fortresses, such as Krak des Chevaliers in Syria, before bringing it back for use at home.

The great advantage of this new design was that an enemy, overwhelming the first line of defence, found himself in possession only of a narrow strip of land in which he was extremely vulnerable from yet higher walls ahead—higher not only to make them harder to scale, but also to enable successive lines of archers to shoot down over each others' heads to the open ground outside the walls. The careful placing of gates could force attackers to cross this dangerous outer bailey at a most awkward angle. Neither gate through the outer wall at Beaumaris is exactly opposite the inner gatehouse to which it leads.

The intellectual pleasure of such an ideal design can be sensed in the lay-out of Beaumaris, but it is even more plain in the pattern of a castle built at Queenborough in Kent in 1361–77 which was unfortunately destroyed in the seventeenth century. On the flat lands of the Isle of Sheppey there was, as at Anglesey, no natural feature to guide the architect. He was free to develop the ultimate logic of defence, and every practical discovery of the previous centuries here achieves its most perfect form. That round walls are stronger than square ones, that a defensive system should be concentric, that gateways are best defended by flanking towers, that entrances out of alignment force an enemy to cross open ground or that a barbican can channel his approach—all these discoveries, carried to their purest conclusion, provide in the ground plan of Queenborough castle a shape as satisfying and self-contained as the most careful of modern abstracts.

A moat with two drawbridges surrounded a massive circular wall. One of these served only a small postern gate (it could be as important to get out of one's own castle in a crisis as to prevent an enemy from getting in), but the other drawbridge, on the opposite side of the circle, led to the outer gatehouse. An attacker who forced his way through this gatehouse found himself, beyond it, in a narrow passage formed by a barbican. If he rushed to the end of this passage, he reached only the blank wall of the inner bailey or keep. To get any further he must turn right or left through a small gap in the barbican, make his way round a half circle of open ground under fire from stout towers to one side of him and possibly from the outer wall to the other, and then re-enter a similar gap in the opposite barbican before approaching the inner gatehouse. The inner bailey or keep (it can logically be seen as either) was itself the ultimate in the use of circles—a perfectly symmetrical arrangement of round towers evenly spaced round a round wall, with the single exception that two of them are more closely bunched together to guard the gate.

The ground plan of this most intellectual of castles may bring to mind one of those irritating games, where a ball has to be rolled between infinite obstacles and hazards from the outside of the puzzle to its very centre. If so, the reason is far from accidental. The designer of Queenborough castle was making matters hard for an intruding neighbour in precisely the same spirit as the maker of the puzzle for the little silver ball.

But if Queenborough represents the perfect castle, it was a perfection which had arrived too late. At the end of the fifteenth century the castle itself was about to become an anachronism. For another hundred years or so a few would still be built, but their military importance was on the wane.

The arrival of gunpowder and artillery, first used in England in about 1325, has often been given as the reason for the decline of castles, but this is very much less than a full explanation. It is true that from a surprisingly early date there were massive guns which could hurl balls heavy enough to do severe damage to castle walls, but they were so expensive, so few in number and so unwieldy that they made little difference to ordinary warfare. It would be centuries before the cannon readily available would be strong enough to make a decisive impact in a siege, and even as late as the Civil War many of the old castles, which had been virtually neglected for two centuries, came suddenly into their own protecting Cavaliers from Roundheads and vice versa. Corfe Castle was able to withstand no less than nine months of battering from Cromwell's artillery.

The real reason for the decline of the castle derived from a change in

The earliest known drawing of a cannon, ms illumination, 1326, Christ Church, Oxford

the conventions of war. A castle, like gold, is only currency if it is generally agreed to be so. In the Norman period such an agreement had prevailed, and war was like a game of chess with slightly reversed rules. The castles were stationary pieces and between them there moved, in ever shifting groups, the kings and queens, the bishops, the knights, and as many peons as they could gather about them. The strength of each side increased with the acquiring of ever more castles, more often by alliance than by siege. A king in his own castle was the strongest unit on the board. A king captive in someone else's castle spelt the end of the game, or at the very least an agreement to revise the rules.

The end was in sight once the men recognized that a long siege might waste a great deal of time and effort and still leave the quarrel unresolved. As armies grew larger there was a new tendency towards battles in the open field, disregarding occupied castles which must sooner or later fall when the entire countryside was in enemy hands. Throughout the Wars of the Roses the great castles did continue to have a function, but largely as safe places in which to keep important prisoners. When Edward IV was captured near Coventry in 1469 he was kept first in the castle at Warwick, and then moved to another at Middleham, just as he himself had earlier placed Henry VI for safety's sake in the Tower of London. Significantly, on the various occasions when poor Henry was taken prisoner, it was not after the loss of a castle but of a battle—at Northampton in 1460, or St Albans in the following year. And it was to be such a battle, at Bosworth Field, which finally settled the matter.

There had always been a conflict, in the design of castles, between the demands of military efficiency and the comfort expected by the lord in what was also his residence. Perching in a narrow tower on top of a mound, or squeezing himself and his family above the machinery of the portcullis in a keep-gatehouse, the bold baron of the earlier centuries had felt compelled to put his comfort second. With the decline in the military importance of the castle, the emphasis could change. The result in a few cases was a more sumptuous castle, as at Bodiam. More often, and more sensibly, the solution was to live in a house rather than a castle and to fortify it as required. The fortified manor-house was nothing new, for there had always been local squires who could not afford a castle but who needed, as did everyone of any wealth, protection from their neighbours. Even Domesday Book records some 'defensible houses'. By the thirteenth century—at the same period as Edward I's great programme of castle-building—a licence from the king to crenellate had become fairly common, and the earliest of England's delightful surviving fortified manor-houses were already in existence. One of the best known and most attractive of these is Stokesay in Salop. The house itself had been built in about 1240.

Some fifty years later the owner received his licence to crenellate it, whereupon he enclosed a bailey to one side of the house with a wall which included a gatehouse and a fortified tower, and surrounded the entire complex of buildings with a moat. He had added the essential ingredients of a castle to his otherwise normal home and had acquired, in the opinion of succeeding generations, the best of both.

For another hundred years a gentleman would need this type of defence against his neighbours. Not until the Tudor period would the stone wall and strong tower become unnecessary, and then the only trace of those harsh days surviving in a fashionable residence would be that most pleasant of all defensive barriers, the moat. The castle had finally yielded to the palace and mansion.

*   *   *

Wandering today among the stark walls of a ruined castle, with its massive and jagged chunks of stone, it is hard to imagine that life in such a pile was anything but extremely uncomfortable. The dank hole of the privy, a mere cavity in the thick outer wall at the end of a discreetly angled passage from the great hall, seems to sum up the atmosphere of camping under difficult conditions. (And as well as the whistling draughts, were there perhaps even graver fears in the use of it? It was not unknown for besiegers to force their way into a castle up through the sewers). Only the great fireplaces seem to give some hint that all may not have been unrelievedly brutal—or the occasional stone window-seat, high above the landscape, where one can well imagine pleasant dalliance on a summer's day.

Accurate details of life in the early castles are rare, but there is one late example which provides so many insights that it is worth describing at some length. From three fortunate accidents—that some of its building accounts survive, that a full inventory was made of its contents, and that it belonged to those most vivid of early English letter-writers, the Pastons—we know more humdrum details about Caister Castle than about any other.

It was built by the man whose name was immortalized by Shakespeare, to the very considerable irritation of his seventeenth-century descendants. Sir John Fastolf began work on his castle in about 1430, and the accounts survive for the years 1432–5, as made out by William Granere, 'master of the new work at Castre'. Most of the details are obvious enough, with prices given for firing bricks at Sir John's own kilns, for purchasing and conveying timber (at one time he owned as many as six ships for supplying the castle), and for buying such necessities as 265 trays of burnt chalk 'to make mortar of', or 1,090 stacks of rushes to cover the bricks. Even in this dry list of figures evocative human details sometimes peep through. Master Granere records with more than a hint of disapproval the financial demands of one of his masons:

Henry Wode, *masoun*, 4s. 1d. for his wage for one week last year, which he asked beyond what is shown by the hostel book, and 12s. 3d., which he asked for half days in coming from Norwich and returning, on which he did no service to the lord—and disallowed to him until he shall speak thereof with the lord.

There is no record of whether Henry found Sir John softer-hearted than Master Granere in the matter of expenses, but the knight was far from miserly when it came to his own comforts. We know the details because on Sir John's death in 1459 a full inventory of the castle's contents was drawn up.

Caister Castle, near
Great Yarmouth,
Norfolk

The first surprise to a modern eye is the colossal amount of gold and silver. It is as though a millionaire today had transferred all his wealth to bullion, and indeed in those pre-capitalist days there was little else to be done with it (the wheel may have come full circle). In coins alone, not all of them kept at Caister, Sir John had £2,643, and his dishes, flagons, candlesticks and chargers added up, with all his other plate, to 98 ounces of gold and no less than 14,813 ounces of silver. From his own cupboards a banquet of over a hundred people could eat and drink from silver or silver-gilt, (at his death there were some 200 gallons of red wine in the cellar), and while they feasted they were protected by the warmest of tapestries from those bare castle walls which are all that we see today.

The arrangement of the main hall in a castle followed an age-old pattern, familiar in England even before the Normans, by which the lord sat at a raised table at one end of the hall while his followers occupied the rest of the room. Behind the high table there was screened off the family's private area, or 'solar', and a similar screen at the other end separated the diners from the buttery (a word more to do with butler and bottle than butter), above which a gallery was later added for the use of musicians. It is an arrangement which can still be seen in Oxford and Cambridge colleges today.

When Sir John entered the hall at Caister to take his seat, there was behind him on the dais a 'cloth of arras' showing a Wild Man, no doubt covered in the traditional green leaves, who carried a child in his arms. At the bottom end of the hall another such tapestry had 'a geyaunt in the myddell, berying a legge of a bere in his honde', and on the west wall was a covering which must often have prompted flattering comments from Sir John's guests; it showed the siege of Falaise, at which he himself had held command during the winter of 1417–18 in the army of Henry V. Impregnable—that was the reputation of the fortress on its high rock, where Henry's mother had been born. They had taken it.

The contents of the hall at Caister, though more lavish than one might expect, are in keeping with the conventional image of a medieval banquet. The inventory of the bedrooms is rather more surprising. Twenty-five bedrooms are listed. Of these all but two are for one person only; all but one are equipped with feather beds; and nearly all have a pair of sheets as well as their fustian blankets. Nor are we talking only of the level of comfort expected by members of the family, or by friends and colleagues. The cook, for example, has a room to himself with the regulation feather bed, one bolster, two sheets, and a red coverlet decorated with roses and the heads of blood hounds. The gardener gets a carpet, and has not only a coverlet of blue but also another 'of better blue'. Even the porter has feather bed, bolster, pair of sheets, blanket, covering cloth, and a curtain of red serge. If, as is probable, the interior walls of the rooms were white-washed, these are far from cheerless lodgings.

Sir John had no heir, but in his later years he had befriended a young man of business, John Paston, whose advice had been consistently of use to him. When the old knight was dying he prayed every day,

according to the friar who attended at his bedside, that 'God send me soon my good cousin Paston, for I hold him a faithful man, and ever one man'. It is not known whether Paston was indeed a distant relation, or whether this cousinship was a figure of affection, but two days before his death Sir John inserted a new clause into his will. It said that Paston, his 'best friend and helper and supporter', should inherit all his estates in Norfolk and Suffolk.

Paston came from a family which had risen fast in the world—too fast for the liking of some—even before the vast Fastolf wealth was added to his own. His grandfather, Clement Paston, had been a yeoman farmer in the village of Paston. By hard work and a judicious marriage he had laid the foundations of an estate and had bought for his son the best possible education in law with which to protect that estate. This son, William, found himself in his turn a rich wife, rose to become a judge, and in his lifetime greatly increased the Paston fortunes. Ambitious and shrewd but always reliable, marrying money and well versed in the law—this had remained the pattern down to the third generation when the grandson, John, met and became friends with Sir John Fastolf and by virtue of his level-headedness gradually became the man on whom the old knight increasingly relied for advice. But inheriting the vast Fastolf estates was one thing. Keeping them, for all his knowledge of the law, was another.

In the early stages of quarrels between fifteenth-century landlords, it was the tenants who suffered. Two of the manors inherited by Paston from Fastolf show the process in detail. The neighbouring Duke of Suffolk took a fancy to them, trumped up some claim, and sent his bailiff to collect rent from the tenants. The tenants objected, so the bailiff carried off the horses of a farmer called Dorlet, just as he was about to yoke them to his plough. The Pastons arrived as soon as possible to hold court on their own account, and removed two mares from the only tenant, by the name of Piers Warin, who spoke against them. Soon a hundred and sixty of the duke's men arrived in armour and removed the plough-horses of the parson and of one other villager. The Pastons retaliated by driving off seventy-seven cattle. Each side was able to argue that all this rustling was legal, being but a form of distraint or security against the tenant farmers' payment of rent—an argument which would have made more sense to the tenants if they had known who was the landlord.

At this stage the dispute began to escalate into something closer to outright warfare. The Pastons moved a garrison of sixty men into one of the two manors, Hellesdon, and armed them with large quantities of guns. They held a powerful position, for Hellesdon was a fortified manor-house with a square keep or fortress on the hillside above it, and their show of strength proved sufficient to turn away without bloodshed three hundred of the duke's men who arrived expecting an easy entry. For a while the duke's tactic changed to plain intimidation, and supporters of the Pastons were liable to find themselves cornered and stabbed in the darker streets of Norwich, but at last a full-scale military assault was launched and the garrison realized that it was futile to resist. The invaders seized all the contents of the manor and set Paston's own tenants to demolishing its walls, while they themselves ransacked every building in the village including even the church. John Paston himself was away in London, and his wife Margaret wrote to him that people 'speak shamefully' of this event and that the Duke of Suffolk 'had been better than a thousand pound that it had never been done'. But whatever the effect on the duke's reputation, one of Fastolf's manors had been lost.

It was another duke who had his eye on Caister, a far richer prize. The young Duke of Norfolk announced that he had bought it from one of the executors of Sir John Fastolf, and this rather feeble claim was soon supported by 3,000 armed men outside the walls of the castle. John Paston himself had recently died, and his widow Margaret was living in Norwich. For maximum confusion, both their sons were also called John—the younger of whom was holding Caister, while the elder lobbied the royal court in London for support in his struggle against this very powerful nobleman. Furious letters were rushed post-haste from Margaret in Norwich to her son in London (the journey seems to have taken two or three days), urging him to send more help:

Your brother and his fellowship stand in great jeopardy at Caister, and lack victuals; . . . and they fail gunpowder and arrows, and the place sore broken with guns of the other party, so that, but they have hasty help, they be like to lose both their lives and the place, to the greatest rebuke to you that ever came to any gentleman.*

She informed her wayward son that the duke's men had sent to the seaside for even more cannon and that a great assault was planned, but the young man seemed to have inherited few of his ancestors' practical qualities. He achieved nothing in London, failed to send reinforcements, and even had the effrontery to write at this critical time asking his mother for money as he was down to his last ten shillings.

Margaret, though she failed to instil a sufficient sense of urgency into her elder son, understood all too well the younger John's plight for she knew what it was to be besieged in one's own home. Nineteen years earlier she had been living in one of the family manors, at Gresham— bought by the Pastons, incidentally, from the son of Geoffrey Chaucer— when a nobleman decided that he had a claim upon it. A thousand of his people arrived,

arrayed in manner of war, with cuirasses, coats of mail, steel helmets, glaives, bows, arrows, large shields, guns, pans with fire, long cromes to draw down houses, ladders, and picks with which they mined down the walls, and long trees with which they broke up gates and doors, and so came into the said mansion, the wife of your beseecher at that time being therein, and twelve persons with her—the which persons they drove out of the said mansion, and mined down the walls of the chamber wherein the wife of your said beseecher was, and bare her out at the gates and cut asunder the posts of the houses, and let them fall, and broke up all the chambers and coffers in the said mansion, and rifled and bare away stuff, array and money to the value of £200.

The technique known as mining, a standard method of attack on a castle in the days before gunpowder was plentiful, was to dig under

---

* Quotations from the Paston letters and from the Caister inventory are from James Gairdner, (ed), *The Paston letters*, Chatto and Windus, London, 1904, 6 vols.

the foundations of the building while supporting them with wooden props, as in the gallery of a coal mine. The cavity was then packed with dry brushwood, which was set alight. When the props burnt through, the unsupported wall fell in—a far from pleasant prospect on that distant occasion for Margaret, trapped in her room above and soon to be unceremoniously bundled out through the gates. Her husband, as so often, was away in London.

Matters never came to this extreme pass at Caister, for when the food ran out the younger John Paston capitulated and the duke graciously granted him and his followers a free pass to 'go out of the seid maneur . . . havyng their lyves and goods, horsse, and harneys, and other goods'. They only had to leave behind 'gonnes, crossebows, and quarrells, and alle other hostelments, to the seid maneur annexed and belonginge'. Even so there was further affront in store. The duke's council later brought a prosecution against Paston for having killed two of the duke's men by firing a gun at them from Caister. The outcome of what would seem to be a singular piece of impertinence is not known.

Yet there was some poetic justice in the story. Six years after the siege the Duke of Norfolk suddenly died, at the age of only thirty. The Pastons were able to walk back into Caister unopposed—no doubt to their own amazement as much as anyone else's. Within another four years the elder of the Paston brothers had himself died of the plague. So the younger John, who had defended the castle against the duke, came to spend the rest of a relatively long and peaceful life within its walls. The family remained there until 1599, when they moved to a more comfortable mansion which they built nearby. Caister, like so many of its kind, was left to crumble.

*   *   *

The Battle of Bosworth Field had put the Tudors on the throne, initiating a new and more settled era in English history. It is significant that one thinks of Henry VIII or Elizabeth not in castles, but in palaces—Greenwich, Richmond, Hampton Court. With this new authority in the land, the castle was no longer needed. It would not be strong enough to shield the subject from the wrath of his monarch; and the monarch had better ways of protecting himself or herself against dissident nobles.

The only so-called castles to be built at this period, which include such splendid buildings as Deal, Walmer and St Mawes, were in fact coastal defences—more akin to elaborate Martello Towers than to true castles. Like Pitt nearly three centuries later, Henry VIII feared invasion from France, and he prepared for it with these exceptionally solid and squat clover-leaf towers in which to house his cannon at strategic points along the coast.

By the early seventeenth century any genuine castle not capable of being turned into a mansion was already on the way to becoming a ruin, sheltering in its strong walls local peasants and their flocks. 'It is a reverend thing', Francis Bacon was able to write, 'to see an ancient castle or building not in decay.' Only the idea remained of the castle, as the ultimate symbol of personal security and independence, and it was the seventeenth century which provided the best known use in

Aerial view of Deal
Castle, Kent

the language of this image. The great jurist Sir Edward Coke, in one of his volumes of interpretation of the common law, argued from the case of a certain Semayne that 'a man's house is his castle, *et domus sua cuique est tutissimum refugium*; for where shall a man be safe, if it be not in his own home?' Ever since, in the popular adage, an Englishman's home has been his castle.

Admittedly the castles did come briefly back into their own for a few years in the middle of the seventeenth century, when it was discovered that however run down an ancient stronghold might be it was still the best available protection against the nearest army of Cavaliers or Roundheads. A settled way of life had erupted into outright civil war and large-windowed mansions, normal for at least a hundred years, had sudden disadvantages. But with the Restoration the unusual circumstances came to an end, and the castles returned—more battered now—to the slow process of decay.

Yet there was one area which even now was making a very positive contribution to the story of the castle, for it was a district where the way of life of the Pastons had continued through the sixteenth and even seventeenth centuries. In the richer part of the highlands of Scotland, between Aberdeen and Inverness, plunder remained almost a normal occupation among gentlemen who, like the Pastons, were in every other way quite sophisticated. The result was some of the most delightful castles that can be seen anywhere in Britain.

The castle consisting of a single tower had for several centuries been a standard feature in Scotland and the north of England, but the form achieved its ultimate expression in these later times. The tower-houses of north-east Scotland occupy hardly more ground than would be necessary for a cottage, but on that tiny base they soar up to six

Coxton Tower, near Elgin, Morayshire, built 1644. *Left*, a photograph of the castle today; *right*, an 18th-century engraving reproduced from D. F. Simpson, *Exploring Castles*, Routledge, 1957

or seven storeys with small turrets projecting at the upper levels to provide extra space and to give the whole the appearance of a miniature castle in a fairy tale. And the enchanting exterior is only half the story. These fine gentlemen wanted—even in such awkward quarters—the full aesthetic pleasures of a civilized life, and so commissioned the startlingly beautiful plasterwork of Craigievar or Muchalls, or the painted ceilings at Crathes. (See pages 178 and 186.)

Yet the very same laird who appreciated such fineries could also accept that it was too dangerous for him to enter his house at ground level. In some places an open stone stairway, on which anyone approaching the first-floor entrance would be singularly vulnerable from above, seemed sufficient security. In others a ladder was all that could be risked, and one of the most seductive of the many thousands of prints of castles is that which shows the owner of Coxton Tower returning home. He is a most dignified gentleman, and in clothes suitable for doing business in Edinburgh he solemnly climbs a ladder to his own front door.

*　　　*　　　*

The following work was found in the library of an ancient Catholic family in the north of England. It was printed at Naples, in the black letter, in the year 1529. If the story was written near the time when it is supposed to have happened, it must have been between 1095, the era of the first crusade, and 1243, the date of the last.

With these words Horace Walpole introduced, in 1764, *The Castle of Otranto*—the preposterous tale of dark doings in castle vaults which, far from having been discovered in an ancient library in the north of England, he had himself concocted in his own rococo version of a medieval home in Twickenham. Strawberry Hill is usually given the credit for launching the style of neo-Gothic in architecture, just as *The Castle of Otranto* is in literature, but Walpole was not alone. Other rich householders were already rejecting the rectangular windows of rationalism in favour of something more mysterious. In the year of *Otranto* the fashionable world was already abuzz over the ancient Gaelic poems of Ossian, which had recently been forged without too much subtlety by John MacPherson. Down in Bristol a twelve-year-old boy, Thomas Chatterton, had invented the fifteenth-century monk, Thomas Rowley, whose poems he would brilliantly compose and then claim to have discovered. The desire to project oneself back into a more romantic age—whether by fraud, imagination or solid research—would not reach its mighty flood for another hundred years, but it was already more than a trickle. By the turn of the century the Gothic novel was the favourite and much frowned upon reading of fashionable young ladies. It was Catherine Morland's fondness for such tales which made her see gruesome signs, where none existed, in the medieval surroundings of Northanger Abbey. The gentle ridicule of Jane Austen could make no difference.

The only change over the years was that authenticity became increasingly in demand. It would no longer be sufficient to claim that one had found an old volume in a Catholic library; nor, on closer inspection, did Strawberry Hill look remotely medieval. By contrast, the medieval tales of Walter Scott were based on extensive research, and theatre directors of the mid-nineteenth century were to become obsessed with the accuracy of every detail in their costumes and settings, publishing elaborate academic justification for results which now look totally unconvincing. The richer landowners, wanting a comfortable new medieval house, carried their longing to its natural conclusion and paid massively for what both looked like and called itself a castle— even, as at Eastnor, going to the extravagance of a massive dry moat spanned by a permanent stone drawbridge.

Mrs Alexander, searching in 1848 for an image to suggest the divinely ordained social structure, settled upon:

> *The rich man in his castle,*
> *The poor man at his gate,*
> *God made them, high or lowly,*
> *And order'd their estate.*

A hymn-writer of the previous century would not have chosen this setting for the rich man. The castle had made its come-back.

No single event sums up so perfectly the neo-medievalism of the early nineteenth century, or the attitudes of those who designed and lived in the modern castles, as that notorious tragi-comic spectacular of 1839, the Eglinton Tournament. In it there came together all the separate attractions of those distant times when Richard had a lion's heart—the seemingly lost sense of chivalry, the sumptuous visual appeal of rich fabrics and skilled craftsmanship, the family pride of heraldry and the personal pride of single combat, the mystery of archaic phrases in long forgotten rituals, the apparent simplicity of days before the words radical or reform had even been coined. This yearning is made touchingly plain in a passage written by Charles Lamb (not, as will be apparent, the essayist). At the age of twenty-two, Lamb was one of fourteen knights who chanced their luck in the Eglinton tilt-yard. He appeared as the Knight of the White Rose. Soon after returning from what had been an undisputed fiasco, he wrote an account of the tournament in a private and suitably illuminated manuscript. He described his own appearance with appropriate care:

Now he was clad in a goodly suit of polished steel. Hys surcote covered over with white roses which were also embroidered upon hys belt, whereon was the legend of *une seule*, and one white rose in hys cap, all in token of his Lady love. Hys shield emblazoned with the arms of Burges, hys father's house. The crest of the same upon his helmet, with plumes of his tinctures and a mightie sword in hys hand readye to do battaille with all comer.*

The tournament had resulted partly from Lord Melbourne's decision to drop much of the traditional but very expensive medieval pageantry from Queen Victoria's coronation. The most famous piece of ritual to be dispensed with was the throwing down of the gauntlet by the Queen's Champion, mounted and fully armed, during the banquet in Westminster Hall. It so happened that Lord Eglinton's step-father had a hereditary right to a fairly prominent place in this ceremony. The young peer, aged twenty-six, was outraged on the older man's behalf—until it occurred to him that he might hold, as if in compensation, a medieval entertainment at Eglinton Castle, a neo-baronial home on his vast estates in the west of Scotland.

The enthusiasm of his friends was immediate, as was the interest of the press and public, and the idea snowballed until a full-scale tournament was planned. Soon young aristocrats were fitting themselves out in full armour at the establishment of Samuel Pratt in Bond Street, and breaking an experimental lance or two, to the vast entertainment of the locals, against a wooden knight in the Finchley Road. Throughout the country hundreds of seamstresses prepared the costumes of the retinues. Up at Eglinton an army of carpenters created a tournament ground looking just like those in ancient miniatures, with a tilt-yard between lavishly draped stands and with spectacular tents for the champions, while the staff inside the castle tried to cope with the flood of letters from the public asking for tickets. Of the many special reasons pleaded for admission by far the most common was support for Lord Eglinton's

---

* For this quotation, as for all details to do with the Eglinton Tournament, I am indebted to Ian Anstruther's enchanting book *The Knight and the Umbrella*, Bles, London, 1963.

well-known Tory views, one applicant even going so far as to mention that 'if political conduct is any inducement to grant such a great favour, it is well known that my wife with a Candlestick and I with my sword . . . nearly killed a Radical at the rising in 1819.'

The great day was August 28. The stands held only 4,000, but the crowd on the hillside behind was estimated at 100,000. A procession half a mile long was to accompany the Queen of Beauty (Lady Seymour, a grand-daughter of Sheridan) to her place of honour overlooking the tilt-yard, but it took longer to marshal than anticipated and appeared before the public some four hours late. Just as it did so, the heavens parted. The rest of the day was a downpour unprecedented even in the annals of Ayrshire. The fine costumes were ruined; it was impossible to admire the rich workmanship of the suits of armour; the knights, encased head to foot in metal, went unrecognized because announcements were inaudible; and when they galloped towards each other on slippery ground all but a few went wide of the mark and floundered past unscathed. Even the roof over the heads of the Queen of Beauty and her companions started to leak, but at least they had the castle to hurry back to. The lesser spectators fared worse. The river had risen to make the driveway almost impassable to carriages, and the cancellation of the evening's part of the entertainment meant that people were leaving hours earlier than they had planned. In the chaos, and the continuing deluge, many spent the most memorable night of their lives sheltering in barns or burrowed into a haystack. It has been calculated that the day had cost each of the participating knights £1,500, and Lord Eglinton himself some £40,000.

Thirty-four years later Disraeli planned to include the tournament as a scene in *Endymion*, and wrote to the ageing Queen of Beauty, now Duchess of Somerset, to ask if she had any souvenirs of it. She replied:

I do not know what I can find of the Eglinton Tournament, except a colored print which I will send you—I had all sorts of relics, points of splintered spears with the colours of the Knights but a stupid old house-maid considered them as 'rubbish' as she said, and burnt them together with a Blessed Palm that I had caught in mid air from the Pope's own hands.

'Lord Waterford in combat against Lord Alford', *left,* and 'The Queen of Beauty, Lady Seymour, surrounded by maids-of-honour and Atholl Highlanders', *right*. Engravings of drawings by James Henry Nixon, published in John Richardson, *The Eglinton Tournament*, 1843

It is possible—through the dotty spelling of poor Charles Lamb, or by dawdling among the suits of armour displayed at Eastnor—to imagine quite fully how people in the early nineteenth century felt about castles. One has only to climb the narrow staircase at Craigievar, between rooms which are lavish and yet infinitely snug in the thick walls of the tower, to know exactly what pleasure a seventeenth-century laird took in his sort of castle. Further away still, the inventory at Caister and the struggles of the Paston family give more than an inkling of what they were fighting for. But in the crucial first years of the British castle we have little except excavation and diagram to fire the imagination. What was it actually like in those early Norman strongholds? We know that they were for the most part small and wooden, totally different from our preconceptions about castles. But how small? How wooden?

A rare glimpse of the scale—human as well as architectural—is given in the surviving details of the siege of Bamburgh by William II in 1095. Inside the castle was Robert Mowbray, the rebel Earl of Northumberland, and with the king's forces were several who had been his accomplices in conspiracy. In a common technique of the day, the besieging army rapidly constructed a so-called counter-castle—a rival fortress, presumably of wood, which rose beside Bamburgh as a base from which to assault it. William gave this creation of his the appropriate name of Malvoisin or Evil Neighbour. While Malvoisin was going up, Earl Robert was on the battlements of his own castle calling by name to his erstwhile friends to remember their obligations. None did. Instead they connived in a trick which brought Robert out of his castle one dark night and led to his capture. In spite of this blow, his wife Mathilda and his nephew held out in Bamburgh. So the royal forces used another technique popular in siege warfare in all countries and at all periods. The earl was paraded in chains below the walls and it was announced, no doubt with a certain amount of fanfare, that his eyes would be put out unless the castle yielded. Mathilda gave in. Her husband, even so, was confined for the remaining thirty years of his life in the castle at Windsor—whether with or without her, history does not relate.

This, in spite of the pleading from the battlements and the intimate demonstrations from below, was a clash over one of the most strongly sited castles in the kingdom between the king himself and a nobleman too powerful to be put to death. It still leaves us a long way from one of those timber strongholds which were run up in a few weeks. Yet, there are still many parts of the world in which people live at a very primitive level in forts (villages in Afghanistan, or even Morocco, are examples), and a description of the home of the rajah of Acheen, in Sumatra, in the early nineteenth century provides a most evocative analogy to a small Norman castle. However different in spirit, his dwelling was composed of precisely the same ingredients—a bailey surrounded by a defensive wall, standing slightly apart from a taller and stronger keep.

The rajah was visited one morning in 1834 by George Bennett, Esq., F.L.S., F.R.S., a highly adventurous surgeon, keen naturalist and author. The residence in which he lived with his wives and attendants was surrounded by a tall and impenetrable fence of waving bamboos. There was a single gateway in this fence, and over it a small room in which His Highness liked to smoke or receive visitors. Mr Bennett reports that he climbed up into the royal presence by a ladder. The furniture consisted only of carved chests, on one of which he was invited to sit before being offered some coconut milk. On the other side the room looked down over the compound—an enclosure formed by the bamboo fence, in which several houses on stilts rose from a lush grove of coconut, banana, orange, mango and custard-apple trees. In these houses were the rajah's two eighteen-year-old wives and the four-year-old child to whom he was already betrothed.

This enchanting bailey was for times of comparative peace. In case of emergency the procedure was to climb to the top of the bamboo fence and then to cross by ladder over the gap which separated the bailey from its fort—precisely the same arrangement as when crossing over the ditch to the security of the mound in a primitive Norman castle. The fort was of stone, about eighteen feet high, with a thatched roof of palm leaves and a look-out post on top. In it Mr Bennett found

several large brass guns, most of which had the arms of the East India Company upon them. . . . From some large rents in the walls of the fort, it was evident that the con-cussion of the guns, if fired off, (which they had not yet been), would bring the whole fabric down about their ears: the minister and 'authorities' thought the same, and said a stronger fort was to be built, when a sufficient number of stones calculated for the purpose could be collected.*

Lesser Norman barons, with their timber castles rapidly becoming out of date, must have harboured precisely such dreams for the future.

It may be readily conceded that the similarity of the young rajah's home to a mound-and-bailey castle does not go beyond the ground plan, for his life within his bailey, smoking languidly among his orange trees and girls, could hardly be further from that to which the Earl of Northumberland was accustomed. He, when in castles less solid than Bamburgh, would have been familiar with defensive towers on stilts—but not (however much the idea might have appealed to him) with the pleasures of the harem. Yet how much he would have given, in 1095, for several large brass guns from the East India Company to point at his Evil Neighbour.

---

* George Bennett, *Wanderings in New South Wales*, 1834, pp. 404–7.

Key

▲ –Castle

⚑ –Castle and town of same name

● –Town

ENGLAND

TO THE ROMANS Britannia was the entire island which includes England, Wales and Scotland, and Britain has remained historically the name for that area. It was dubbed Great Britain in 1707 to celebrate the political union of the three countries and became the United Kingdom when linked with Ireland in 1801.

Within Britain England was the first country to be dotted with castles—specifically Norman symptoms, contracted in the late eleventh century by direct contagion from northwestern France. It is in England therefore that the most ancient and venerable of all British castles are to be found. Nor are they only impressive ruins, such as Colchester— the largest keep in Britain, founded in 1080 but only recently re-roofed to become a museum. Windsor, Warwick, Dover, the Tower of London: all these have remained going concerns, incorporating over the centuries each new defensive technique or domestic convenience and becoming in the process little less than private townships. They celebrate now almost nine centuries of continuous use.

While the royal family and the great barons were improving their existing castles, new men at each period were building more modest ones. Nunney can stand as an enchanting example of what the fourteenth-century gentleman hoped for from a small castle. Eastnor, nearly five hundred years later, provides an equally intriguing glimpse of the nineteenth-century idea of a large castellated house. And then there are the oddities—brick castles (Caister) or clover-leaf coastal forts (Deal, St Mawes). There are the peculiarly romantic castles of the Northumbrian coast (Bamburgh, Lindisfarne), hybrid but practical homes such as the fortified manor of Stokesay, and so many others. Both Welsh and Scottish castles possess a special type of unity. England counters with age and diversity.

Alnwick NORTHUMBERLAND

11th-century castle, much extended by successive generations of the Percy family, dukes of Northumberland, whose principal seat it has remained since 1309. Above, *the Prudhoe Tower and the Chapel, erected 1854;* right above, *the castle seen from the banks of the River Aln;* right, *the 15th-century gatehouse with stone figures carved in 1764*

A short distance to the west of the castle, at the main entrance to its surrounding parkland, there is a stone which marks the spot where William the Lion was attacked by a party of English barons, unexpectedly and—according to a chronicler—at dinner without his helmet. It was also near here that Malcolm Canmore, king of Scotland, had been killed in 1093. In this border country such encounters were commonplace, and it is hardly surprising that Northumberland has more castles, towers, peles and other fortifications than any other county in Britain.

When Henry Percy acquired the castle and barony of Alnwick in 1309, he found himself in possession of a stronghold already some 200 years old and of great strategical importance. The existing shell keep, begun by his Norman predecessors in 1096, he rebuilt in the form of seven semi-circular towers around the courtyard. The outer gateway and the greater part of the curtain walls survive today and are also his work.

The Percy family was engaged in incessant warfare —against the Scots or on occasion against the king, as in their rising of 1403 which was made so vivid by Shakespeare in *Henry IV, Part I*—yet Henry Percy's son found time to improve the fortifications at Alnwick. The striking barbican and gatehouse date from about 1440 and are probably the work of the 2nd Earl of Northumberland, son of Harry Hotspur, though the full-length stone figures ready to spring from the battlements were only put up during extensive restorations by the 1st duke in 1764, and it is not certain whether they were then an innovation or a replacement. It was he who effected a major transformation in the appearance of the castle. Over the years the influence of the lords of Alnwick had been somewhat enfeebled by a succession of misfortunes, brought about by their Lancastrian sympathies, their position as leaders of the northern barons and their Roman Catholic loyalties, and for a century after the Civil War they had even lived elsewhere. In 1750, however, when the 1st duke inherited the estates, a new era was introduced. Robert Adam was summoned, and the renovation of the castle progressed until 1766, by which time a magnificent ducal residence had been created, totally different from the medieval castle of the early Percys but quite in the fashionable 'Gothic' style of Strawberry Hill. In the next century, however, when Sir Walter Scott visited the castle, he commented on the lack of a dominating feature in the profile of the keep, and it was to render the castle more imposing that the 4th duke built the great Prudhoe tower in 1854.

Today like Arundel, whose shape and plan it somewhat resembles, the original layout of Alnwick is still clearly apparent beneath an accumulation of stonework fitted ingeniously together to suit the requirements of succeeding centuries. The castle's extraordinary patchwork of styles is curiously suited to the many different administrative and educational activities that are now carried on within it. It has often been involved in warfare, but only of a skirmishing type; over the years the real threat to the medieval castle was not the enemy's mines or bombardment, but the work of the improving architect.

Arundel WEST SUSSEX

The original castle dating from the 11th century had a mound and two baileys, all of which survive today. Top, the Barbican Tower built c. 1295; above, the 19th-century façade and south tower; right, the Bevis Tower, built 1170–90, during the reign of Henry II

Seen from the ramparts of the great circular Norman keep at Arundel, the South Downs roll and curve below, an open and inclement territory to the creeping enemy. The chalk spur on which the castle stands runs to a commanding height above the River Arun; a few miles to the south lies the sea, where the danger of attack from France was always to be anticipated. Thus when William the Conqueror conferred the earldom and castle of Arundel on the Norman knight Roger de Montgomery, it was no empty privilege, but one with specific responsibilities in the chain of his new kingdom's coastal defence. Earl Roger accordingly built a strong stone castle on the site of an earlier Saxon fortification, and he and his family enjoyed the tenure of Arundel until 1102. The expected attack from the seas, however, has never come; and of three recorded sieges, two were provoked by direct rebellion of the castellans against the monarch.

At the time of the first siege Arundel was already a castle of some considerable robustness, for it held out for three months against a strong force led by Henry I in 1102. Its owner at that time, Robert de Belesme, was probably responsible for starting the building in stone of the excellent keep, a circular building with thick walls on the top of a 70-foot-high mound. Henry I, when the castle was in his hands, continued the work, and it may have been completed by Henry II, whose building at Windsor it closely resembles, though nothing now remains inside the keep of the king's chambers and other rooms, nor of the garden which he made outside his own apartment. Though the outcome of this siege was a decisive triumph for the Crown, it was the policy of the time to mortify only the castellan, not the castle. Robert de Belesme forfeited his lands and died in prison, but the castle was not in any way dismantled.

The second siege occurred when it was held by a powerful knight, William de Albini, who supported and indeed harboured within his castle at Arundel the Dowager Empress Matilda, with her rival claim to that of King Stephen. Stephen's inevitable attack on the castle seems to have been a strangely half-hearted affair, for he soon raised the siege; Matilda was allowed to depart and the de Albinis were confirmed in their tenure as earls of Arundel until the male line died out. The inheritance passed through a daughter to the Fitzalan family, and thence through the female line again to the Howards, dukes of Norfolk. These were the only interruptions in the family's line of descent, and there still live in the castle today the descendants of William de Albini, who received the Honour of Arundel in 1138—a continuity rare in English history, rivalled only by Berkeley or the less well-known castle of Dunster.

The Fitzalan family proved energetic builders. It was Richard Fitzalan, 1st Earl of Arundel, who remade the upper part of the gatehouse to the west in about 1295, also the two flanking barbican towers, and the four similarly shaped towers beyond the keep. This splendid sturdy gateway to the castle remains today defended by a portcullis, a two-leaved door and a drawbridge. His great-grandson, the 4th earl, built the beautiful chapel known still by the family name, which though restored in the late 19th century still retains the atmosphere of its 14th-century origins. It fell into disrepair at the time of the Dissolution of the Monasteries, and was later used as a stable by Cromwell's men. To the south of the high altar there remains a magnificent chantry worked in Purbeck marble, the monument of William, 9th Earl, and his countess, who died at the end of the 15th century.

The male line of Fitzalan died out in 1580 and Arundel passed with the marriage of a daughter to the dukes of Norfolk. Future crises in the history of the castle derive from the increasingly unusual fact that this major stronghold was held by a Catholic nobleman. In the reign of Henry VIII the 3rd duke, Thomas, had been the leader of the Catholic party and as such was imprisoned and condemned to death. By an amazing stroke of luck the king himself died on the day before Thomas's execution was to have been carried out. The family, however, continued to suffer because of their religion, and the 3rd duke's son was less fortunate than his father, for this time it was the king, Edward VI, who outlived his prisoner by the shortest of margins. Henry Howard was executed in 1547 at the age of 30 and Edward died nine days later, ushering in a reign when Catholics were to find high favour, and the Protestants went to the Tower. In the next reversal under Elizabeth his son fared no better and was executed in 1572 for plotting to marry Mary Queen of Scots, while his grandson was also imprisoned by the Protestant queen and died in the Tower in 1595 after refusing to abandon his faith, for which he was beatified after his death and canonized in 1970. Thereafter the Howard heir to Arundel wisely left the country and played no part in political affairs. It was during his absence abroad that the castle suffered its last and only crippling siege. In 1643 the Parliamentarians under Sir William Waller bombarded it for nearly a month from the security of the neighbouring church, until the garrison surrendered: and when Cromwell's forces finally left in 1648 they ensured that the already considerable damage was made even greater. After the Restoration Charles II, who knew all too well the discomforts of exile on the Continent, restored to the family all their titles and lands. It was he who confirmed to them as a hereditary privilege the Earl Marshalcy, the great office of state with the highest authority on royal ceremonial occasions. The Howards returned, however, to find a castle so roofless and shattered that for 70 years they preferred to live elsewhere. Fortunately the Barbican had survived, but marks of cannon can still be seen on its towers.

By the time Horace Walpole visited the castle in 1749 it had in part been made habitable by the 8th duke; nevertheless Walpole found it 'now only a heap of ruins, with a new indifferent apartment clapt up for the Norfolks when they reside there for a week or a fortnight.' Could he have seen it 40 years later he of all people would have approved. In the 1780s the 10th duke employed the architect Hiorne and began an immense restoration in the fashionable Gothic style, which cost a total of £600,000. A later descendant, the 15th duke, swept away most of this architectural fantasy, and at the end of the 19th century undertook a more straightforward reconstruction of the early Norman stronghold, though what the many visitors find today are the scanty remains of early buildings almost smothered in the impressive but nonetheless very different masonry of the late Victorian period.

Fitzalan Chapel in Arundel Castle, erected 1380 by Richard Fitzalan, restored 1886

Bamburgh NORTHUMBERLAND

Bamburgh Castle, seen from a distance along the shore across stretches of wet black rock and empty dunes, seems no more than a chunky irregularity in the pattern of the landscape—a part merely of the disorderly volcanic outcrop on which it stands. But this remarkable affinity with its own austere surroundings is only the effect of distance and light—those in search of the romantic and picturesque should look no closer, for much of the castle is modern, its restoration having been very fully undertaken by Lord Armstrong and completed in 1903. At close range the new stones, some bought by Lord Armstrong from a distance of nearly 30 miles by great convoys of horse-waggons, are even-coloured and disappointing. Their surface will perhaps need a few more years of harsh Northumbrian gales to weather and fret the bland-looking slabs, but at least in true castle tradition the new work looks solid enough to last the course.

Today nothing remains of the earliest stronghold at Bamburgh. In the 6th century, when it was the centre of the kingdom of Bernicia, and thus a most powerful part of Britain, the fortress on the rock was immensely important to whomever could hold it. Its name derives from the wife of King Ethelfrith, Queen Bebba. Reference is made in the Anglo-Saxon Chronicle under the year 547 to the stone walls with which the castle was fortified. And it was presumably against these that William II arrived in 1095 to build his wooden counter-fort, the *malvoisin*, in what was to be the castle's most famous siege. This 'evil neighbour', which rose up intrepid alongside the ramparts of Bamburgh, achieved nothing, for William found the great citadel impregnable and had to content himself with a baleful but impotent observation of its activities. He finally left others in command of the siege and went south. Robert de Mowbray, the turbulent 3rd Earl of Northumberland and Lord of Bamburgh, made his escape from the castle leaving his young bride in command of the defence. When he was at last captured and paraded before the walls of Bamburgh under threat of having his eyes torn out, his wife Matilda agreed to surrender to the king.

Over the next 100 years a new castle gradually developed, replacing the early wooden buildings and whatever stone walls there may have been. By the reign of Henry III the castle was well established over an area of five acres, and was a very much more secure and congenial place to live than at any earlier period.

The steep curving way, called in the Middle Ages the Vale Tipping, is today a well-maintained tarmac road essential for the many admirable uses to which the castle is now put. It leads on through the re-fashioned gatehouse to the top of the crag where the great mass of the Norman keep, the oldest and least altered part of the castle, confronts somewhat uneasily the new generation of residential buildings. The keep has itself been restored; its 18th-century windows and widened loopholes make it look unprepared for bombardment, but the plinth on which it stands is still solid enough to deter would-be attackers from nibbling away at it from underneath. The nail-studded door into the keep is curiously sited, for the entrance was usually set inaccessibly on the first floor and reached by an external staircase. Inside the walls, which vary in thickness from nine to 12 feet, is a deep ancient well mentioned in a chronicle of the 8th century, round which the keep must have been built. The basement was also probably used for hostages and prisoners—the Scottish king David Bruce among them in the Border Wars.

During these upheavals of the 13th century the stone walls stood up most successfully against cannon and bombardment. Later, in the Wars of the Roses, the castle fared less well. The Earl of Warwick, leading an army for Edward IV, brought to Bamburgh a new weapon and a dubious distinction—that of the first stronghold in England to be breached by gunfire. The two cannons, Newcastle and Dysion, by far the largest so far seen in the region, made a bigger hole in the walls than the occupants could have believed possible. Capitulation followed as a matter of course. Some may have considered it none too soon, since the garrison had already eaten all their horses.

The castle remained in a sorry state of disrepair until the 18th century, when Lord Crewe, Bishop of Durham, bought it from the Crown. He eventually left it to charity, and it came under the trusteeship of the Archdeacon of Northumberland, Dr John Sharp. The archdeacon not only spent much of his own money on restoration work, but also set up a model welfare community with cheap or free distribution of food to the poor, a hospital, a school, a library and the use of the castle windmill for grinding corn. Perhaps most to his credit, he set up a coastguard station for the warning and rescue of ships in distress, and gave over part of the castle for a rehabilitation centre for shipwrecked sailors. It was from Bamburgh that the first boat built for life-saving was tried out in 1786, and it would have pleased Dr Sharp to know that 40 years after his death Grace Darling was to make Bamburgh the scene of the most famous life-saving exploit in England's history.

Nail-studded doorway to the keep which is probably of a much later date than the original Norman stonework. See Colour Plate II

Berkeley GLOUCESTERSHIRE

Berkeleys have lived in this pastoral landscape since the middle of the 12th century—the only family to have lived for so many years in a castle of their own name. The castle, a patchwork of dappled grey and pinkish stone, somewhat mossy and sprouting red valerian, stretches along a small wooded escarpment and overlooks the luxuriant grazing of the water meadows to the south west. From this side there are magical views of the castle with wide grassy steps at its base, which become on closer approach remote terraces and hanging gardens high as unreachable shelves. Unlike many of the great castles such as Bamburgh, Harlech or Stirling, intended to command the countryside from the top of a crag, Berkeley Castle has been built on a graceful rather than imposing site. It is good hunting rather than fighting ground. Here Edward I granted Thomas, Lord Berkeley, the special privilege of hunting fox, hare, badger, and wild cat, with his own dogs—presumably the start of the famous Berkeley Hunt, now still distinguished from the others by the yellow rather than the pink coats of its hunt servants. The meadows, however, may also have provided a small extra defence, in that they could be flooded to protect the long southerly façade. The river is now much smaller, and there is no longer water in the immediate Berkeley landscape.

Little else has happened to alter the appearance of the castle since the 14th century. The Norman shell keep, probably replacing an earlier wooden structure, was built about 1156. It comprises a circular wall built round the base of the earlier walls, enclosing various buildings within a central courtyard. The floor of the courtyard is some 40 feet higher than the ground outside the walls—an arrangement quite unlike the other kind of keep, a single tower block on top of a hill. To this were added four semi-circular bastions, today no longer remaining—one was replaced by the 14th-century Thorpe Tower, another by the gatehouse, and the two others were incorporated into buildings inside the keep. Thomas, 3rd Lord Berkeley, undertook large-scale remodelling between 1340 and 1350, and in the inner bailey his 14th-century buildings, including the Great Hall, survive almost intact. This was in spite of a devastating attack by Parliamentary troops in the Civil War, when the castle surrendered after three days of siege and a break of some 35 feet was made in the west wall. Perhaps the long tenure of the castle by one family accounts for the faithful retention of the early fabric. Apart from a few windows which have appeared in the façade, and the inevitable alteration of details in the internal arrangements, the castle remains virtually unchanged. Even the breach in the walls remains as it was in 1649.

The Domesday Book records that the first tenant of Berkeley after the Conquest was Roger, who held the land in 1086 and took the name de Berkeley. He must have had some form of castle on the present site as Henry I spent Easter there in 1121. The descendant of Roger de Berkeley was dispossessed about 1152 and Berkeley was granted to Robert Fitzharding by Henry II in 1155, whom he confirmed as lord of Berkeley. A marriage was effected between this family and the earlier tenants, and thus the ownership of the castle seemed to be set fair for the rest of time. But if this marriage created a new family harmony, two later ones were to undo it.

The first crisis resulted when the younger brother of the first marquis married the daughter of a Bristol alderman, and the narrow-minded peer, appalled at the thought of a connection with the middle classes, settled his lands on the king rather than on his brother, the rightful heir. An alternative and perhaps more likely version of the story was that he sold the castle and inheritance to Henry VII in return for the marquisate, thus earning the name of Waste-All in the family chronicles. Fortunately for the Berkeleys their line continued longer than that of Henry VII and as there were no surviving male Tudors, they were able to claim back the castle on the death of Edward VI.

If there were doubts as to the suitability of the worthy alderman's daughter, the third famous Berkeley marriage must have shaken the county to its foundations. The 5th earl took up with an enchantingly pretty girl called Mary Cole, whose father was butcher and publican in nearby Wotton-under-Edge and whose portrait by Hoppner hangs today in the morning room of the castle. She may have grown up under the appreciative eye of her future lover, for there is a tradition at Wotton even today that the largest of the houses in the steep main street of this charming little market town was where the earls of Berkeley used to keep their mistresses. The couple proceeded to raise a family together, and when Mary Cole was pregnant with the fifth son, they married in Berkeley in 1796. Before his death the earl tried to establish the legitimacy of his first four sons by testifying to an earlier marriage with Mary at Lambeth, but as a result of the decision going against him the curious situation arose of the fifth son inheriting the earldom and the first son the castle. The eldest son tried to maintain that his possession of the castle gave him an automatic right to the title,

---

Norman shell keep, remodelled in the 14th century, its stonework since then surviving virtually intact; seen from the meadows to the south

The King's Gallery, the small room in the keep where Edward II was imprisoned. Right, *carved Italian doorway, entrance to the castle from the courtyard*

but the House of Lords found this unsubstantial and pronounced all peerages to consist of an hereditary and inalienable quality fixed in legitimate blood. This case and its judgment established the principle, and the Berkeleys took their place in English lawbooks. But it was not the first such distinction achieved by the family for they were already famous for having engaged in the longest lawsuit in English history. The daughter of Thomas, Lord Berkeley, an early supporter of women's rights, was so outraged at the thought that her inheritance must go instead to a nephew, that she sued, and thus started a family contest that lasted two centuries. Hostilities at times burst out of the courtroom into violent arms, and in 1470 even into a pitched battle at Nibley Green, in which Berkeley claimants from the two branches of the family actually killed each other, in what is thought to have been the last private battle in Britain.

In 1916 the elder line of the Berkeleys died out and once again the earl was in the castle, but only for a brief quarter of a century before that branch too came to an end. The inheritance of the castle devolved on a junior line which had separated from the main branch before the earldom was even granted, so the dilemma came to a natural end. As an ironic finish to all the disputes, the Berkeley who has legitimately inherited the most glamorous and aristocratic of English castles—has quite appropriately perhaps in the mid-20th century—no title at all.

The most famous single event in the castle's history concerns not marriage but murder. Such secrecy enveloped the arrival of Edward II at Berkeley Castle sometime in April 1327, and his death there in September of that year, that the precise circumstances of both events are unknown. After his deposition he remained some months at Kenilworth Castle, but his continuing presence in mild custody there remained a threat to the usurping government of his wife Isabella, and his removal to Berkeley was undoubtedly in order to bring about a swift but discreet death.

What is now known as the King's Gallery is the small room in the keep in which Edward was imprisoned, while subjected to all manner of deprivation, in the hope that he would die in a seemingly natural way. But he was physically strong, and he survived the initial assault, which was perhaps too sophisticated a device to overcome his robust constitution. Rotting animal carcases were thrown into a pit in the corner of his small room in the hope that the ensuing vapours would either infect or asphyxiate him. Some five months later he was still alive and his plight was becoming known to his sympathizers; it is even thought that an attempt to rescue him was made. For Isabella his immediate death had become imperative, and quite suddenly on 21 September 1327 it was officially announced that Edward of Caernarvon had died of natural causes. When Jean Froissart visited Berkeley Castle in 1366 he was told that Edward had died 'for someone cut his life short'. Those responsible were undoubtedly his jailors, Sir John Maltravers and Sir Thomas Gurney, but more mysterious is the manner of his despatch. A contemporary chronicle maintains that his death was a dire one, 'with a hoote brooche putte thro the secret place posterialle'. The apparent idea behind this macabre method of death—so lacking in outward marks of violence, so apt in its homosexual imagery—was merely to avoid detection. The more conventional means of poison or suffocation would have been equally effective and discreet, but less lurid, and it may be that the whole tradition of how Edward died derives more from popular fantasies of his perversion than from any historical reality.

Berry Pomeroy DEVONSHIRE

In the warm moist air of the Devon valleys the vegetation is lush and rampant, and the ivy prone to climb and cling to rough masonry. Photographs taken in the early part of this century show the castles in this county—Totnes, Restormel, Launceston—almost smothered to extinction by this grasping weed. Berry Pomeroy for many years defied the efforts of antiquarians eager to verify statements of their predecessors that once, under it all, beneath the leaves and roots, there were features of architectural distinction. But then this was a ruin with a particularly heavy overmantle. Even today, though cleared by its owners of the worst impertinencies of the vegetation, the forbidding authority of its great gate tower is somewhat lessened by the tufts of grass and sproutings of colour that burst deliciously from its flanking turrets. Without that characteristically spic-and-span appearance of its contemporaries in the care of the Department of the Environment, with their beautifully mown lawns and municipal seats, Berry Pomeroy retains an atmosphere more darkly evocative of the mystery that people once found in ruins.

Two families have lived in the castle. Ralph de Pomeroy appears in Domesday Book as owner of dozens of manors in the county. These, like his original castle on this site, have vanished, but it was he who first chose this inaccessible darkly-wooded knoll above a rivulet on its way to the Dart, leaving his descendants to consolidate the family holding by reconstructing it in stone during the 12th century and later. All those parts which can be called medieval stretch along the façade from the gatehouse to St

12th-century gateway leading to a great mansion, begun in Elizabethan times but now in ruins. Right, a detail of the mansion. See Colour Plate VI

Margaret's Tower, and were built by various members of the Pomeroy family. They lived the comparatively modest lives of prominent members of the Devon gentry (as opposed to the nobility), and could pursue a relatively settled existence for some 500 years.

Nevertheless the record survives of some dangerous moments for the family. Henry de Pomeroy, as a rebel against Richard I and supporter of John Lackland, accomplished the astonishing feat of seizing St Michael's Mount. He then died: one tradition says by suicide, specifying surgical bleeding or driving his blindfolded horse over a ravine as possible methods; another, less glamorous, claims that he died of fright at the approach of Richard Coeur de Lion. Sir Thomas, the last of the Pomeroys to inhabit the castle, mustered a force of 2,000 malcontents during the reign of Edward VI and besieged Exeter for a month. In defeat he narrowly escaped the dire punishment of being hanged, drawn and quartered at Tyburn. Soon the purchaser of his property in 1548, the Duke of Somerset and Lord Protector, would also find himself languishing in the Tower under sentence of death. In his case no reprieve came and he was executed in 1552. His heirs were only to enjoy the benefits of the new property for 100 years.

It was, however, during the period of their ownership that perhaps the most interesting and surprising development occurred to the appearance of the castle. Within the quadrangle of the ancient walls, they set about building a fine mansion typical of the ostentatious display of wealth so popular in the late 16th and early 17th centuries. Here at Berry the financial aspect seemed to present no problem, and the Seymours are said to have spent £20,000 on their building—a massive sum for the period, resulting in a mansion of such conspicuous opulence that in 1701 the Vicar of Berry Pomeroy wrote a reverentially amazed account of the former splendour of its alabaster statues, polished marble and other rich adornments. Unfortunately for the Seymours the place was never lived in the style they had intended. The Civil War interrupted work on the mansion when in the final stages of completion; further damage to the unfinished structure was done afterwards by the Parliamentarians, and although better days were in store for the Royalist families, the Seymours abandoned Berry in about 1688.

It is thought that towards the end of the 17th century a fearful thunderstorm set its roofs on fire, but this may well be a tale to match the dramatic beauty of its eerie frontage, with now only the sky showing through its many mullioned windows. Wind and rain would have worked more slowly the same desolation.

Bodiam EAST SUSSEX

In the late 14th century when the French were raiding at will in the English Channel and sweeping on glorious forays in and out of the south coast ports, Richard II was doing little to discourage them from thoughts of invasion and even another conquest. In 1377 they had sacked Rye, Yarmouth and Newport, and there was consternation along the south coast at the likelihood of their plunging further inland. Bodiam is in the valley of the Rother, which was in those days a bigger river and navigable this far by quite sizeable ships. Sir Edward Dalyngrigge, a well-known knight at Court and a veteran of Edward III's wars abroad, was aware of the danger and applied for a licence to crenellate the mansion of Bodiam inherited by his wife. Permission was granted on the understanding that the castle would protect the immediate countryside from an invading enemy. It may be that this important proviso enabled Sir Edward to interpret 'crenellation' in a very broad sense, for the existing manor was abandoned and a new site chosen nearby half way up the slope of a hill. Thus Bodiam came to be one of the few examples of permission given to a private citizen to build a castle of his own.

Several castles, such as the Edwardian strongholds of Wales, had already been built at a single date and in a single style, and it seems that Sir Edward took as a model the French ones he must have seen as a soldier, just as Edward I had done 100 years before. But although externally Bodiam reflects the style of earlier buildings with its symmetry of walls and towers, the inside is a departure into something much more sophisticated—a properly designed fortified court-yard house with splendid private suites, separate servants' quarters, chapel and other amenities remarkable for their number and extent. Lord Curzon, the last of its private owners and the man who gave it to the National Trust, managed to count 33 fireplaces and 28 lavatories built into the walls, all with drainage into the moat. The builder of the castle also designed a complicated approach to it as an additional ingenious defence. The main entrance is now reached along a modern causeway with an octagonal island in the middle of its length, like a pretty stepping stone, apparently there only to adorn the lake. Originally, however, the approach to the castle was at right-angles to the main gate along a wooden bridge. Thus an advancing enemy would be exposed on his unshielded right flank all the way to the octagonal fortified island in the middle of the moat before he could turn the corner and proceed across a draw-bridge to the barbican. This was also on an island and consisted of a strongly fortified tower with guard rooms, and a further system of bridges to the castle itself—altogether three portcullises, three draw-

bridges, two fortified bastions and three doors, a unique multiplication of defences. On the opposite side of the castle there were almost equally elaborate devices.

Another particular feature of the design was in the arrangement of the living quarters. The new gangs of hired mercenaries with which the noble had to make do, instead of calling on old ranks of feudal retainers, were obviously as dangerous as the gunpowder they handled. It was thought preferable to isolate them in their own quarters, and in Bodiam these could be sealed off at a few controllable entrances in case the hired soldiery turned violent. There was no communicating door through to the adjacent rooms of the lord and his family, nor one to the gatehouse at the other end. This precaution had the added advantage of minimizing the risk of an accidental fire spreading. As a further safeguard the gatehouse and water supply were under the owner's control.

These splendid theories of defence were never really put to the test. Bodiam today is a ruin, but not because it was ever destroyed by siege. It was attacked twice, once in 1484, and once in 1643 by Parliamentary troops. It would seem that the castle surrendered without much ado on both occasions, as the walls were not breached. The castle was incapable of being defended against the heavy cannon that was then beginning to be used—its walls were thin and tall and not of the immense thickness of later forts. The only attempt to prepare for this modern kind of warfare seems to have been the adaptation of existing arrow-slits by inserting portholes for guns beneath them. The guns, however, would only have been of a small kind.

The Parliamentary forces were ordered to dismantle it and the moveable materials were presumably sold. The castle remained in a picturesque state of dilapidation, the perfect 18th-century ruin, until it was partially recovered by Cubitt in the late 19th century. Lord Curzon bought it in 1917 and with immense energy and academic seriousness undertook its restoration, even to the extent of draining the moat for structural work on the foundations. The ivy, undergrowth and weeds were eliminated; trees were removed from the crevices of the masonry and planted in more appropriate places to form parkland which surrounds the castle today.

This beautiful 14th-century moated castle was carefully restored by Lord Curzon in the early 20th century. Right above, *seen from across the moat;* below left, *the main portcullis and* right, *aerial view showing the elaborate fortification plan*

Carisbrooke ISLE OF WIGHT

When King Charles I fled from the army at Hampton Court his intention was to sail via Portsmouth Harbour to Jersey, trusting the brother of his chaplain to help him in the undertaking. But his faith proved ill-founded for instead Colonel Hammond conducted him to his own castle at Carisbrooke where the king's confinement, after two ill-managed attempts to escape, soon became as rigorous as at Hampton Court. The room where the king stayed is thought to have been in the Governor's House at the south end on the first floor. Presumably his two children who were brought to Carisbrooke were also kept here. On one occasion the king's remarkable self-confidence and lack of imagination led him to announce to his rescuers that he could certainly insert himself through the bars of his window, for he had tested the size of the opening with his head, and that wherever this could pass his body would undoubtedly follow. It was in the event only after fearful exertion that he managed to dislodge his crest-fallen person from the unyielding grille.

These were the last dramatic events to colour the castle's history—a longer one than most, for the stone wall visible in the steep earthen bank suggests a late Roman origin. Little is known of its pre-Norman history except that the Jutes settled in the island and presumably took over the Roman fort, and that the West Saxons took it from them in the late 7th century. The earthworks of the present castle belong to the end of the 11th and early 12th centuries, but none of the domestic buildings of the original Norman castle still exist. The great dominating feature of the gatehouse with its drum towers dates partly from the 14th century and partly from the 15th. At both periods there was grave alarm in the island at the possibility of foreign invasion. In 1377 the French landed but the castle was not taken. Again in the reign of Elizabeth I the south coast was alerted to the threat from Spain, but the nearby battle against the Armada turned away any subsequent danger. The castle was nevertheless considerably altered to resist the new artillery. An eminent Italian engineer, Federigo Gianibelli, was commissioned to build outer lines of defence, enclosing the old castle, and to his design the curtain walls, bastions and bulwarks were built—all still in very good condition. No further structural additions were made to the castle, other than modernizations. It remained the occasional residence of the governor of the island until Princess Beatrice, the youngest daughter of Queen Victoria, succeeded her husband as governor and lived there.

*A Norman castle whose earthworks incorporate part
of a Roman stone wall. This 14th-century gatehouse
has ports for hand-guns in its upper storey*

Clifford's Tower   NORTH YORKSHIRE

When in the year 306 Constantine the Great was proclaimed emperor in the fortress town of Eboracum, the Roman legions might well have seen fit to change its name to something more celebratory and appropriate to the occasion. The present city of York might even now be known by the splendid name of Constantinople, or some Roman equivalent. In the event there remains little of Rome's past in the city except two stone towers, marking its former western and eastern extremities.

Instead it was the Danes who established a more lasting reminder of their presence here, for not only do many of the street names date from this period, but the word 'York' itself derives directly from the Danish 'Yorvick'. Facing each other across the river Ouse near Skeldersgate Bridge the great earth mounds of William I's two castles still recall the grim days when the Danes were challenged by the Normans for possession of this valuable strategic centre at the junction of two rivers. The Danes, since their capture of York in 867, had provided useful and welcome trading links with Scandinavia, and the local population was loth to see them replaced by an unknown and reputedly ruthless enemy from France. In 1069, the year after William had built his first wooden tower to dominate the city, he visited the north again; and in response apparently to the hostile and turbulent atmosphere with which he was met, he immediately ordered the erection of a second castle to reinforce the authority of the first. Part of the city was demolished and York's other river, the Foss, was dammed to provide the necessary moats for the defence of the castles—thus a great artificial lake was created complete with water mills and fish, and known as the King's Pool. These elaborate precautions served only to provoke the Danes, for within the year they had entered the Humber estuary and were sailing towards York. The enthusiastic townspeople rose to support them and promptly dismantled the hated Norman towers. They were rebuilt, but again in wood rather than stone.

It may have been during the next century that the eastern tower, known since the 17th century as Clifford's Tower, developed into the more prominent fortification. It was here that the Jewish population of York congregated in 1190 to escape the harrassment of a violent mob, but the riot ended in a fearful holocaust and the tower was burnt down. Again it was rebuilt on an even higher mound and again destroyed, this time by the great gale of 1228. A record exists of the sheriff paying out two shillings for the gathering up of all the scattered timbers, but this time they were not put back and in 1237 the castle could still be described as 'prostratum'.

So it remained until the summer of 1244, when Henry III visited York and commissioned two eminent craftsmen to undertake its reconstruction. Over the next years Master Simon the carpenter and Master Henry the mason set up a fine keep of magnesian limestone at the considerable cost of £2,600. Its shape was quatrefoil, a design common in France rather than England—where the conventional plan was either round or rectangular. A fore-building was set between two of the great curves to contain the entrance with portcullis and heavy doors, and a wooden staircase rose up the side of the mound, much like today's modern flight of 55 steps. It was probably during the course of these works that a stone wall was built round the large bailey to the south-east of the keep. Once completed it stood fortified with about five stone towers and two gateways—altogether a magnificent complex that was to survive practically unaltered throughout the 14th and 15th centuries.

During Edward I's Scottish campaigns York assumed a role of great importance, for it virtually became the temporary capital of the country: the royal courts and exchequer accommodated themselves in buildings inside the castle bailey, and it was here too that the town assizes took place. After the death of Edward II the exchequer returned to Westminster and the castle's main function was thus removed. It lay abandoned, used once by Queen Isabella but thereafter spurned as a royal residence, for the monarchs preferred to stay in more modern accommodation in the nearby archbishop's palace. Though the keep and walls needed constant maintenance and attention, all available funds were consistently absorbed into the more urgent work of repairing the dam and its mills. By 1360 the walls of the keep were reported to have cracked from top to bottom in two places—an inevitable hazard in building such a heavy stone structure on an artificial mound—yet nothing effective was done to stop the slipping, sagging masonry from collapsing into the moat. Just before the Battle of Bosworth Field it was hastily dismantled for reconstruction, but Henry VII on his accession to the throne in 1485 never took up the work planned by his predecessors. Further and more effective demolition was caused in 1596 by a predatory gaoler, who managed to remove and sell a good part of the internal stonework before being apprehended. Somehow the decrepit masonry was encouraged to hold together for the duration of the Civil War. It was fortified and garrisoned for the king, and subsequently bombarded into surrender in 1644. After the restoration of Charles II in 1660 the damaged fore-building was replaced, and the royal arms and those of the Clifford family were placed in panels over the en-

On the mound set up by William I, the stonework of the keep dates from the 13th century. The present entrance was built in the 17th century and the staircase is modern

trance. It was at this date that the tower received its present name, though unofficially its association with the Cliffords had remained a strong memory since 1322 when the body of the Lancastrian leader, Sir Robert Clifford, was hung in chains from the top of the ramparts. The split and tilting fabric of the tower suffered its last assault in 1684, when a resident garrison appears to have set fire to their quarters, presumably in the hope of receiving something better.

The castle bailey has been perfectly preserved in outline by three magnificent 18th-century buildings. On the far side from Clifford's Tower is the Debtors' Prison, and to its left and right the assize courts and female prison—an open-sided quadrangle, with Ionic columns and loggia echoing cupola and clock-tower opposite and together forming one of the most interesting and monumental civic compositions in the country.

IV Windsor, Berkshire

Round Tower, probably built in stone by William I about 1075, extensively remodelled in 1175 by Henry II and finally heightened in the 1820s by Sir Jeffrey Wyatville. *See* p. 130.

V Acton Burnell, Salop

Edward I's bishop of Bath and Wells and favourite chancellor, Robert Burnell, received from the king a licence to crenellate in 1284. Acton, the small Shropshire manor where for a century the Burnells had lived as minor landholders, flowered briefly into quite a grand estate. The chancellor's manor is a simple, elegant building of red sandstone. A central two-storey block contained all the principal rooms. Projecting towers at the corners provided stairways, service rooms and a chapel.

By 1420 the male Burnell line had died out and the building was left uninhabited and became ruinous. Although it passed into the hands of various other owners, the house retained in its name the original association with the Burnell family.

VI Berry Pomeroy, Devonshire

Founded by the Pomeroys who came over with William the Conqueror, in 1066, the castle was reconstructed in stone during the 12th century and later. Damaged by the Parliamentarians during the Civil War and then by fire, it was finally abandoned by its owners, the Seymours, in 1688 and left to its fate, becoming an eerie and romantic ruin. *See* p. 52.

VII Eastnor,
Hereford and Worcester

Built for the Earl of Somers in 1812, the family ·
assembled a fine array of eminent 19th-century
architects and designers to embellish this medieval-
style castle. A. W. N. Pugin designed the Gothic
drawing-room. *See* p. 78.

Colchester ESSEX

When Boadicea and her people the Iceni arrived at the gates of Camulodunum, they came upon a city apparently echoing with fearful portents and already proclaiming its own imminent destruction. Tacitus writes a lively account of how unearthly cries and other wailings were heard, and, most shocking of all, the statue of Victory in the Temple of Claudius fell down. It was to this temple that many of the citizens fled while the Britons sacked the town, but this too was eventually stormed and burnt. Marks of the conflagration remain today in the temple's foundations, carefully preserved by the masonry of the next great structure which 1,000 years later grew up on the same site. The vast size of the Norman keep of Colchester (152 feet long × 111 feet wide), bigger than any other in Europe, can probably be attributed to the fact that it is built round the platform of the Roman temple—a ready-made foundation to support the immensely thick walls that the Normans liked to build. Colchester was also a particularly suitable site for a major Norman fortress, for in Saxon times it had recovered some of its former Roman importance as a strategic and commercial port on the East Anglian coast.

The exact date of the erection of the keep is not known, but it is associated with Gundulf, Bishop of Rochester, William I's great builder-priest to whom the construction of the Tower of London and Rochester castle is attributed. Work is thought to have started in about 1080. With plentiful supplies of Roman stone available building probably progressed quite fast, and by 1085—when the King of Denmark was known to be planning an attack—the walls may have stood high enough to be fortified with battlements. As it turned out, the Danes never came; and

work could be resumed, raising the building to an impressive height of three or more storeys. The early battlements can still be seen some way up the face of the outside walls.

By 1101—when Henry I issued a charter granting to Eudo the Steward 'the city of Colchester, and the tower and the castle and all the fortifications of the city, as my father had them and my brother and myself'—the keep with its inner and outer baileys, ditches and ramparts was probably complete. Thereafter the castle remained as the gift of the monarch in the hands of successive stewards, an arrangement which led to some swift changes of ownership in the baronial wars. In 1215 it was occupied by the troops of King Philip of France, sent to assist the barons' cause. In the following year this led to a bitter and successful siege waged by King John in person. But the French proved hard to discourage and not till the accession of Henry III in 1216 did they finally withdraw.

As might be expected the castle was too sombre a place to hold many attractions as a royal residence, and as a prison it inevitably played a humbler role than its much grander neighbour further down the coast, for most captives of distinction or power ended their days at the Tower of London, and it was usually only the common felons and local pirates who found their way into the gaol at Colchester. But in the 16th and 17th centuries, when religious persecution was at its height, this castle in no way fell behind in providing its share of martyrs, nor were the conditions of its prisons a whit less revolting than those found in London.

The present building is much lower than it once was, though not as a result of violence or warfare. After the Civil War, in which the whole town of Colchester sustained a twelve-week siege by Cromwell's troops, the castle appears not to have received the usual dismantling of the battlements; the Royalist officers on the other hand were savagely punished, and two of the three were shot in the castle bailey, where there is now a commemorative obelisk. Some years later, in 1683, there came to the castle keep the greatest threat in the whole of its quiet history. A certain John Wheeley bought the building for the sake of its raw materials and proceeded to pull it down. Fortunately the task proved harder than anticipated and only the top part of the keep could be removed. It then passed through various hands until the mid-19th century when Charles Gray, a lawyer and antiquarian, fostered local interest in the neglected building. Over the next century it gradually became established as a museum, and in 1931, as if to confirm it in this worthy purpose, the main building was roofed in and galleries were built to display Colchester's collection of Roman and British antiquities.

The 11th-century Norman keep, the largest in England, narrowly escaped demolition in the 17th century. It is now used as a museum

Conisbrough SOUTH YORKSHIRE

This 12th-century castle was one of the first to have a non-rectangular keep; its massive buttresses rise to a height of 86 feet

When Ivanhoe and Richard Coeur-de-Lion arrived at the 'rude yet stately building of Conisborough', it was to witness the improbable raising of Athelstane from the dead, an outrageous turn of events suggested to Sir Walter Scott by his printer's grief at the character's untimely death. Scott was clearly very much captivated by his first vision of the castle: 'there are few more beautiful or striking scenes in England than are presented by the vicinity of this ancient Saxon fortress'. A Saxon fortress for his Saxon thane—but again Sir Walter is in the realms of fantasy, for although the name Conisbrough may well be a modern version of the Saxon *Cyningesburh*, meaning king's *burh* or defended site, yet the superbly finished masonry of the castle's ashlar walls is clearly the work of its later Norman owners.

In Domesday Book Conisbrough formed part of the vast lands held by William de Warenne, 1st Earl of Surrey, and builder of the castle at Lewes. Whether he erected the great earthworks on which Conisbrough stands, or simply inherited an existing earth and timber defence of his Saxon predecessors, is not known. At Lewes he had built in stone. Here, it seems, he contented himself with wood, for the castle was most probably converted to stone only in the latter years of the 12th century by the half-brother of Henry II, Hamelin Plantagenet.

The castle is of a most interesting and unusual design. After the first great rectangular keeps of the early Norman years in this country, a second generation of towers sprang up, not square but round, where the assailant could find no easy edges for his pick or battering ram. Conisbrough belongs to this second type, and is probably the first such structure to be built in England. Perhaps its designers hesitated in their total commitment to a new cylindrical form, for six wedge-shaped buttresses protrude from the exterior like cogs on a wheel. They appear to serve no real practical purpose, for all are solid except for one into which a small chapel is set. The base of the keep all round is splayed out for extra stability and to cause stones dropped from the top of the walls to ricochet out at the enemy. Partially enclosing the keep, a roughly semi-circular bailey is contained within a 35-foot-high curtain wall, again strongly splayed out at its base, and again supported with solid towers. Here the projecting towers would be of enormous value on the great stretches of wall, enabling the garrison to cover the enemy below with the minimum of risk. This again is perhaps the earliest such use of round towers in the country.

Only three of the wall's buttresses remain, and the original gates and bridge no longer exist, but the castle is considerably less ruinous than it might have been. It played no part in the Civil War, for its decay in Tudor times was already so far advanced that its possibilities as a stronghold were thereafter ignored.

Corfe DORSET

The large placid village of Corfe Castle with its many stone roofs lies peaceful enough today, a quiet survivor after the deadly explosions that once shattered the summit of the hill above and sent tumbling down its slopes in fearful cascades the towers and turrets of Corfe's magnificent castle. Of all the devastations of the Civil War there was none other so wilful or so effective. Normally the 'slighting' of a Royalist stronghold consisted of dismantling the fortifications and sometimes breaching a wall. Very often the castle remained habitable. In the case of Corfe something quite different occurred. On 5 March 1646 Parliament voted that Corfe Castle should be 'demolished'. The building was first thoroughly plundered and then reduced to its present ruin by a hefty combination of gunpowder and mines. Many other castles were equally stubborn in their loyal support of the king, but at Donnington and others the garrisons had marched out with full military honours in recognition of their bravery. The vindictive anger felt by the Parliamentarians against Corfe is curious, except that there were certain unusual circumstances which perhaps distinguished its two sieges from those against other castles. On the first occasion in 1643 it was Lady Bankes who defended the castle in her husband's absence, and stood so resolutely obstructive in the face of all the enemy's engines of war (a contemporary document lists such varied equipment as scaling ladders, culverin, demi-cannon, two sakers and a certain Boar and Sow) that the 500 assailants fell back ingloriously having lost one-fifth of their number. The second siege in 1646 was wisely timed when Lady Bankes was in London. It was nonetheless again stoutly resisted. This time the enemy resorted to treachery, and infiltrated the garrison with a seemingly friendly body of troops who later admitted the besiegers. Whether made vindictive by the lady's heroism or their own response to it, they left little behind them of this great royal fortress—once said to be the strongest castle in England.

Heroism apart, the 13th century was perhaps the time of Corfe's greatest splendour. King John considered it his favourite residence and spent over £1,400 on improving the royal accommodation and the defences. Within the inner bailey immediately to the east of Henry I's keep, he built a fine unfortified complex of hall, chapel and domestic offices, known as the Gloriette. Henry III spent a further £1,000 on additional walls and towers, including two gatehouses, and whitewashed the exterior masonry—an improvement which he also carried out at the Tower of London. Edward I was to complete his father's fortifications. The castle continued through successive reigns as the important administrative centre of the whole of the royal domain of Purbeck, and the constable's absolute authority in the area ensured a most satisfactory inflow of tithes and other loyal payments in kind to provide for the king, his household and their well-laden tables. The castle's other notable function was as a state prison for important enemies of the monarch, and it acquired a gloomy image as the place where King John starved to death 22 knights from Anjou and Poitiers. Its reputation was apt for the secondary role which it played in another horrific event in the annals of English castles. It was a staging post on the final journey of Edward II to Berkeley.

Corfe Castle was the favourite residence of King John and was once thought to be the strongest in England; it was blown up in 1646 during the Civil War

Donnington BERKSHIRE

William Camden, the first man in England to make a comprehensive topographical survey, found Donnington 'a small but very neat castle, seated on the banks of a woody hill, having a fair prospect and windows in all sides very lightsome'. But that was in 1586, when the castle was still only 200 years old, and before the great mortars of the Roundheads finally reduced it almost to its foundations in one of the most remarkable of 17th-century sieges. The tall and beautiful gatehouse, which stood midway on the east wall of what was once a roughly rectangular enclosure, is now all that remains of this late 14th-century castle. Like other castles of its period it was built primarily as a fortified residence—designed to deter raiders and other dangerous small enemies—but otherwise was not a building of any great strength. Its last resident owner, a Mr John Packer, found it easily snatched from him by a party of Royalists at the start of the Civil War.

When in 1643 Colonel John Boys was entrusted with the castle by Charles I, its tall elegant walls must have seemed eggshell security to a military man and quite unsuitable to withstand cannon. He promptly set about constructing an outer defence with great star-shaped projections, in keeping with the latest thoughts on fortification in Italy and the Low Countries where the fashion for round bastions had been superseded, and the new sharply-angled walls were found to offer maximum coverage of those without and minimum exposure of those inside. By 1644 Donnington was superbly fortified, and with some justification; for it sat, like a tethered hound, where the London to Bath road intersected the route from Southampton to Northampton, thus forcing an enemy on the high road either to take action or give it a wide berth.

Its long siege started in July of that year with the usual polite exchange of letters, testing the resolution of both sides. There then followed, over the next 20 months, an amazing series of bombardments by the Parliamentarians and astounding sallies from the castle by Colonel Boys and his men. King Charles himself on two occasions effected a relief, but it seems that he was more impressed by the castle's loyalty and dogged determination than by its material security, for he collected his crown and treasure which he had previously left there, and moved on elsewhere 'to refresh his men for the ill lodging they had endured at Donnington'.

Soon the castle was in a sorry state with four of its towers in ruins and one of its wells poisoned by the besiegers. The incident of the well offers a curious insight into siege etiquette, for Cromwell's commander immediately gave notice to Colonel Boys of his ungentlemanly action and seems to have allowed the castle's garrison to clean the well without firing on them. Colonel Boys, by now knighted as Sir John, quite rightly commanded the immense admiration of his enemies, for whom it had become a matter of prestige to reduce the castle only by assault. Parliament in 1646 thought fit to vote the sum of £6,600 for this task, although the castle was already largely demolished, and a mighty force was sent bearing with it a 15-inch mortar. Donnington was finally reduced in 1646. Sir John was allowed to communicate with his king, whose cause was by then lost and who advised speedy negotiation. Honourable conditions for the garrison were obtained. They marched out with full honours, and the unfortunate Mr John Packer was free to reclaim the shattered remains of his former home.

Destroyed by mortars in the Civil War, the ruined gatehouse is the only surviving part of this late 14th-century castle

Dover KENT

Above, *the Constable's Gate, c. 1227, main entrance to the castle;* right, *the keep and outer defences on the west side of the castle*

For nearly 2,000 years would-be invaders of England have been confronted by a strong fortification on the high cliffs above Dover. It is quite likely that the outer bank and ditch of the present castle were already in existence as part of an iron-age hill fort when the Romans arrived, and that they built within it their pharos or lighthouse, originally a flint-rubble tower some 80 feet high. Very little is known about precise details of fortification in Saxon times, but the church of St Mary-in-Castro by the side of the lighthouse dates from the late 10th or early 11th century, and must have been built as a chapel for the castle garrison. Certainly a reference to the castle is made in the Anglo-Saxon Chronicle when Eustace, Earl of Boulogne, attacked it and was driven off with great loss. No other fortification in Britain has such a long recorded history, nor occupied such a central position in the country's line of defences against Europe. It is significant that this castle was mentioned as a prize possession by Earl Harold in his supposed oath of allegiance to Duke William, and it was here that the Normans proceeded immediately after the Battle of Hastings, to spend eight days strengthening what was to be a key fortification for nearly 1,000 years. William entrusted his royal castle to his half-brother, the militant Bishop Odo of Bayeux, and to Hugh of Montfort. Since then the list of constables in charge of it includes many prominent names—princes (Henry V, Henry VIII, James II and George V, before their accession to the throne) and distinguished subjects such as William Pitt, the Duke of Wellington, Lord Palmerston and from 1941 until 1965 Sir Winston Churchill.

At the time when the castle was held for King John by Hubert de Burgh, the single most dramatic event in its history occurred. Prince Louis, heir to the throne of France, arrived in England, having been invited by a number of English barons to overthrow their king and seize the Crown. He laid siege to Dover Castle, a position of prime importance, described at the time as the 'key of England'. But the target was a formidable one and seemingly impregnable. Its defences were then the most up-to-date in the country and an unprecedented amount of money had been spent on their erection. Henry II had embarked on a complete reconstruction, carried out between 1168 and 1188, costing the prodigious sum of £6,000 which had provided the castle with three important new features—the towered walls of the present inner bailey, the beginning of an outer wall, an early precursor of Edward I's famous concentric fortification, and, most important of all, the great square keep, one of the strongest and largest of its kind in the country in the 12th century. His son Richard had continued the expensive work, though most of the spare revenue in his lifetime was lavished on his even more magnificent Normandy castle at Les Andelys and finally King John, after his French losses, had spent a further £1,000. The army of Prince Louis was thus confronted by a castle, unrivalled in its finished strength and splendour, but the result of the siege was disturbing. Despite a gallant defence by Hubert de Burgh, the invaders were able to seize the barbican and undermine the gate itself, the east tower of which collapsed. The breach was repaired with wood, but the French would certainly have soon penetrated the inner ward. Fortunately for the besieged garrison the life of King John, who was at that time heading northwards with the royal treasure, came to an unmourned end, after a surfeit of peaches and cider in Newark Castle. His son, Henry III, had the backing of the Church and a number of influential barons, as well as the continuing loyalty of the castle at Dover, a factor of vital importance. In the face of this new unity the wider aims of Prince Louis seemed likely to be thwarted. He wisely retreated to France.

Clearly the castle's defences were not as strong or as modern as had been imagined, and during the reign of Henry III a further £7,500 were spent in an attempt to make the structure more solid. By about 1256 the castle had reached its maximum strength and size. Its unusually great number of towers were for the most part completed, and an interesting underground passage was constructed through the chalk rock to provide a covered access for the garrison to the furthest outwork. The splendid Constable's Gate had replaced in about 1227 an earlier gateway, and it is here that the various constables have had their official residence while ostensibly safeguarding the all-important entrance.

It is perhaps not surprising that the subsequent history of this bristling stronghold was comparatively quiet in Plantagenet and Tudor times. Edward I came here briefly before his accession as a prisoner of the barons, and then again in 1274 as a royal crusader returning from the Holy Land. Some Tudor fortifications were added, but otherwise its history was uneventful until it was seized in a surprise attack by a small party of Parliamentarians at the outbreak of the Civil War in 1642. It remained in Cromwell's hands until the Restoration, and thus escaped the usual slighting which caused the ruin of most of England's castles.

It has, however, suffered certain drastic alterations since the 18th century, particularly at the time of the Napoleonic wars which were causing general alarm along the south coast. Ditches were deepened and earth ramparts were formed behind the walls: today great trees spread out from this heightened ground, dwarfing the mutilated vestiges of the towers of the outer curtain wall, most of which were cut down to provide suitable platforms for artillery. In this new form the castle was expected to hold fast for 14 days after the landing of an enemy, but fortunately this claim was never put to the test. Even in the modern period the threat of invasion from the sea has necessitated the maintenance of these fortifications, and the bastions were rebuilt as recently as World War II, so that heavy guns could be mounted over the harbour. Thus Dover ever remains the mailed fist which England shows to the Continent, but one which has rarely needed to be used against a foreign invader.

Dunster SOMERSET

'William of Mohun holds Torre, and there is his castle', records Domesday Book. Nothing of this early keep on the hill of Torre at Dunster has survived except for a portion of curtain wall, but the gatehouse which the Mohuns built in the 13th century remains today almost intact, and a descendant of their family lives on in the castle. The Mohuns sold it in 1404 to the Luttrells, whose male line continued unbroken until 1737 when the estate was left to a daughter. The Mr Henry Fownes whom she married, however, was descended—by a happy genealogical accident—from the original Mohuns. He merely added the name of Luttrell to his own. Thus the continuity of tenure represented by the present descendants of the two families is unrivalled in Britain.

Dunster, stands forth, like Berkeley, on a wooded escarpment, clustered round by patterns and hues of elegant trees, whose mottling of greens and seasonal variants of flame and copper enhances the pale graceful silhouette rising from their midst. The castle dominates a neatly concealed little town, with its approach along a wide main street of dainty Elizabethan houses and past the octagonal market hall built by George Luttrell in the 17th century. To the right is the Norman church, with monuments to the many Luttrells who lie buried there.

The final entrance is through an early 15th-century gatehouse to the north-west. The façade of the inner castle, like many of the houses in the town, is largely Elizabethan; indeed the main front of the residential buildings was the work of George Luttrell in 1589, with only traces of the medieval masonry remaining. Entering the main door and proceeding from the outer to the inner hall, and thence to the dining-room, the continuity of the Luttrell presence is emphasized by the prodigious number of portraits. These elegantly-clothed persons look down calmly on the architectural changes which their long line of descendants has worked on this family seat. Amongst them is a picture by Eworth of remarkable interest and beauty. Sir John Luttrell, who died in 1551, wades naked through the waves of a stormy sea. Behind him is his wrecked ship flailed by the tempest, to the side floats a drowned companion, and above him in a solidly-built cloud a diminutive Peace comes to his rescue. Sir John was taken prisoner by the Scots in 1550, and the English Government paid the large sum of £400 for his ransom—a tribute which the family quite rightly wished to celebrate.

Dunster's history, like that of its owners, has been a comparatively peaceful one. The handsome Sir John of the portrait died of a 'sweating sickness', (not apparently an ill-effect from the shipwreck) and the Luttrells lying in the neighbouring church were not sent to the Tower, or executed for treason. The castle's only major crisis was, as for so many, the Civil War. It first resisted the Royalists in 1642, then was held as a garrison for them until 1645, the last in the county to contain the king's troops. When Colonel Wyndham finally surrendered the castle and his six guns to the Parliamentarians it was after a siege of 150 days and the loss of 20 men. The Luttrells might have paid dearly for this Royalist allegiance, and orders were sent for the castle to be demolished. Happily they were not carried out, nor was it even slighted beyond the dismantling of the battlements. Instead it was merely garrisoned for five years by Parliamentary troops before the Luttrells were able, on payment of a fine, to take up once more their residence.

The earliest surviving building of this originally Norman castle dates from the 13th century. The main portion is Elizabethan, much restored by Salvin in the 19th century. Right, Sir John Luttrell, portrait by Hans Eworth, 1550

Thereafter the Luttrells set about energetically renovating and improving the comfort of their home. Certain drastic changes took place in the 19th century, when the architect Salvin was employed to embellish it inside and out. A new tower was added and other structural alterations were made to the walls, so that many of the windows now have that romantic Gothic appearance fashionable with the Victorians. Its appearance today is less ancient than that of Berkeley and its history is not so famous, yet in one respect Dunster, in its own quiet way, outdoes Berkeley by nearly a century—the descendants of its Domesday Book owners still live on in the castle.

Durham COUNTY DURHAM

The holiness of St Cuthbert and the memory of his community of monks, wandering uncertainly through the north-east of England with their saint's body, still lives on in the present-day city of Durham. That they finally chose this great rocky peninsula as the safe and permanent sanctuary for their precious burden lent fame and religious importance to the site, giving such prestige to the Bishop of Durham that even today—by immemorial precedent—he stands at the right hand of the sovereign at the coronation.

This early spartan community would have been astonished by the glories and political power that the later ecclesiastics of the city were to acquire. In 1092 Bishop William of St Calais began to build the present cathedral and the monks of St Cuthbert were re-established as Benedictines. Meanwhile the Normans had also replaced whatever Saxon fortifications they found beside the cathedral, on the site of the present castle, and the Bishop of Durham was invested with charge of the new stronghold. It suited the king remarkably well to have this strategic fortress in the hands of a bishop rather than a baron, for the bishopric was non-hereditary. In recognition of the importance of its loyalty the king lavished great privileges on the see.

Durham became a palatinate, and the prince bishops had full administrative rights within their bishopric and along its coast. In return for this absolute power over their own territory, the bishops of Durham were expected to levy an army and even to ride out at its head, particularly if there were any threat of the Scots moving south. From these remarkable twin strongholds of spiritual and temporal power, built side by side over the river gorge, the arm of the Church Militant held sway over a most crucial length of the invasion route between the two countries.

Little survives of this early Norman castle except for the chapel and part of the undercroft of the Great Hall, but the general layout of the keep, with its spreading courtyard, still follows the original pattern. Once through the gatehouse the buildings of the various bishops extend ahead and around, each rivalling its neighbour in craftsmanship. On the walls, over the doorways, in whatever conspicuous place could be found, the prelates left their mark. Like an artist singing his work, each of the later bishops carved his personal coat of arms in the stone, though in most cases after doing no more than renovate or restore the work of predecessors. Bishop Fox proclaims his own merits (after adapting the Great Hall in 1499) with a pelican piercing her breast to feed her young with her own blood. Nathaniel, Lord Crewe, outdoes them all in the 17th century by surmounting his arms with coronet as well as mitre. In spite of this extravagant attention to the embellishment of their castle, the bishops nevertheless found time to maintain its strength as a centre of military operations, for there is no record of it ever having been taken by force.

During the Reformation the bishops lost some of their political powers, and the military importance of the castle dwindled away on the union of Scotland and England. The last substantial architectural additions were made after the Civil War, and thereafter it passed through the hands of successive bishops as a most comfortable and well-appointed palace. The changes in episcopal life-style were finally acknowledged when William van Mildert, the last prince bishop of Durham, gave it to the newly-founded university as a residential college. Bishop Hatfield's keep was almost totally reconstructed and much other adaptation of the old buildings took place.

In the 1930s a vast rescue operation was set in motion to underpin the subsiding foundations. The early monks had been more felicitous in their choice of site for the cathedral, for it rests in good biblical style on solid bedrock. The castle it seems had been foolishly built on more treacherous, shifting ground. Its imminent collapse was fortunately prevented, and it remains today high on its promontory alongside the cathedral. Together they represent, however much patched, propped and refaced, the splendid surviving nucleus of a medieval city.

The hall keep of Durham Castle which stands above the River Wear. Originally built by the Norman prince bishops of Durham, alterations were made until the mid-17th century

Eastnor HEREFORD AND WORCESTER

Above *and* right, *two aspects of this mock-medieval castle built in the 19th century.* See *Colour Plate VII*

In the mid-19th century the 3rd Lord Somers, who travelled extensively on the Continent, brought back rare shrubs and trees for his family home, Eastnor Castle, which have now grown massive and lush, improving the severity of its large grey unweathered stones. The castle was built by the 2nd Earl of Somers, starting in 1812 during the Napoleonic Wars at a time when many were making similarly exuberant architectural gestures, and Regency villas were the fashion. Lord Somers was more ambitious than most in commissioning Sir Robert Smirke, R.A., already famous as the architect of Covent Garden, to build him something similarly theatrical, and he designed the mansion as a replica of a medieval castle. Smirke progressed from grand to grandiose and in 1822 built the British Museum in the style of a Greek temple.

Mules were found to bring the stones from the Forest of Dean at the reputed cost of £12,000: a lake was hollowed out of the landscape and the foundations of Eastnor were laid in front. When it came to constructing the roof the current shortage of timber, which was being claimed for the war effort, led Smirke to improvise with a successful new technique, using cast-iron stanchions instead of the traditional wooden ones for the roof trusses.

From the windows there are fine views out over the Malvern Hills. The beautiful ornamental lake somewhat dissipates any military effect, but when Lord Somers was taking tea and cinnamon toast in the drawing-room he was able also to gaze at the British Camp, an early fortified earthwork castle, itself an echo of a stormier way of life when defence was a serious business.

The Great Hall is a huge lofty room designed by George Gilbert Scott. In the context of a modern castle, where the original functions of a great hall are catered for by the addition of drawing-room and dining-room, it is hard to devise a particular use for such a vast cavernous space—60 feet long, 30 feet wide and 55 feet high—except as a repository for the bulkier items handed from branch to branch of the family tree. Here the walls are hung with suits of armour and weapons, including large two-handed swords of the 15th and 16th centuries, broadswords, halberds, daggers, maces, shields, scabbards and pistols. Suspended rather disturbingly are 33 legless (or technically 'three-quarter') suits of armour, while four other standing suits wait stiff attendance on a magnificent Italian jouster mounted and ready for tourney. The decoration on the walls is aptly based on the design of a Saracen banner from the Crusades. The pleasing curved motif of birds is echoed above in the arches of the high gallery.

Above, *the Long Library, designed by G. E. Fox;*
right, *the Great Hall, by George Gilbert Scott*

The Long Library was designed by G. E. Fox and
the theme of the decorations and furnishings is
Renaissance Italy. It is a light and very long room
(63 feet) reminiscent less of a library than of one of the
galleries at Versailles. The woodwork of the book-
cases, windows and doors is Italian walnut inlaid with
boxwood, and is based on that in the sacristy of
Santa Maria delle Grazie in Milan. On the ceiling are
paintings of the Virtues and Vices based on illustrations of the 15th century. The tapestries on the long
wall are Flemish but their heroes are Roman. They were
commissioned by Catherine de' Medici in memory of
her husband and were brought by the 3rd earl from
a palace in Mantua. A lighter contemporary touch

amongst the classical allusions is a portrait of Garibaldi
carved on the stone mantelpiece, possibly slipped in—
in authentically medieval fashion—by some radical
immigrant among the workmen.

The Somers family assembled at Eastnor an impressive cast of leading 19th-century designers, and
the decoration of the Gothic drawing-room is among
the last work of Augustus Pugin, shortly before his
death in 1852. Above the fireplace is a heraldic tree
showing the family pedigree from the 16th century,
embellished with their motto 'Prodesse quam cons-
pici' which must have greatly pleased the solemn
Pugin. 'Be useful rather than conspicuous' is, however, for today's streamlined tastes a surprising cap-
tion to this amazingly ornate and lavish drawing-room
—itself an unusual departure from Pugin's normal
undertakings of seriousness, whether religious or
secular (a lifetime of churches and the Houses of
Parliament). The theme he most loved to preach was
that architecture should be judged by and inspire
the highest standards of morality. It would be interesting to know what persuaded him to embellish
a nobleman's drawing-room—because he found high
morality there, or hoped to introduce it, or was it
that Lord Somers had an urge to sit in something very
akin to a cathedral of an evening? Whatever the reason
the finished result is a richly brilliant and flamboy-
antly decorated room. Great gilded fans sweep upwards from the thinnest of Gothic columns and tiny
carved capitals, to give support to a curving barrelled
ceiling intersected by triangular ribbing. Every flat
surface displays an heraldic device—even the inter-
vening spaces between the ribs of the fan vaulting
manage to sport the letter 'S'. The raised surfaces are
gilded and gleam in the light of the great brass chan-
deliers, also designed by Pugin after the original in
Nuremburg Cathedral, and exhibited at the Great
Exhibition in 1851.

In this delightfully elaborate context the extremely
fine French tapestries of the 17th century still
manage to make their own conspicuous contribution,
and Pugin must have found them useful in that they
saved him from covering an even larger wall-space
with family emblems. The four seasons flank the
fireplace and windows, and at either end of the room
Alexander the Great is dealing with his foe Darius in
modestly heroic fashion. The room altogether shows
an imaginative use of materials in a harmoniously
designed whole—a technical accomplishment of
great skill.

Framlingham SUFFOLK

Framlingham has the distinction of having been dismantled as early as 1177. Alnodus the engineer and his masons and carpenters were paid £14. 15s. 11d. by Henry III for demolishing the castle, though it would seem that this rather modest sum was insufficient to cover the cost of any serious destruction, and that little more than the outer defences was affected. Hugh Bigod, Earl of Norfolk and owner of the castle, died the following year, but his son Roger lost no time in making good the king's damage and more. The resulting massive towers and walls of today's castle, together with defending earthworks and ditches, must have seemed a resounding proclamation of Bigod independence to King John when in 1213 he stayed there as a guest. Three years later he besieged and captured it. The Bigod family, however, continued as rebels and were not crushed until Edward I removed the last of them from the office of Marshal and formally received their entire estates.

Thereafter it became for a while the chief seat first of the Mowbrays and then of the Howards, dukes of Norfolk, with periodic forfeiture to the Crown. It was during one of these interludes in the Howards' ownership that Princess Mary—threatened by the uncertainty which followed the death of her brother Edward VI—came here to stay in 1553, and it was here that the Earl of Arundel arrived to inform her that she was Queen of England. Mary then raised her standard over the gatehouse and assumed the title. Meanwhile the dukes of Norfolk, when they were not under sentence of death in the Tower for their

Roman Catholic loyalties, lived in their more modern and comfortable properties of Arundel and elsewhere, and little use was made of the castle except by Elizabeth as a prison for recusant priests. The main entrance, which is basically the work of Roger Bigod in the 12th century, was considerably altered and the bridge was built by the 3rd Howard duke, whose family arms remain in the panel above the arch. Many of the Howards have their tombs in the church of the local market town of Framlingham, and there still survive various interesting architectural features in the castle which date to their tenure—the splendid ornamental chimneys sprouting from most of the towers are an amusing 16th-century addition, and there was apparently a garden outside the curtain wall to the north-west.

Unlike most other castles Framlingham played no part in the Civil War. As a result its battlements are well preserved. It did, however, come in for a fair share of demolition in the 17th century, for in 1636 it was bequeathed to Pembroke College, Cambridge, with the proviso that 'all the Castle, saving the stone building, be pulled down,' so that a poor-house could be erected on its site. And thus it was that the Great Hall and other internal buildings were gradually demolished. The poor-house survived some 200 years and was then used as a county court and drill hall.

This late 12th-century castle was built without a keep, its defence consisting of a circuit of 13 strong towers linked by a wall

Helmsley NORTH YORKSHIRE

The ruins of Helmsley Castle, one of the many private strongholds that came into being in the 12th century, stand just to the west of the town on a slight rocky eminence in the valley of the Rye. Two moats, once filled by the river, surround the rectangular complex of keep and outer walls. The only parts of the castle still in a good state of preservation today are the west tower and the later Elizabethan mansion, with many of the windows glazed and part of the roof intact. This was built by Edward Manners, 3rd Earl of Rutland, who owned Helmsley from 1563 to 1587.

Behind this is the keep, built about 1190 by Robert de Roos, who was largely responsible for all the oldest parts of the surviving castle. It is not as large as other more famous English keeps, though it does rise some 100 feet above the bailey, and is of a curious and enterprising design. Instead of the usual rectangular shape, it was given a rounded external face with no dangerous corners for the attackers to undermine; but inside the walls the more useful four-square shape was preferred for the domestic arrangements.

Small 12th-century stronghold. The western façade shows the keep on the right; the Elizabethan mansion added in the mid-16th century is on the left

Helmsley's history was pleasantly uneventful. When in the first half of the 12th century Walter l'Espec built his original castle, of which now no trace remains, he was fortunate in his choice of site— or perhaps more skilful than fortunate, for he was also the founder of Rievaulx Abbey, not far off in the same valley, and was clearly a man with a sure eye for a beautiful, peaceful situation. The only time in its history that the castle changed hands by sale was in 1689 when a London banker, Sir Charles Duncombe, bought it for £95,000. In spite of this vast sum of money, it must already have been in a sorry state of repair, for the only siege to the castle ever recorded had been in 1644, when for three months it was held for the king. After its surrender the fortifications were destroyed, including the rounded eastern half of the keep.

Herstmonceux EAST SUSSEX

In 1675, when the Royal Observatory took up its new quarters in Greenwich, built by Sir Christopher Wren, it was with the definite purpose of improving navigation. Nearly 300 years later, in search of purer air for the delicate and advanced work of charting the heavens in the 20th century, the Observatory moved south to Herstmonceux, where the climate turned out equally unfavourable but the new home even more distinguished of its kind—one of the most splendid early brick buildings in the country.

This palatial manor house rising tall and sheer from its wide moat was probably built on the site of an earlier house. Roger de Fiennes, a member of the second Norman family to hold the lands, received a licence to crenellate in 1441. Like his powerful contemporary, Ralph Lord Cromwell of Tattershall castle, he too had a hand in managing Henry VI's finances (as Treasurer of the Household), and he built himself a magnificent home in keeping with the dignity of his high office. Though he is not known to have been so flamboyant a character as Lord Cromwell, Sir Roger nevertheless constructed a comparably stylish and elegant fortified mansion with a very imposing gatehouse. Its two lofty towers, surmounted by a double row of battlements, rise to a height of 84 feet on either side of the entrance and drawbridge. The castle walls are too thin for serious resistance against heavy artillery, but are laden with all the paraphernalia required for defence with either firearm or crossbow. In similar fashion each of the octagonal and semi-octagonal towers is provided with both gun-loops and bowslits.

In the event Herstmonceux saw very little military action: few incidents of any kind are recorded in its history. It passed from the Fiennes family and was received by one neglectful owner after another until it reached the ruthless hands of the Reverend Robert Hare, who immediately recognized the castle's potential—as the raw material from which to build himself a brand new house in the 1770s. His devastation of the interior of this majestic medieval building was as efficient as anything that Cromwell's men could have achieved, while nearby the new house grew apace with all the confidence of a rapacious young cuckoo. Photographs taken a century or more later show a mournful ruin in a dry tree-filled moat, the exquisite symmetry of its walls intact but all the delicate features of turrets and windows obscured and confused under a dense blanket of ivy. In this sorry condition it might well have attracted the attention of Lord Curzon before he started on his great task of recovering the castles of Tattershall and Bodiam. As it turned out it was Sir Claude Lowther, a new owner, who began a complete restoration in accordance with detailed plans still in existence, and this work was completed by his successor Sir Paul Latham. All the castle's imposing military effects were put back into place. Its beautiful brickwork, so simple at the level of the moat, flourishes upwards into a great fanfare of corbels, turrets and machicolations. All is as Sir Roger de Fiennes would have wished. The only strange sight in this medieval landscape are the curious domes standing sentinel on the crest of the nearby hill as the one reminder of the castle's modern function.

This magnificent castle built of Flemish brick in 1441, of which the 84-foot-high gatehouse and drawbridge are shown here, was completely restored in the early 20th century. It now houses the Royal Observatory

Hever KENT

When Sir Thomas Boleyn died in 1538 he was buried quietly, but with a magnificent brass to commemorate his name, in St Peter's Church, Hever, a little to the south of his castle. It was also in a church dedicated to St Peter that two years earlier his daughter Anne had been disposed of, but with much less ceremony—in a common elm chest, a mere container for arrows, her head severed from her body. Her brother too was executed for alleged adultery with his sister. Thereafter with the decline of the Boleyn family their castle at Hever, where Anne had grown up and been courted by Henry VIII, was appropriated by the Crown.

Since its licence to crenellate in about 1340, Hever had passed by marriage and purchase through several families. For a time all looked set fair for the rising fortunes of the Boleyn family and their continuing tenure of the castle, but after the death of Anne and her brother the castle reverted to its earlier pattern. A confusing succession of owners came and went.

It survived all, however, as a working farm house, and although there was nothing very military about the ducks and geese in the moat, its exterior at the end of the 19th century was apparently still in good condition, its fine 14th-century battlemented gatehouse no doubt cutting a certain dash amongst the neighbouring Kent farmsteads.

In 1903 it was bought by William Waldorf Astor, and within a short space of time the castle was a mansion again and the home-farm and dairy had been transferred to a brand new Tudor village at decent remove. Hever was soon resplendent with examples of Edwardian craftsmanship, including panelling and wood decoration in oak, teak, walnut, holly. Expense was no object in the restoration of the castle to its former glory, and more. The gardens too were transformed as if by magic from the modest sprawl of orchard, meadows and marsh, into a vision of the Italian lakes, an Isola Bella in the surprised Kent countryside. Statues, vases, columns, porphyry and marble, the public and private myths of a dozen cultures mingling together as freely as the nymphs splashing in the sculpted fountain.

Other innovations are perhaps less successful. Hever has the doubtful distinction of being the only castle in Britain to have replaced the function of its portcullis by a traffic-light at its otherwise splendid gatehouse.

13th-century castle, later the home of Anne Boleyn,
lavishly restored in the 20th century

Kenilworth WARWICKSHIRE

The holding of Kenilworth that Henry I had granted to Geoffrey de Clinton was a pleasing gift. The Warwickshire countryside was an agreeable one, gently rolling and thickly wooded. It was land with more obvious merits as a hunting ground than as a site for a stronghold, and as a gift from the king to his chamberlain and treasurer it was eminently suitable. Yet it is for the castle they built that the Clintons are remembered there today. Kenilworth's massive square Norman keep still bears their name and was probably built by the son or grandson. The conversion of what had been a simple manor into a conspicuously strong fortification prompted Henry II to appropriate it for the Crown, and the Clintons were compensated with lands in Buckinghamshire. Henry II and his successors, John and Henry III, all spent considerable sums of money on expanding and improving the defences. It was early in the 13th century that Kenilworth's great lake was made by damming the streams which flow through the valley, as a protection for the castle to the south and west. A further safeguard was provided by two lines of moats on the north side. This vast water fortification covered over 100 acres, a larger area even than that at Caerphilly, and with the completion of the mural towers in the outer ward, the castle was incomparably defended, one of the most unassailable in the country.

It is curious that such an intuitive understanding of military strategy as Henry III must have possessed should be accompanied by what would seem a total lack of political foresight. When his stronghold was completed Henry was unwise enough to give it as a residence for life to his sister Eleanor and her husband, the man who was to become his greatest enemy. Sixteen years later at Kenilworth this same Simon de Montfort, Earl of Leicester, based his revolt against the king, and imprisoned there the king's son, Prince Edward, and his brother Richard—events which were to lead to the castle's famous siege of 1266, perhaps the greatest in this country's history.

Edward, having escaped from Kenilworth and slain Montfort at the Battle of Evesham, appeared before the castle gate, where Montfort's son, also Simon, had rallied the last of his father's supporters. The long and arduous siege began. Surrounded on three of its four sides by water, the castle could not be undermined and it was against the only part not protected by the lake that the royal troops, under both Edward and his father Henry, directed their attack. Two wooden towers—one so large that it could contain 200 archers—were constructed, and eleven catapults were set up. There began an intense bombardment of the castle, but one returned with such fury by the besieged from within their walls that, according to a chronicler, boulders flying from the mangonels and other engines were constantly in shattering collision overhead. A night-time attempt was then made to approach the castle, with barges brought overland from Chester, but this proved ineffective. Another improbable thought which occurred to the royal party was to use the authority of the Church against the rebels, and the Archbishop of Canterbury, accompanied by two of his bishops, appeared in person before the castle and excommunicated those inside. They were met with the mockery of men convinced of their own invulnerability, for the rebels produced on top of the walls a figure similarly clad in white ecclesiastical garb, who pronounced the same sentence on the archbishop. It was not for another six months, by which time the besiegers virtually admitted the impossibility of storming the castle, that they decided instead to negotiate a surrender. The Dictum of Kenilworth was a treaty offering lenient terms based on the payment of fines, but this the rebels also rejected. Only after two more months, when privation and epidemic disease threatened their annihilation and hope of relief from outside had finally waned, did the garrison surrender. By the agreed terms they were allowed to march out under amnesty, and the young Montforts were able to leave for Italy. From the military point of view there has been nothing in the castle's history comparable to this great siege.

Other events, however, fulfil all expectations of the chivalrous and heroic, and combine to make this the most romantic and proud of castles. In 1279, Roger de Mortimer—at that time in charge of the castle—held a famous tournament on the dam of the lake and invited to it 100 knights with 100 ladies, for three days of tilting and the introduction of the new military game of the Round Table. In the first part of the next century it was here that Edward II learned of his deposition, and signed his abdication. In Marlowe's play *Edward II* it is just outside the castle that the king's jailors shaved him with water from a puddle. Its history was further enlivened by frequent visits of royalty, most famous of all being the reception which Robert Dudley, Earl of Leicester, as castellan lavished on Queen Elizabeth. These summer festivities of 1575 continued for 19 days, and the entertainment consisted of an expensive and relentless round of dancing, plays, contests, pageantry and other pleasures, the provision of which allegedly cost Leicester £1,000 a day. Altogether he is thought to have spent about £100,000 in providing the magnificent accommodation necessary for the queen and her court. The great gatehouse to the north is his, likewise those buildings known as the Leicester Buildings and the very beautiful Long Barn, with its ground floor built of stone, and timbered above. The slightly

modern appearance that the keep has today is perhaps due to the large windows he inserted in place of the earlier Norman ones.

Leicester was the last of the great builders at Kenilworth; after his death the castle declined. During the Civil War it changed hands, but without much fighting, and in 1649 Parliament, perhaps fearing the splendour of its historic and royal associations, decided to destroy it. Actual demolition was prevented, but the subsequent slighting was so savage that the castle is now nothing more than a vast ruin. Of all its many buildings only Leicester's gatehouse remains habitable.

Perhaps the saddest relic is the great banqueting hall, built in the second half of the 14th century by the most illustrious of all the castle's owners, John of Gaunt. In spite of his many other properties he was known to be particularly fond of Kenilworth, and spent an enormous amount of money transforming it into a magnificent palace, which with its beautiful lake and surroundings was to become a favourite residence of his successors, the Lancastrian kings. Though Shakespeare portrays it as happening in London, it was probably in this great hall that Henry V received the mocking gift of tennis balls from the French ambassador. All that remains today of John of

Gift of Henry III to his sister Eleanor who married Simon de Montfort, the castle has many royal associations. The massive stone keep was the first part to be built in the early 13th century. See Colour Plate III

Gaunt's lavish apartments are free-standing walls, their roofs gone, but with graceful oriel windows and their splendid decoration almost intact. Had it survived in a good state of preservation it might well have compared in excellence with the magnificent hall of his nephew Richard II at Westminster.

Sir Walter Scott could be set musing by any castle, but Kenilworth stirred him more than most with the contrast between its glorious past and sombre remains. In the novel which he names after it, *Kenilworth*, he writes:— 'The bed of the lake is but a rushy swamp; and the massive ruins of the castle only serve to show what their splendour once was and to impress on the musing visitor the transitory values of human possessions and the happiness of those who enjoy a humble lot in virtuous contentment.' Modern visitors may well share Sir Walter's intimation of the wheel of fate without being quite as sure of the merits of poverty.

Kirby Muxloe LEICESTERSHIRE

The castle begun by Lord Hastings at Kirby Muxloe in 1480 as part of an ambitious building programme, such as only a man of great wealth and power could indulge in, was never finished. In the early summer of 1483 when work on both this and his other great Leicestershire mansion at Ashby-de-la-Zouch was nearing completion, and when John Couper, the foremost architect of his day, was already putting the finishing touches to lead pipes and gutters, William Lord Hastings, former Chamberlain of the Royal Household, Master of the Mint, Chamberlain of North Wales, Receiver of the revenue of the Duchy of Cornwall, Lieutenant of Calais, Knight of the Garter, in short a man of some substance, was seized and summarily executed by the usurping Richard of Gloucester. His moment of doom is famous in Shakespeare as one of the swiftest sentences of death ever passed, a brutally rapid intimation of mortality in the midst of the apparent calm of a counsel meeting:

'Thou art a traitor:—Off with his head!—now, by Saint Paul, I swear I will not dine until I see the same'. *Richard III*, Act III, Scene II.

Kirby Muxloe is one of the few private buildings of the period whose building records survive in such minute detail. These records indicate that after the death of Hastings work was continued only in a very limited way by his widow, and that the roofs, except for that on the west tower, were never more than thatched to give protection from the weather. The three-storeyed west tower where the roof was leaded, shows signs of having been completely finished and is the only well-preserved building of the castle. If the tradition is correct that Edward IV's mistress Jane Shore came here after his death, then it would no doubt have been in this completed west tower that she stayed.

Elsewhere the castle has become totally ruinous. The gatehouse, to the right of the photograph, once its most important defensive feature, survives only partially to the second storey, and the other three towers which would have completed the rectangular shape of the castle have now almost vanished.

These defences were typical of the fortified manors of the Middle Ages. Unlike Ashby which was made of dressed stone, Kirby Muxloe was built almost entirely of thin red bricks varied in places with elaborate patterns in black, a material starting to gain fashion at the time, with stone used only for doorways, windows and string courses. It consisted of a rectangular courtyard, enclosing the principal living rooms of an earlier manor house, the whole protected by towers, a gatehouse and a moat—made possible by the regular supply of fresh water from the connecting brook. The entrance across the moat was defended by a drawbridge, portcullis and two pairs of folding doors. The gunports in both the gatehouse and the west tower seem somewhat ill-placed: many of those in the west tower would point down the barrels of their opposite numbers, while others are below the normal water line of the moat. To give Lord Hastings the benefit of the doubt, maybe his plan was a truly devastating surprise to an enemy attempting to drain the moat, who would find cannon wheeled in to point at him from what had previously been below the water-line. But all in all Lord Hastings appeared to be more interested in the social than the military responsibilities of a chatelain.

The only remaining part of this castle which is relatively well preserved is the three-storeyed west tower, an early example of the use of brick

Launceston CORNWALL

The 13th-century stone keep is all that remains of this early Norman castle

The great feature dominating the thriving market town of Launceston is the very abruptly rising mound on which stands the castle of the earls of Cornwall. Dunheved, as it was called in Domesday Book, was their administrative centre, and as such its castle would have been a stronghold of some considerable importance. Quite surprisingly, however, the early Norman earthworks were not replaced by stone defences until the mid-13th century, and by then the high-and-dry kind of refuge was thought to be unstrategic. This natural hillock at Launceston nevertheless provided an excellent all-round view of the countryside, and a most interesting use was made of the small circular space on top of it. Around its crown a wall, or shell keep, was built. Concentric within this a tower rose up, one storey higher, and the space between the two was roofed over to provide a lofty platform from which to rake the enemy with fire. A bailey extended below it, and the only access to the mound was up a steep, well-defended flight of stone steps.

Arriving so late on the military scene, the working life of the castle was correspondingly short. By the end of the 13th century its attraction as a stronghold was clearly insufficient to keep the earls of Cornwall in Launceston, and it fell into such disrepair that in 1353 the swine of the town are reported as having jeopardized the foundations by trampling the moat. By 1409 the walls were so overgrown with ivy that two special hooks had to be cast to deal with it. Thus as a military post it became increasingly inadequate; it nevertheless retained its importance as an administrative centre for the area, and in the Civil War it was repaired sufficiently to hold out as a garrisoned fortress, and changed hands on several occasions.

During the Commonwealth it was not dismantled by Parliament, as were most other castles, which suggests a state of decay so advanced as to render further efforts unnecessary. It was, however, still used as a prison when in 1656 George Fox, the founder of the Quakers, was confined there for eight months, though the whereabouts of the 'noisome den' in which he was locked cannot be identified. Today the only well-preserved part of the castle is the stonework of the keep and an excellently maintained public garden occupying the former bailey.

Lewes EAST SUSSEX

When John de Warenne, 8th Earl of Surrey, died in 1347, his several children were all illegitimate, and none could claim the castle of Lewes which had been the chief residence of the Warenne family for nearly 300 years. From this date the castle remained untenanted as part of the property of the earls of Arundel. The stonework was considerably damaged in a riot of the citizens of Lewes in 1382 and was thereafter readily plundered as a useful source of building material by the local inhabitants, until by 1620 the castle was so decayed that much of it was pulled down and the flints sold off by the load. The magnificent barbican, built in the 14th century as the last contribution of the Warennes, was granted in 1733 as waste of the manor to Thomas Friend, a wool merchant, who fortunately allowed its beautifully built flint walls to stand unharmed. In 1774 the keep was converted into a summer house, and in the 20th century became the property of the Sussex Archaeological Society. Thus for the last 600 years the castle's history has been uneventful.

Yet the original building of William de Warenne, one of William I's most distinguished followers and Chief Justiciar, was an important and interesting one. Most unusually the Norman knight built himself a castle with two mounds, each consisting of large rough-cut blocks of chalk, the first on high ground above the valley of the River Ouse and then a second more imposing one linked to the town wall by ditch and fence. The shell keep built on this second mound remains in part and dates from about 1080.

The fine 14th-century barbican is the best preserved part of this Norman castle, begun in the 11th century

Lindisfarne HOLY ISLAND, NORTHUMBERLAND

Six miles north across the sands from Bamburgh, the great outcrop of rock known as Beblowe crag—on which the neighbouring castle of Lindisfarne stands —has been eroded by the gales to a smooth and beautiful mound. It was on the sheltered south-west of the island, away from the north sea, that St Aidan's monks, arriving from Iona in 635, built their abbey, no doubt in a place they thought quite exceptionally safe since the island is inaccessible except at low tide and then only by an enemy experienced in the lie of the mud flats. But it was from the sea that danger came. When the Vikings landed and destroyed their abbey in 793, it may have been the first that the monks had heard of these wild men of the north. They rebuilt their church, but their refuge was no longer a safe one and they left it in 875. For two centuries afterwards the island remained uninhabited. The relics of the Celtic saints and the Lindisfarne Gospels had been carried off by the monks in search of a sanctuary which they eventually found in Durham. In 1082 it again became a holy island, when a Benedictine priory was founded, and it is from this time that its modern name derived.

Despite the obvious suitability of the crag as a post of defence on the north sea coast, it was not until 1542 that the first fortification was raised, when gunposts were set up to defend the harbour against the Scots. This was only five years after the Dissolution of the Monasteries; thus there was on the island a ready supply of fashioned stone to be purloined from the abandoned priory a short distance away. The church became the garrison's main store-house. By 1550 the Tudor fort had been completed, and was maintained by a series of colourful governors, but the

expected attack from the Scots or their allies the French never came. Its only dramatic action was in a distinctly minor key. When its garrison had dwindled to only seven men, the castle was seized by a ruse of two Jacobite supporters, who flew their flag for one night before being ejected. In the early 19th century, after only 250 years of what can hardly at any point be called military service, it fell into modest disuse and in 1819 its guns were removed.

The possibilities of this romantic island, however, were eventually developed in an interesting way by Edward Hudson, who summoned the leading country-house architect of the early part of the 20th century, Sir Edwin Lutyens, and between them these two energetic Edwardians built a splendid decorative castle, with vaulted chambers and rock passages. The task of turning a fortress, even such a comfortable one—as by all accounts it was—into a domestic castle was by no means easy. In spite of its many bedrooms and living rooms and wonderful views, the accommodation conformed to romantic literary standards rather than those of convenience. After 1968 it was no longer inhabited, but has been kept by the National Trust just as if lived in.

The monks never returned, but the island continues as a gentle sanctuary even today for seals and for the many species of wheeling, crying sea-birds that nest on the crag.

Most romantically sited of all the northern castles, this Tudor fort was built in 1542 to combat the Scots. Complete rebuilding was carried out by Sir Edwin Lutyens at the beginning of the 20th century

Ludlow SALOP

Perched on a cliff overlooking the River Teme, Ludlow has an ideal site for a fortress. Right, the Norman chapel from the east, seen from the site of the chancel

The transformation of Ludlow's castle from a simple Norman stronghold of only average interest into the most important strategic holding of the Welsh borders derives partly from its impressive site on a hill overlooking the river Teme, but more particularly from the series of lively and pugnacious tenants who for five centuries after the Conquest defended and expanded it as their fortified residence. Probably begun in 1085 by Roger de Lacy before his rebellion against William Rufus and consequent exile, the castle was soon to acquire a remarkably beautiful round chapel in the middle ward—part of the improvements made in the 1130s by Sir Joyce de Dinan,

an enemy and rival claimant to the Lacy castle. The 20 turbulent years of his tenancy and the heroic recovery by the Lacys of their home are described in gory detail in the 13th-century *Geste of Fulk Fitzwarine*—a document written for the hero's Lacy descendants, and the only such family chronicle to have survived.

The male Lacy line flickered out in 1240. Seventy years later Roger Mortimer, the wicked Earl of March and murderer of Edward II, held the castle and recognized its potential. Five generations of Mortimers lived there, and they were probably responsible for the impressive 14th-century buildings of the north front.

Ludlow became royal property when one of the Mortimer family was crowned Edward IV, and it is after his two sons, the Prince of Wales and his brother, that the north-east tower is named. The two young princes lived here from 1472 until they set out eleven years later to their death in that other Tower. Some 20 years after, in 1502, another ill-fated heir to the throne was to be commemorated in the castle. The north-west tower is known as Arthur's because it was there that the elder brother of Henry VIII died.

Thereafter the castle was lived in sumptuously by the Lord President of the Council of Wales, of whom the most illustrious was Queen Elizabeth's favourite, Sir Henry Sidney, father of Philip. The building of the gatehouse on the north side in 1581 was part of the extensive architectural improvement carried out under his tenancy (originally the entrance to the castle had been through the keep). The splendid great hall and its furbishings, still in existence until the Civil War, must have made a perfect setting for the famous event of 1634. To celebrate the entry of the Earl of Bridgewater to the presidency of Wales and the Marches, Milton presented his pastoral entertainment *Comus*. As if in a spectacular last fling to close the castle's long history, shepherds, water-nymphs and an enchanted lady delighted an elegant courtly audience a brief few years before England, and Milton, so abruptly changed their tune.

The castle was not seriously damaged in the Civil War, but almost immediately afterwards, in 1651, the defences were deliberately dismantled. Vandalism in the reign of George I, when the lead was removed from the roofs, contributed to its decay, which continued throughout the 18th century.

Newark NOTTINGHAMSHIRE

When King John arrived at Newark in 1216 it was as a broken and dying man. Two days later dysentery, fever, the gnawing loss of his treasures and regalia in the waters of the Wash, and the famous surfeit of peaches and new cider, accounted for his swift and unmourned death. In the circumstances his surroundings were probably of no consolation, but had things turned out differently he could hardly have chosen a more agreeable place to convalesce than this elegant bishop's palace overlooking the River Trent.

The wooden manor of Alexander, Bishop of Lincoln, had become a fortified residence sometime between the years 1123 and 1135, when Henry I gave permission to the bishop to turn his fishpond into a moat, and surround it with a rampart. The manor was soon described as 'a magnificent castle of very ornate construction', and as such came to the attention of King Stephen. In 1139 he determined to take into his own possession this and the other properties belonging to the bishop, and to this end imprisoned him without food. There is no evidence that this bishop ever received back his castle, but it returned in time to the see of Lincoln and in 1173 Bishop Geoffrey Plantagenet set about building the first stone stronghold on the site.

The castle was an oblong building with huge square towers at the four corners. Little remains of this Norman structure except the main gate, the west tower and various small areas of masonry where the oolite stone can still be seen. The red sandstone with which it joins distinguishes the major rebuilding work of the 13th century, undertaken by Henry III after his devastating assault in 1218 on the group of barons who had seized the castle at the death of King John. Henry arrived outside the walls with 'great engines', which battered the castle into such bad shape that after eight days it was surrendered. Restored and rebuilt, it became again towards the end of the 13th century a magnificent fortified mansion, and one that continued until Tudor times under the control of the see of Lincoln. It was Henry VIII who finally took it from Bishop Henry Holbeach into the possession of the Crown, where it remained.

During the Civil War the town of Newark was particularly staunch in favour of this royal association, and was besieged four times by the Parliamentarians. Following his defeat at Naseby, Charles I took refuge in the castle before retreating finally to Oxford. After his capture by the Scots in 1646 Newark surrendered, and its garrison was allowed to march out with their arms, horses and goods. The subsequent dismantling of Newark was very harsh. In 1649 a survey describes it as 'soe ruined that it will never be made habitable haveinge nothinge left but Ruinous pieces of Walls'. A stirring reminder of the important part Newark played in the Civil War is the collection of interesting lozenge-shaped coins in the castle's museum, minted from silver vessels to pay the troops during the last siege.

The Bishops' Palace on the banks of the River Trent was fortified as a castle in the early 12th century. Famous as the place where King John died

Nunney SOMERSET

The parish church of Nunney is built on a small hill overlooking the village. It contains the tombs of the Delamere family, one of the long reclining marble effigies being of the builder of the castle opposite, and another the donor of a chantry in the church. The castle sits on lower ground beneath it, hemmed in by the thatched roofs and farm buildings of this tiny Somerset village, thus reversing the position of the traditional castle built to command its territory. Nunney, however, was a late venture, started only in the reign of Edward III, and the church had already taken the better site. When Sir John Delamere obtained a licence to crenellate in 1373, it was clearly not with a view to contribute to the king's coastal defence, nor even to safeguard his own small parcel of land, but more perhaps as a celebration of a new-found feudal status. Until 1373 his land had belonged to the Bohun earls of Hereford, but when their male line died out, the tiny estate—'one knight's fee in the Manor of Nony, held by John de la Mere, valued at 100 shillings'—reverted to the Crown, and Sir John became tenant-in-chief.

The castle he built was one of great refinement and interest, as befitted a knight who had served in the French wars and who had no doubt amassed there, like others of Edward III's soldiers, a vast amount of ransom money. The castles with which he would have been most familiar were those of France, for his family in England had lived in modest circumstances. In this little Somerset village the result of his efforts seems quite extraordinary. Sir John took his licence to crenellate very seriously; instead of the low moated manor that he might have built, he set up a tall and splendid rectangular castle roofed like a French château, four storeys high, with a large drum tower at each corner. But the site was rather too small, so the towers at either end are close enough almost to meet, and his beautiful polished ashlar walls were hardly sufficient to withstand the new cannon just coming in. Moreover there was no portcullis and, although the machicolation was up to date, the loops could never have been used for guns, only for bows or cross-bows. The only time it had any serious duties as a castle it failed lamentably: when the Civil War came to Nunney, Cromwell's men simply placed their cannon on the rising ground conveniently overlooking the castle, and almost immediately breached the north wall above the entrance. In 1910 this damaged wall fell down, but the moat has been re-excavated and is once again filled with water from the stream which runs through the centre of the village.

In his own time Sir John must have created with his curious and pretty building more than a mere quixotic impression, for his later career was almost spectacular, bringing him the high positions of Sheriff of Somerset and Knight of the Shire.

This grandiose residence of a smallholding Somerset knight was founded in 1373 when he received a licence to crenellate

Old Wardour WILTSHIRE

Originally built in 1393, a major reconstruction was carried out in 1570 by Robert Smythson, architect of Longleat. It was abandoned as a ruin after the Civil War. Above, *the 16th-century entrance to the hall*; right, *the remains of the castle itself*

Nothing suits Old Wardour Castle so well as its approach along the narrow Wiltshire lanes. As the crow flies, it is a mere two miles from Tisbury but the puzzled traveller must go much further as he copes with the maze of hedges that circuit every field with a relentless purpose of their own. The valley eventually opens out to wider prospects on the west. Ahead the slow meandering of the lanes ends abruptly at the foot of a small hill thick with the cedars, yews and other trees of a formal parkland. The castle is partly concealed by the trees and by its enclosing curtain—a regular hexagon in outline, except where it digresses on the north side to incorporate the gateway. Once inside the precints all is suddenly delightful, a world of picturesque surprises: to the left is a grotto, its porous, drooping plasterwork caught at the perfect moment of volcanic convulsion; at the other side of the bailey a charming Gothic pavilion is reflected in the waters of a still dark lake, and nearby —most deliciously improbable of all—is a three-seater closet with pretty carved panelling and other decorative details. One might be in James Thomson's Castle of Indolence which had been created not long before:— a pleasing land of drowsy head it was' where the weary pilgrim is so enraptured that he sinks into a balmy torpor.

Like its own surrounding bailey the castle is hexagonal, with two flanking towers at the entrance. Inside, the rooms are grouped around a central courtyard echoing the outer symmetry. Only the great height of the castle's walls prevents it from masquerading as a Summer Pavilion or Temple of the Winds, an inspired contribution to the perfect 18th-century landscape. Old Wardour Castle, however, is not of that period. It was built in 1393 by John, 5th Lord Lovel, a veteran of the Hundred Years War, who returned from France and in common with many of his contemporaries obtained a licence to crenellate his home. He interpreted this permission rather freely; like the owner of Bodiam only eight years before, he took it to mean that he could abandon his existing home and build an entirely new castle nearby. He seems to have chosen as his inspiration the castle of Concressault in central France. It is doubtful whether the old campaigner can have conceived of his new home as anything but a quiet place for retirement—a castle in name only, for its situation is secluded rather than strategic and its appearance aesthetic rather than military.

In the event his family lived in the castle for only some 60 years; as Lancastrians they forfeited their property on the accession of Edward IV. For a century the castle passed through the hands of a succession of owners and tenants until Sir Mathew Arundell bought it in 1570 and began a major reconstruction. His architect, Robert Smythson, who had previously worked on nearby Longleat, greatly altered the appearance of the house by replacing the narrow medieval windows with his own larger 16th-century version of Gothic ones—groups of two and three mullioned lights set regularly into the façade. He also formalized the entrance by removing the portcullis and surrounding the doorway with columns, the family coat of arms, a Latin inscription and a bust of Christ. Within the central courtyard the medieval architecture was mostly allowed to survive. The approach from the courtyard up to the hall on the

first floor is splendidly announced by a handsome pair of columns and entablature, but adjacent to it the 14th-century doorways with their simple pointed arches make their own eloquent contribution to the pleasing aspect of the building—in itself a most successful combination of the Renaissance imposed on a Gothic tradition.

The Arundells were a staunch Royalist and Catholic family, who in 1643 drew to their gates Sir Thomas Hungerford, the Parliamentary leader in Wiltshire. Lady Arundell, in the absence of her husband, mustered her small garrison of 25 men and for six days resisted the onslaught of the Roundheads until forced to capitulate by the explosion of a mine in one of the castle vaults. Wardour's second siege some six months later was more prolonged and involved Lady Arundell's son, Henry, who resolved to recover his family property at whatever the cost. In the end the price he paid was a heavy one—four months later

he too was mining the walls. The Parliamentarians finally surrendered, but much of the state of total ruin to which the south-west sides of the castle have been reduced must be attributed to this siege, the rest of the damage being caused by Parliamentary action at the end of the Civil War.

The castle was never repaired. At the Restoration in 1660 the Arundells chose to build themselves a much smaller house on the south side of the bailey wall. A later scheme in 1756 considered the possibility of a reconstruction, but in the end the then Lord Arundell contented himself with building a totally new house of vast proportions, a mile to the northwest, to be known as Wardour Castle. James Paine was commissioned, and as the massive columns, colonnades and pilasters took shape, Old Wardour was relegated to the status of a romantic amenity at pleasant walking distance through the landscaped parkland and formal gardens.

Orford SUFFOLK

One night during the summer of 1841 the peaceful Suffolk countryside was shattered by a tremendous crash, announcing the collapse of the last fragment of the curtain wall which once enclosed Orford Castle. Today a criss-cross network of little white paths meanders disrespectfully over and about the rolling grassy outworks, and even up to and around the great stranded monster on its hillock, as if to inspect it lest, like the naked merman brought to the castle's first constable in the 12th century, it 'secretly fled to the sea and was never afterwards seen'.

The great annual rolls of the medieval exchequer make no mention of the Orford Merman, but provide instead an extremely relevant documentary account of the building of the castle in 1165, the earliest in the country for which this survives. When Henry II became king in 1154, the authority in East Anglia of Hugh Bigod, Earl of Norfolk, was in effect supreme by virtue of the great castles he held there, but three years later Henry felt secure enough on his throne to confiscate all his castles from Earl Hugh. In 1165 Hugh managed by payment of a fine of £1,000 to receive back Framlingham and his castle at Bungay. But it was a barbed deal that Henry was offering the aged earl, for in the same year he established his own royal castle in Suffolk at Orford, specifically between Framlingham and the sea, and at a cost of only £400 more than the money he had received from the earl. Royal authority, however, was not something Earl Hugh tolerated lightly, and, although some 80 years of age at the time, he became one of the leaders of the revolt of 1173 against King Henry. The king's new castle was not apparently attacked, though Flemish mercenaries were brought over by Bigod and fighting occurred near it.

The advanced new design must have acted as a considerable deterrent. It was one of the first castles in the country, even earlier than Henry's work at Dover, to employ a series of mural towers projecting from the outer curtain wall, a development of the greatest importance in the military architecture of the later 12th century. The systematic placing of towers on a long stretch of wall enabled the garrison to command the field with cross-fire without dangerous exposure. The design of the keep was equally interesting and experimental: instead of the traditional rectangular tower of the 12th century, Orford's keep is cylindrical within and its outside shape is that of a polygon with the addition of three projecting rectangular towers and a fore-building. It thus represents a development towards the later keeps of the 13th century, which were usually cylindrical, offering no easy angle under which the assailant could set his pick or his mine. Orford's design, however, although it impressed the enemy, was not popular enough to be repeated very widely elsewhere. Conisbrough was also a keep of transitional shape, neither round nor square, but Henry II's great keep at Dover, built about ten years later, is still solidly and straightforwardly rectangular.

The present impressively intact stonework of the keep relates to its comparatively uneventful military history. After the death of King John, it was taken almost without damage by the French contender for the throne, Prince Louis. It likewise changed hands frequently during the continuing baronial wars of Henry III's reign. The fortunes of the two parties concerned, however, were so varying that any lack of conviction on the part of their supporters was hardly surprising. The castle was maintained in good condition by the Crown so long as it proved its worth, but by 1336 it had obviously declined in importance to such an extent that Edward III could afford to give it in perpetuity to Robert of Ufford—an act of generosity which as it turned out cost the Crown nothing, for it was handed down the generations just as a piece of ancient fabric, and saw no further military action.

The polygonal keep which is all that remains of this castle built by Henry II between 1166 and 1172 when Orford was a busy port on the River Alde

Raby COUNTY DURHAM

When Canute was styling himself 'Emperor of the North'—and not without justification, for his rule extended over Norway and Denmark, and included the whole of the north of England—Raby is mentioned as being in his possession, and the present site of the castle is traditionally that of Canute's mansion at Staindrop. The Neville family, who lived there until the mid-16th century, were descended from a niece of Canute but took their name from a later Norman ancestress, Isabella de Neville, whose wealth and

Raby's early associations are with King Canute, but the oldest surviving parts date from about 1380. Above, the kitchen; right above, view from the south; right below, the east façade with Bulmer's Tower

possessions were such as to promote the change. It may be that Bulmer's Tower, the curiously shaped bastion at the south-east angle of the castle, is partly of Danish construction, but the bulk of the castle dates from about 1380, when the manor of Raby was fortified by John Lord Neville. It was he who built the great vaulted gateway, Neville's Tower, which was the only entrance to the inner court of the castle. The other towers and buildings are grouped rather piecemeal round the small interior courtyard. The castle, in spite of its very thick walls does not have the compact strength of the more specific fortresses of the 13th century. It resembles them because of its size and the nature of its masonry, but it remains essentially a large fortified manor of the late 14th century, designed for domestic rather than military use. It was provided with a fine kitchen—large and lofty, with a gallery running round the walls and three wide fireplaces.

The Nevilles continued at Raby during the Wars of the Roses in which they played a prominent role. As Earl of Westmorland, Ralph Neville was instrumental in placing Henry IV on the throne; and Cicely, 'the fair rose' of Raby, became the mother of Edward IV and Richard III. Their fortunes finally waned during the rebellion of 1569 against Elizabeth, when the nobles of the north attempted to restore the Roman Catholic faith and as a result lost their lands and titles. The Nevilles fared only slightly better than some: Charles Neville, Earl of Westmorland, escaped to Flanders, but died there alone and in poverty. The Neville lands were seized by the Crown and were only returned into private hands in 1626, when the states-man Sir Henry Vane bought the castle. It survived intact the troubles of the Civil War, for Sir Henry and his son were both staunch republicans. It was, how-ever, at the hands of Sir Henry's grandson, Christo-pher, created Lord Barnard, that Raby came nearest to destruction. Angered by his son's marriage, he determined to demolish the castle, and it was only after 200 workmen had finished stripping the roofs, the flooring and windows, and were starting to raze the walls that his son obtained an injunction against him, and the damage was eventually put right. By an intriguing coincidence the castle is again in the hands of the family who first built it, for the grand-mother of the present Lord Barnard was a Neville.

Restormel CORNWALL

The simple circular keep was built in the second half of the 13th century and is still in an excellent state of preservation. Top, *the entrance;* above, *aerial view*

After the Civil War, during which Restormel endured a brief siege, a Parliamentary Commission in 1649 reported that the castle was 'utterly ruined, nothing but the outer walls thereof remaining, which are not where they stand worth the taking down.' Standing where it does, high and inaccessible on the crest of a hill, continued to prove its strongest safeguard against demolition. Instead, during the 18th and 19th centuries it survived, an unexplored, ivy-smothered mass of greenery, quite invisible from below its thickly-wooded site, and it was only uncovered for inspection at the end of the 19th century.

Although the first mention of the castle is in 1264, its origins date from a much earlier period. Its large, almost perfect circular shape, so evocative of the simplest, essential ingredients of a stronghold, was most probably built first in wood shortly after the Conquest. Then in about 1100 a square projecting gatehouse was added to the south-west, and finally the timber palisading itself was replaced in the second half of the 13th century. All round the ring wall there are battlements and a complete walk behind them, still in an excellent state of preservation. The internal wooden buildings were the last to be replaced with stone, and this seems to have been done at the end of the 13th century by Edmund, Earl of Cornwall, who built himself a handsome two-storeyed residence against the inner circle of the wall, with a hall, chamber, kitchen, stable, barracks for the garrison and a chapel in an adjoining tower to the east.

Thereafter the castle's history is associated with the Crown, for in 1337 it was handed over to the Black Prince as 1st Duke of Cornwall, who put it in good repair and kept court there twice. It remained until this century as part of the Prince of Wales's titular possessions, but in 1925 the Commissioner of the Duchy of Cornwall handed over the castle into the care of the then Ministry of Works.

Richmond NORTH YORKSHIRE

On its cliff above the River Swale, Richmond Castle would seem to command a vast tract of country stretching to all sides, and yet the high moors surrounding it for many miles isolated it from the mainstream of events in the country's history, and have in effect curtailed its sphere of influence to the relatively small area of Swaledale. The land on which it stands belonged to the Saxon Edwin, Earl of Mercia; the first Norman holder was Alan the Red of Brittany, son of the Count of Penthievre, and relation to the Duke of Brittany. It was this last title and the ensuing clash of loyalties between two countries often at war with each other that was to cause constant trouble for the owners of Richmond over the following 300 years. Each time they fought for France the castle became forfeit to the Crown, though always only as a temporary punishment, for the monarch could ill afford to cultivate wealthy enemies. It was not until the death in 1341 of John III, Duke of Brittany, that the long and provocative liaison with France began to be severed, and to be replaced by an elaborate and intimate association with the throne of England. John of Gaunt, son of Edward III, held the castle as Earl of Richmond for 30 years until 1372. It reverted for a final 25 years to the Duke of Brittany, but the usual difficulties of allegiance occurred. Thereafter its links with the Crown, anxious to retain this great fief, became very close. The Honour was held by Henry VI's half-brother, Edmond Tudor. His son styled himself Earl of Richmond, after his father, though meanwhile Edward IV proceeded to bestow the castle and title on his own brother, George Duke of Clarence. Naturally the third brother, Richard of Gloucester, took over the earldom once Clarence had met his death in the Malmsey wine, and he continued to hold it after his accession as Richard III. Thus only when the hereditary Earl of Richmond became King Henry VII was the Honour finally and completely absorbed by the Crown. In this same reign Richmond lent its much older name to its present counterpart in the south, for when Henry VII rebuilt the royal palace on the Thames at Sheen, it too became known after his dukedom as Richmond. The title itself, the Dukedom of Richmond, remains today with the Lennoxes, descendants of the natural son of Charles II.

Apart from its royal associations, Richmond's most interesting feature is the early date of most of its

Aerial view showing the 12th-century keep, seen top right. Much of the other stonework dates from the early years after the Norman Conquest

masonry. Its curtain walls, replete with rectangular flanking towers, follow an unusual triangular pattern owing to the castle's curious-shaped site. They were the work of its first Norman owners in the twenty years following the Conquest; they include the Robin Hood Tower, where William the Lion is thought to have been imprisoned in 1174.

Scolland's Hall, the large two-storey building overlooking the river on the right of the picture, was the work of Alan of Brittany in about 1075. Before the 12th-century keep was added to the north of the castle this hall would have fulfilled the keep's function. Together with the similarly placed building at Chepstow it is considered the oldest of its kind in Britain.

Despite its devastated appearance today, the castle's history has been a quiet one. Most unusually it was not involved in either the Wars of the Roses or the Civil War, and indeed there is no recorded siege of the castle, nor any account of warfare in or about it. Its remote situation proved even more effective than its elaborate defences, and its present ruin dates from the mid-16th century, when it was left to decay.

Rochester KENT

It is a commonplace that in the days of the Crusades the Church Militant was living up to its name, but there were few places that this was more apparent in England than at Rochester, a castle not only built by a bishop but jealously guarded by the see of Canterbury until the end of the 12th century.

The present castle, one of the earliest in the country to be constructed in stone, was built by the Bishop of Rochester in about 1090, using some of Rochester's Roman walls for a foundation. The great four-square tower of the keep, 125 feet high and the tallest in England, was added by Archbishop William de Corbeil in 1127, to whose see at Canterbury the castle was granted 'in perpetuity' by Henry I.

Perpetuity, as it turned out, lasted until the end of the 12th century. After a succession of archbishops had enjoyed the custody of Rochester, clerical control came to an end in the most famous episode in the castle's history and one of the best-documented sieges of the Middle Ages. In 1215 Archbishop Langton disregarded King John's instructions to yield the castle to the Bishop of Winchester, who, unlike Langton, was one of the king's close supporters. For two months King John in person besieged the castle but his five great stone-throwing engines failed to breach the walls and he resorted finally to undermining them. This was a matter of digging out earth from under a corner of the walls and propping the masonry up with posts, which were then fired to bring about the collapse of part of the tower above. An urgent writ went out from the royal encampment: 'send to us with all speed by day and night forty of the fattest pigs of the sort least good for eating to bring fire beneath the tower.' Whether these animals were driven squealing into the fiery furnace or rendered down more discreetly, their excessive fat was a material of such combustible nature that a whole section of the tower came tumbling down. Yet even then the siege was not over. The barons retreated behind a great cross-wall, the traditional precaution in some keeps against exactly this eventuality, and continued their resistance. Starvation, however, at last forced their surrender after what had been to that date the greatest military operation of its kind in England.

Repaired, besieged and damaged again in 1264, allowed to decay, restored by Edward III, and improved in minor details by Richard II, allowed once more to moulder into disrepair—the castle's subsequent history was never again as dramatic as the great siege of 1215. In the 18th century there were plans for its demolition. Fortunately this drastic action proved uneconomical, likewise an attempt to turn it into a barracks, for it was clearly less well adapted to keeping soldiers in than keeping them out.

Seen here from the north bastion is the 12th-century keep

Rockingham NORTHAMPTONSHIRE

Originally square, these magnificent entrance towers were adapted to their circular shape by Edward I

Rockingham's great moment in history came in 1095, when after two years of dispute the English bishops sided with William II against their archbishop of Canterbury, Anselm. The Council they held in the Great Hall at Rockingham was one of the earliest recorded assemblies of State. Since then little of comparable importance has happened in the castle's history to justify William the Conqueror's rather curious siting of this impressively large Northamptonshire stronghold, one of the few to be built seemingly at random in the middle of the countryside —neither on the bank of an important river nor in the immediate vicinity of a town. Doubtless it proved an exceptionally fine hunting-lodge in the vast expanse of Rockingham Forest, for the Norman kings often held court there. John in particular was a frequent visitor. When, later, the business of ruling Britain became more complex the castle was gradually neglected. Edward I at the end of the 13th century was the last king to undertake large-scale repairs. Thereafter it was turned over to the royal womenfolk, who lived there at intervals throughout the 14th and 15th centuries: Isabella, Philippa, Anne, Joan of Navarre and Margaret of Anjou, all maintained an interest in Rockingham. Nevertheless it declined rapidly in importance, becoming very dilapidated, and had it remained a royal property would probably by now be nothing more than a ruin.

In 1530 a most fortunate event occurred to alter this

sorry situation. Edward Watson, a local landowner, succeeded in leasing the castle from Henry VIII. His portrait hangs conspicuously today in Rockingham's large Tudor hall, as well it might, for the Watson family thereafter consolidated their tenure, restored the Norman castle to a proper condition and have continued to live there to the present day. A particular characteristic of this energetic family was the practical use to which they put the old Norman masonry. The entrance towers, already adapted by Edward I from square to their present more useful curving shape, were kept as the castle's main defence. The Great Hall was divided into two rooms and Edward Watson put in a first floor. The cloisters became part of the library. Although the family decided to retain the Norman keep, it was soon demolished in 1646 by Parliamentarians, who used the castle as one of their major garrisons in the Midlands and handed it back to the family in a sorry state of repair. The Watsons fortunately survived these troubles, made good most of the damage and continued to live there. In the 1840s that strictest of all authorities on medieval military architecture, Anthony Salvin, was summoned to give to Rockingham its Plantagenet face-lift.

St Mawes AND PENDENNIS, CORNWALL

One of the best preserved of Henry VIII's coastal fortifications, St Mawes was designed in the mid-16th century specifically to resist cannon. Top, the castle; above, part of the eight-sided gun room. Each recess has its ammunition cupboard and smoke vent

While Pope Paul the Third in the late 1530s was preaching his crusade against the iniquities of the English king, Henry VIII, for his part, was taking decisive action against possible invasion. With the incomparable wealth amassed from the Dissolution of the Monasteries he undertook the creation of a vast scheme of coastal defence. By 1546 the coastline of England, where it faced the Continent, offered a front so bristling with fortifications that the only revisions found necessary in the 20th century to cope with possible invasion were protection against aerial bombardment. Henry not only refortified existing castles such as Dover and the Tower of London with great impregnable gun-proof bastions, but built a number of entirely new strongholds. The interesting pair of Cornish castles guarding Falmouth Bay, St Mawes and Pendennis, were by no means the earliest of the network to be built, but they are among the best preserved. Work started first on the more immediately vulnerable areas of Kent and the Isle of Wight, and it was not until after the alarms of the Armada in Elizabeth's reign that all the defences were completed.

Originally the two castles must have been of similar size—St Mawes consisted of a central tower entirely engulfed by three great lobes splaying out into the form of an ace of clubs, while Pendennis was simply a round tower and gate enclosed by a lower curtain wall. Later, in Elizabethan times, an encircling wall with bastions was built at Pendennis to include an area of over three acres. Of the two St Mawes is visually more pleasing, with its interesting symmetry and ornamental inscriptions and coats of arms on the outer wall of the keep—a splendidly lavish touch by the architect on such a military establishment.

In 1595 the Spanish arrived in Cornwall: a raiding party of four galleys succeeded in burning Penzance and two neighbouring small towns, and the threat to Falmouth and its great estuary became very menacing. Further defences were hurriedly erected and the garrisons reinforced, but the Spanish invasion never came, and the only attack in the castle's history was during the Civil War and from the land.

It was then that the interesting differences between the siting of the two castles became a factor of crucial relevance. Pendennis, on the highest available ground and built to dominate the whole of its peninsula, held out for six months in 1646 against the Parliamentarians; apart from Raglan Castle, which resisted for two days longer, it was the last in Britain to surrender to Cromwell. The struggle had been so prolonged and so debilitating that the full honours of war accorded to the garrison proved too much for the famished and enfeebled soldiers, many of whom died after the celebration. St Mawes, on the other hand, in spite of its massive bastions and eleven guns ready to sweep the enemy out of the sea, was weakly placed on the landward side, half-way up the slope of a hill. The governor made the decision that his defensive position was a preposterous one and handed over the keys without more ado.

Since then both castles have been used as barracks. During both wars in the 20th century they were included in the system of coastal defence and occupied by the army.

Scarborough   NORTH YORKSHIRE

World War I had barely begun when Admiral Franz von Hippen, on 16 December 1914, reached the English coast at Scarborough. A misty morning had enabled the forward cruisers of the German fleet, *Der Fflinger* and *Von der Tann*, to steam into shore before they were sighted. A fierce bombardment of the castle followed, and the barracks, constructed in 1746 after the Jacobite risings, were almost totally destroyed. This was the last of an extraordinarily varied history of assaults and alarms to trouble the citizens of Scarborough, a town that received its name 1,000 years ago from a Viking invader Thorgils, nicknamed Skarthi, the hare-lipped. In prehistoric times its great headland had been the site of an Iron Age settlement, and during the Roman occupation a look-out and signal station. In 1066 it was raided by Harald Haardraade, but it was not until the reign of Stephen that Scarborough's port was protected by a great stone castle. Although begun by a Norman knight, William Count of Albermarle and Holderness about 1140, it was soon appropriated by the Crown and remained from 1154 until the reign of James I as a royal castle. Of the ruins that today crown the rocky promontory the most substantial part is the work of Henry II, who built the great keep and probably the curtain walls. Later King John, who visited Scarborough four times, was to spend more than £2,000 strengthening the fortifications. The castle, thus completed on its formidable site, was a very powerful stronghold, and though besieged on several occasions it was never taken by assault. When in 1312 Piers Gaveston, Earl of Cornwall, immured himself here against the barons, it was only because of the threat of starvation that he eventually surrendered, and was swiftly taken to his execution. This has perhaps become the single most famous event associated with the medieval history of the castle, but there were other fierce sieges including the assault made for three weeks by a detachment of the Pilgrimage of Grace. Queen Mary's marriage to Philip of Spain caused much outrage and was angrily opposed by Thomas Stafford who in 1557 surprised the castle with a troop of companions disguised as peasants, but their triumph was short, and within a week Stafford was despatched to Tower Hill. Its capitulation in the Civil War so excited the Puritans that they decreed that 19 August 1645, should be held as a special day of thanksgiving, though such

Built on the site of an Iron Age settlement, first the Romans, then the Normans used Scarborough's great headland for this castle. Only the east wall of Henry II's great 12th-century keep survives today

rejoicings may have proved premature, for in 1648 they had to start on a fresh siege.

Today the east wall of the keep stands almost intact, but the west wall is completely demolished. The destruction caused by Cromwell's men in 1645 has been steadily increased by the storms of the North Sea. Piece by piece, great wedges of the curtain wall have fallen down the cliff. The tower where George Fox, founder of the Quaker movement, was kept imprisoned for a year in 1665 collapsed into the sea in the great fall of 1890, and perhaps more will eventually follow. The keep, however, stands well back and, though battered and hollow, is still on reassuringly solid land.

Skipton NORTH YORKSHIRE

Norman in origin, most of the present castle dates from the early 14th century with restorations of the mid-17th century. It was the last northern castle to resist Cromwell. Above, *the gatehouse;* right, *the Conduit Court which provided the castle's water supply*

Edward II's gift in 1307 of this great Yorkshire stronghold to his favourite Gaveston was only one of the contributory causes of his friend's death, but it was sizable and important, and a gift that many must have coveted. Three years later Gaveston was dead, killed by the king's enemies, and Robert de Clifford commenced his tenure. 'Desormais' was the family motto, and indeed the Cliffords, famous as the castellans of the castle of York and builders of Clifford's Tower, continued thenceforth at Skipton for 14 successive generations, and the great gatehouse bears their inscription on both sides. Edward II's gift to the Cliffords proved a judicious one, for the family was consistent—to a quite unfashionable degree—in its loyalty to the Crown. Robert de Clifford had fought bravely as a young man for Edward I against the Scots, and was finally killed at Bannockburn in the service of Edward II. His descendants of the 14th and 15th centuries likewise fought and were killed in France, Scotland and Germany— wherever the English monarch conducted his wars— and Shakespeare's Clifford in his *Henry VI* was the 8th baron, killed at the battle of St Albans. Their support of the Lancastrian cause was total and their losses disastrous, with the result that for 24 years their castle and lands of Skipton were confiscated, and the 10th baron had to be brought in 1485 from the Cumberland Fells where he was living as a shepherd, a name by which he was subsequently known, and under which he fought with distinction at the Battle of Flodden. During the Rising of the North the Cliffords remained loyal to Elizabeth, and finally their

most notable Royalist endeavour was under Lady Anne, the last of the Clifford owners of Skipton. In 1642 the castle was held for the monarch for three years, and was the final stronghold in the north of England to resist Cromwell.

Such consistent dedication to the Crown was on occasion, however, alleviated by less well-mannered behaviour. In 1250 William de Clifford, having quarrelled with his sovereign, managed to force one of his unfortunate officers physically to 'eate the King's Writ, waxe and all.' The royal displeasure was predictably so great that 'while he lived he was made the lesse able to feede himself, paying to the King a very great summe of money, and hardly escaping without confiscation of his whole patrimonie.' Most flamboyant of all the family was George Clifford, 3rd Earl of Cumberland, a buccaneer of irregular life-style, who staked his money and that of Elizabeth I with a splendid extravagance and presumably a fair measure of success, for he stood in high favour at Court. It is thought that his only addition to the structure of the castle is the decoration of the Shell Room, a tiny grotto-like chamber encrusted with a myriad plenitude of pretty-coloured shells. Last of all the direct Clifford castellans was Lady Anne, Countess of Pembroke, who throughout the 43 years in the mid-17th century when the castle was hers, repaired and replaced with such energy all the dismantling done by Cromwell's men that much of the castle in its present form must be attributed to her.

Though Norman in its origins, there are only fragmentary remains of this period apart from a barrel-vaulted passage of 1178, and the commanding site over the river below. The massively bulging towers of the gatehouse were of the early 14th century, likewise the seven round towers inside the bailey—all perhaps the work of Robert, first of the Clifford barons at Skipton. Elsewhere the work of Lady Anne abounds. Her passion for bricks and mortar together with her piety sustained her until her death at almost 90 years of age, by which time she had played her part in restoring and building— not only Skipton but five other castles elsewhere, seven churches and chapels, two almshouses and various other monuments. The crest and initials AP carved on the stonework in various places are decorative reminders of this prodigious lady.

Very few castles recovered in this splendid way from Cromwell's destruction. Skipton has remained in an impressive state of repair, and, though now empty of furnishings, seems likely to continue so, for it was bought in recent years by someone born locally, a private citizen of the town, whose long-standing interest in the castle's history is reflected in the care and affection with which it is maintained.

Stokesay SALOP

Seven miles north of Ludlow on the Onny river stand the small and enchantingly pretty group of buildings known as Stokesay Castle. The moat has long been dry and the original gateway has disappeared, likewise most of the outer wall, leaving the castle today quite unmilitary in appearance, and suggesting in every way that it has survived since the 14th century as a peaceful manor house in a quiet Shropshire valley. Yet this was the dangerous border region of the Welsh marches, one of the most explosive and violent parts of the country, and even for a private house defence was essential.

Laurence de Ludlow, a great wool merchant whose father had bought the manor in 1281, obtained nine years later from Edward I a licence to crenellate. He lived only a few more years, but before his death in 1296 he had built a strong high tower at the south end of the west front. The north tower had been built by an earlier owner in 1240, and is the oldest surviving structure in Stokesay; to this Laurence added a top storey with fine projecting timber-work. Being a man of quite considerable wealth, he could afford to pull down the earlier hall and set up what must have been a most splendid new building measuring 31 feet wide × 52 feet long with glazing in the upper windows, a sign of opulence, for this was a period when glass was so expensive that families with several houses tended to take their window-panes with them from one manor to another. Though some of the timber-work may have been modified in the 19th century, much of it is original, and the great blackened tree trunks, which support the roof, show how the smoke usually made its way upwards and out through the louvres. This elegant complex of buildings Laurence surrounded with a moat and curtain wall of stone and lime as his outer system of defence.

The Ludlows held Stokesay for more than 300 years. Thereafter it was sold and resold, but suffered only minor reverses. During the Civil War it was garrisoned for the king as an outpost of the neighbouring crucial stronghold of Ludlow Castle, but surrendered promptly in 1645 to the Parliamentarians, thus avoiding a siege. The subsequent slighting was nominal and left the north tower intact but without battlements. It may have been at about this date that the pretty timber-framed gatehouse was added to replace the original 13th-century entrance. The castle's gradual decline was less damaging than it might have been. It became run-down rather than ruined. It was put to various unseemly uses, such as a granary and a cooper's workshop, but since the 19th century has been well cared for.

Top, Stokesay seen from the small lake to the west of the castle; above, the Great Hall. The 13th-century stonework and original timbers incorporate later modifications. Right, the North Tower, begun about 1240, with the timber-framed 17th-century gatehouse on the left

Tamworth STAFFORDSHIRE

In the year 913 Ethelfleda, daughter of Alfred the Great, defeated the Danes and built a wooden stronghold at the junction of the rivers of the Tame and the Anker. This remains the site of the present castle, though the wooded country that surrounded this former capital of Mercia has given way to the coal mines and industry of which this area is the profitable centre.

The Norman castle that exists today was most probably built by Robert de Marmion, the exploits of whose descendant were so to inspire Sir Walter Scott in *Marmion*. He was the first Champion to the King of England, a position of great power and privilege which he handed on to his descendants, and the shell keep he set up on top of this great mound was a suitably massive red sandstone rubble fortification, with walls some 7 feet thick. Connecting it to the town there is a wing-wall which remains as a fine example of early Norman stonework, known as herring-bone. Near the entrance gateway there is a square tower added in the 12th century and projecting slightly outside the keep wall.

As the keep has been lived in almost continuously since Norman times, rebuilding and refacing to the outer structure was carried out whenever necessary. But by the time the castle had passed from the Marmions to the Ferrers in the 15th century, it was the original interior that had totally vanished. Most of the buildings now inside the courtyard are of brick, and were built somewhat at random from the 16th to 18th centuries. The splendid open-roofed banqueting hall is Tudor, and in the upper storey there is beautiful panelling and carved decoration of the 16th century.

When Defoe visited Tamworth in the early part of the 18th century, his comment was brief:— 'a fine pleasant trading Town, eminent for good Ale and good Company, of the middling sort.' The castle goes unmentioned, but by now it too fits his description—extremely pleasant in its municipal park, but very much of the middling sort, tamed at last by the town.

*Detail of the magnificent 16th-century carved oak
panelling in the banqueting hall*

Tattershall LINCOLNSHIRE

In 1911, when Lord Curzon of Kedleston bought Tattershall Castle, its four magnificent sculpted fireplaces bearing the heraldic shields of Ralph, Lord Cromwell, and his wife had been prised from their settings and taken to London for immediate despatch to the USA. Lord Curzon's timely intervention secured their return to their original beautiful brick surrounds, where they remain today as the chief ornament of the tower's great vacant rooms. One of the motifs of the stone panels is a purse tightened with draw-strings attached to a belt, the emblem of Treasurer of England, and it was no doubt to celebrate his appointment to this high office in 1433 that Lord Cromwell built his magnificent keep at Tattershall.

An earlier castle belonging to the Cromwell family was built originally in the 13th century. Since then various inheritances had steadily accumulated, and when the 3rd baron came to assess his wealth, the small squarish home of his ancestors may have seemed too modest an establishment for a man of state at the climax of his career. So, happily, he commissioned a lavish extension to it in the form of a tall square tower and other adjacent buildings, all surrounded by two moats and to be made from the small dark red bricks that were beginning to find favour in the new buildings of the day. In the event well over a million of them were made in Lord Cromwell's kilns and were used at Tattershall. The four storeys are built over a vaulted basement and rise to a height of 100 feet, including the hexagonal corner turrets. The roof gallery is built out on corbels and is probably unique. Its rectangular shape too was something of an exception in England at the time: the great square keeps in this country, such as Rochester or the Tower of London, were all built much earlier, and the erection of one in the 15th century by a lesser man might have been considered curiously old-fashioned. Lord Cromwell's travels with the English army in France and his introduction to the architecture of the Continent, where this kind of keep was still in vogue, must have stimulated him to brighten his new home in England with a little borrowed drama from abroad.

The keep rose magnificently from the flat Lincolnshire landscape, replacing the former stone house. Instead of the small protected openings of the Middle Ages, Lord Cromwell's home was provided with large ornate ground-floor windows, gaping invitingly towards the enemy but providing wonderfully light airy rooms for the family. His household was indeed a sumptuous one, for he lived with an entourage of over 100 people in what was a castle in concept rather than practice—a 15th-century equivalent of the romantic Gothic of 300 years later. 'Nay je droit' was the splendidly arrogant precept by which he ran this elegant establishment, and fortunately the enemy

Above, *the Great Tower (1432–48), part of Lord Cromwell's castle, restored by Lord Curzon.* Top, *the Treasurer's Purse, a detail of the carved stone chimney-piece* right

never came. Little is known about the later history of the castle, but it appears not to have been involved in the upheavals of the 16th and 17th centuries.

Following the example of his king, Henry VI, at Eton and Cambridge, Lord Cromwell founded his own collegiate chapel. He rebuilt on a lavish scale in stone the old parish church, intending the new building to serve both parochially and as a college of priests. He and his wife were in the end buried there long before the scheme was completed. Fortunately of all the buildings erected by Cromwell the two most important, the keep and the church, still stand today in good condition.

Lord Cromwell died without children, and the castle passed to the Crown, then to the earls of Lincoln, and was finally bought—like Bodiam—by Lord Curzon on his return from India. Nothing remained of the original 13th-century stone castle, for the entire complex had become derelict and a bricklayer had been commissioned to remove all the useful materials, level the castle yard and fill the inner moat. This was clearly carried out to the satisfaction of those involved, for a brewery had been built from the spoils. Lord Curzon, when he took on the work of restoration, found himself confronted with an enormous task. The tower was derelict and had been struck by lightning, farmstock wandered through the ground floor. He set about re-excavating the moat and did much restoration to the floors and to the top of the building. On the whole the actual fabric of the walls remained in good condition, justifying Curzon's claim that it was 'the most splendid piece of brickwork in England.' 2

Tintagel CORNWALL

In Geoffrey de Monmouth's narrative romance of how Arthur was conceived in Tintagel Castle, Merlin the Magician sits out the proceedings in a cave, which lies at the bottom of the cliff and passes under the castle from one side of its promontory to the other. Presumably the foaming waters which flood through at high-tide were nothing to him for it was by his magic that Uther, the British king, had changed his likeness to that of the castle's owner, Gorlois, and could thus ravish his wife, Igraine. When Geoffrey de Monmouth published his *History of Britain* in 1139 the interest in the Arthurian legend had been growing considerably over the past century, and so plausible an endorsement of popular belief could only be well received. Later romances identify as owner of the castle Arthur's villainous kinsman, King Mark, who caused the death of Tristram and the beautiful Queen of Ireland, Iseult.

Access to the castle is still difficult, half on the mainland and half on a peninsula, and the storms which lash into the North Cornwall coves periodically sweep away parts of the jagged slate rock of the coastline. In Geoffrey de Monmouth's time there was a narrow causeway joining the mainland 'which three armed men shall be able to defend against the whole power of the kingdom', or so he thought, though there would have been little even in his day that Tintagel could have done to resist the long-ranging siege engines that were already in current use. A further weakness lies in the castle's division into two parts: the gate and upper ward, once captured, would leave the isolated island ward vulnerable and open like a pinioned duck. The causeway has now

flaked away into the sea, leaving the castle almost as remote as the legends with which it is associated.

Architecturally there is also little left to give substance even to the authenticated history of Tintagel in more recent times. When Reginald, Earl of Cornwall, the illegitimate son of Henry I, built a stronghold here in 1145, he may have found the remains of an earlier fortification as well as the cells and monastery established by the community of St Juliot, the Celtic missionary, who had arrived there at the beginning of the 6th century. It is to Reginald that the Great Hall and Chapel are attributed. The buildings were later extended by Earl Richard, younger brother of Henry III, in the middle of the 13th century, and the main part of Tintagel, such as it is, dates from his lifetime. It passed in the 14th century with other castles in Cornwall to the Black Prince, and remains today part of the Duchy of Cornwall. A certain amount of restoration was done, but after his death the castle fell into ruin and was never again used except as a prison at the end of the 14th century. The present nature of its shapeless state is perfectly suited to a site whose main appeal is now mythological, and whereas in most castles the visitors are grappling with problems of bastion and barbican, here the mind can float unimpaired to the dark romantic areas of Celtic legend, for even without the ruins the drama of the site would be enough.

Built in the 12th–13th centuries on a site famous for its association with the Arthurian legend and for its dramatic situation over the cave in the cliff below

Tower of London GREATER LONDON

To be sent to the Tower has represented through much of this country's history the ultimate disaster. 'No sadder spot on earth' is how Lord Macaulay describes the Chapel Royal of St Peter's ad Vincula, for of the 63 people said to lie within the crypt, only nine were buried with their heads on. The present appearance of the chapel is the work of Henry VIII, but it was founded in the 12th century, probably by Henry I; it derives its name from the chains thought to have bound the Apostle that now lie in Rome in a smaller neighbour of the great St Peter's. Henry VIII is associated with the whole of the Tower, not only for the memorable number of people he managed to send there to their death, including two of his wives, the martyrs Thomas More and John Fisher, the poet earl of Surrey, and his adviser Thomas Cromwell, but also for the sterling additions he made to its structure. It was he who built as a royal residence the pleasing half-timbered King's House in the south-west corner, and the angle turrets on the White Tower. Indeed it was he who brought the Tower of London virtually to its present form nearly five centuries after William the Conqueror had founded it on the site of a Roman fortification.

The south-east corner of the Roman wall enclosing the City of London was where the Normans chose to build their fortress. The wall was probably then in sturdy shape as King Alfred had rebuilt it in 885, but today only fragments survive, where the Normans set up the bastion known as the Wardrobe Tower. Otherwise of all the huge complex of towers, baileys, domestic buildings and outworks, only the White Tower, the original nucleus of William I's magnificent stronghold, survives. Some 12 years after he arrived work began on this great keep to improve the temporary fortifications of 1067, for the Normans understandably were wary of 'the fickleness of the vast and fierce populace'; even more dangerous, there was the ever-present threat of the Danes. Gundulf, Bishop of Rochester, was entrusted with the task, and set about building for William a massive, fortified royal residence, 90 feet high, complete with a great hall and chapel, and with walls 15 feet thick to resist all manner of known ballistic devices. Little is known about the building of the keep except that its white stone came from Caen, and that its appearance continued even whiter when Henry III in 1241 applied paint to the whole of the exterior. William I died before his fortress had been completed, for there are indications that building was continued in the reign of his successor. It was, however, presumably finished when in 1097 William II built a wall round it, thereby incurring much hatred for his oppressive levy of money and men. Gundulf may have lived to see other additions, for he survived both

these kings and lived on until 1108 in the reign of Henry I, having built the similarly magnificent keep of Rochester.

At this early period, although impressive for its massive strength and solidity, it was clearly not yet the unshakable prison it was later to become. Ralf Flambard, Bishop of Durham, its first recorded prisoner, effected his escape to Normandy from there in 1101. As the building of the outer fortification continued, so did its security, and others were not so lucky.

The successive stages of its fortification are not clearly identifiable in the 12th century, but work was evidently in progress, for there are records of the expenditures. Particularly remarkable was the vast sum of £2,881, spent in 1190 by Richard I. It is not, however, until the time of Henry III that more fully documented work occurred. As he enjoyed using the Tower as a royal residence, and yet was aware of the continuing hostility of the people of London, it was understandable that he should improve the defences, and it is he who built most of the great circle of flanking towers that still form the inner curtain, thus turning the stronghold into a very early concentric castle, famous otherwise as the innovation of Edward I. Henry III also undertook extensive redecoration and rebuilding of the royal apartments, and his programme of royal whitewash extended from the exterior of the great keep to every room inside. Even the beautiful chapel of St John, part of Gundulf's original work with its great cylindrical columns and simple arches, was given a new coat, decorated and fitted with stained glass windows. The most surprising of his additions to the Tower was the building within its walls of an elephant house to accommodate an unfortunate animal presented to the king by Prince Louis in 1255, and said to be the only elephant seen in Europe since the time of Hannibal. Interesting animals have always found favour with royalty, and the elephant, which survived only as long as might be expected, was the precursor of many strange and curious gifts that ended up in this most unlikely of menageries. A tower, which formerly existed at the main entrance, was assigned to them and became known as the Lion Tower.

The bridging between the work of Henry III and the last additions to the defences made by Henry VIII was effected by that most assiduous of castle builders, Edward I. Today the castle is approached by his

The White Tower. The central keep, begun about 1078 and once painted with whitewash, is that part of the castle after which the whole is named

Inscriptions by prisoners carved on the wall, in Beauchamp Tower

entrance from the City through the Middle Tower, across the bridge over the moat and through Byward Tower; more famous though is the river entrance, also built by Edward I in about 1280, known as St Thomas's Tower or Traitors' Gate. A former gateway in another part of the castle had been linked in the popular imagination with St Thomas à Becket, for a tower built by Henry III at great expense suddenly 'fell as if it had been struck by an earthquake'. To the medieval mind the most likely available cause would have been the revenge of the martyr visiting, in good biblical fashion, the sins of the fathers on the children. Edward's new water-gate perpetuated the link by including an oratory to the martyr. It was under this wide-spanning arch that high-ranking prisoners, brought by river from trial at Westminster, would enter first St Thomas's, then the Bloody Tower, and find themselves admitted to perhaps Beauchamp or Bell Tower as their final place of confinement. This was how Queen Elizabeth I would have arrived when as a young princess she was imprisoned here in the Bell Tower, where before her Bishop Fisher and Sir Thomas More had been kept. Each of the towers has had its quota of famous prisoners, for up to the 17th

century the risk of arrest and confinement there was an occupational hazard of those who entered the deadly game of politics, or who were unfortunate enough to be born too close to the Crown.

The Tower, although the symbol of this ever-present threat, had perhaps less gruesome an image than might be imagined, for the royalty of England seemed happy to maintain a residence there. Henry III clearly favoured it and was a frequent visitor with his queen. Edward IV used it as a residence even more than his predecessors and sometimes kept splendid court there. But Henry VI, confined and killed (probably in the Wakefield Tower), is the only king whose memory is ceremonially observed. His two great foundations of Eton and King's College, Cambridge, send respectively a sheaf of white lilies and white roses every year on 21 May. It was James I who finally broke the old custom of staying in the Tower before his coronation.

Edward I's other major work was the setting up of the outer curtain wall and towers, and the digging of the present moat beyond it, which continued until 1281 and cost upwards of £4,000. Thus the Tower expanded to its present extensive area of twelve acres, with even an encroachment on the river itself by an artificial embankment. (Today's stone wharf, stretching along the whole riverside length of the castle, probably dates from the end of the 14th century, when Geoffrey Chaucer was Clerk of the King's Works). It was at this period too that the Royal Mint was set up in the Tower, where it remained until 1811.

Since Edward's time 700 years ago the Tower has needed the constant attentions of the country's best masons and engineers, who have patched, restored, crenellated, buttressed the fabric, and done everything financially possible to primp and preserve this aged creature of medieval England. The moat, were it still filled with the tidal waters of the Thames, would no doubt be a more picturesque feature today than it was in the Middle Ages, since the garbage, for which it was then the immediate repository, now goes elsewhere. Edward III, perhaps with a view to curbing outbreaks of plague and other infection, introduced the death penalty for those caught bathing in the Tower's moat. After the introduction of artillery, it ceased to be an impregnable fortress; nor was it used as a royal residence after Cromwell, a man of logical thoroughness where it concerned royalty, had demolished the ancient palace. However, its function as a State prison was one maintained until the 18th century, when Jacobite supporters were confined in its cells. The last execution took place there after the 1745 Rising, but it was twice used as a prison in the 19th century, and again in the 20th when the

Irish leader, Sir Roger Casement, convicted of treason, was sent there in 1916, and Hitler's deputy, Rudolf Hess, in 1941.

The present entirely cheerful atmosphere—visitors queuing to see the Crown Jewels, the Yeoman Warders in their Tudor regalia and the extraordinary ravens—is largely due to the Victorians, for it was in 1875 that the Tower, much restored by the architect Salvin, had its first free opening to the public, whose interest and imagination had already been fired by the best-selling romance of Harrison Ainsworth, *The Tower of London*, in 1840. It is perhaps appropriate that this last work inspired by the Tower should have been written from outside it, and not, as were so many before, by some languishing prisoner. The remarkable number of these mournful and moving works bears witness even more than the Tower itself to the sombre plight of those who dwindled away there, or went out to a brutish and public death on Tower Hill. In a curious way the monastic solitude and discipline of life in the Tower seems to have inspired a few of those confined there. Sir Nicholas Carew, lent a translated Bible by a keeper before his execution, thanked God 'that ever he came into the Tower, where he first savoured the life and sweetness of God's most holy Word'. Sir Thomas More

wrote here his *Dialogue of Comfort against Tribulation*, and his *Treatise upon the Passion*. Although paper and ink were removed from him and he had to continue writing with charcoal, his spirits had never been higher, and it was a much more anxious King Henry who sent urgent word that More was not to speak too much at his execution in 1535. So More restricted himself to a few encouraging words to his executioner: 'pluck up thy spirits, man, and be not afraid to do thine office: my neck is very short.'

Many poets flourished in the Tower, soaring in word and spirit where they physically might not go: Charles, Duke of Orleans, Robert Southwell, Sir Walter Raleigh were all busy men who found more time here than elsewhere to write verse. Raleigh also wrote his *History of the World* here while others such as Edmund Dudley, Stephen Gardiner and Sir John Eliot produced treatises ranging freely from politics to theology. During the long hours of confinement many prisoners carved for themselves and for posterity all manner of moving inscriptions and memorials. Particularly fine is the sculpture and poem by John Dudley, Earl of Warwick, in the Beauchamp Tower. In the Salt Tower there is a remarkable astronomical clock and calendar with Zodiac signs, inscribed by its imprisoned maker Hew Draper of Brystow. Most moving of all perhaps is the simple anonymous inscription: 'close prisoner 8 monthes 32 weekes 224 dayes 5376 houres.'

Aerial view of the Tower. See Colour Plate I

Warkworth NORTHUMBERLAND

Crossing the River Coquet at the north end of the village is a fine medieval bridge complete with fortified tower, a rare survival in Britain. At the time when the castle was the main seat of the Claverings and later of the great Northumberland family of Percy, who built the magnificent cruciform keep, this fortified bridge would have been an essential part of the outer defences of the castle, for although excellently sited in a loop of the river, it is vulnerable from the village. Not as grand or as well known as the great strongholds of Alnwick and Bamburgh, with which it formed part of a chain of resistance to the ever-threatening Scots, Warkworth is nevertheless more lovely in its wooded valley and as ancient in its origins.

In 737 Geolwulf, the king of Northumbria to whom Bede dedicated his chronicle, gave its tithes to the Lindisfarne monks of St Cuthbert, who maintained possession of it through the pillaging of the Danes only to lose it to Osbert, the last king of all Northumbria. Thereafter it remained a baronial rather than ecclesiastical property, but the castle, which came into being during the first part of the 12th century, was not of great strategic importance until the early 13th. It was then that Robert of the family of Clavering, who had received the estate from Henry II, first made the castle into a serious stronghold. His splendid gatehouse and towers, known as the Carrick-fergus and West Postern, greatly added to the existing stone fortifications, which had failed shortly before in 1173 against the Scottish king, William the Lion, during the castle's first recorded siege. His alterations to the Great Hall and chamber, chapel and other household areas must likewise have improved the quality of daily life. Next time the Scots laid siege— which they did twice in 1327, once under the leadership of Robert the Bruce—the defence was sustained. It seems, however, that the Clavering family became rapidly less capable of managing their affairs, and in 1332 the estate slipped through their fingers into the grateful hands of the Percys, for whom it soon became the favourite residence.

The splendid late 15th-century tower gives entrance to the Great Hall, and is decorated with a stone carving of the Percy lion and motto 'Esperance'. Hope was certainly a dominating theme in the restless exploits of the 3rd Percy, Lord of Warkworth, and his son Harry Hotspur, when they risked all—first to win the crown for Henry IV, and then four years later in their bid to deprive him of it. Shakespeare in *Richard II* sets three scenes of this great conspiracy inside the castle walls. Only two years after Hotspur's death in 1403, his father was again eager to pledge his hopes to another imprudent cause. The rebellion was that of Archbishop Scrope; this time when it failed Henry marched swiftly north to Warkworth and,

with seven discharges of the royal cannon, forced the castle to surrender.

Thereafter the Percys came and went from Warkworth as they paid for their misdemeanours. Each time they were restored to their lands, and made important additions and alterations throughout the 14th and 15th centuries. A coat of arms on the keep-gatehouse shows that it was probably built by about 1390, the work of the 3rd Lord Percy. This is the remarkable sequin-shaped building overlooking the river. It provided accommodation for the lord, quite separate from his garrison who lived in the recently built domestic buildings on the west side of the castle, once the palatial mansion of the Claverings. It was probably also the 3rd Lord Percy who laid the foundations of a large church across the centre of the courtyard, no doubt intended to be a great collegiate church such as accorded with the dignities of a wealthy and pious family. Its scale and situation suggest that it would have resembled other such magnificent foundations as St George's Chapel at Windsor, or that which the Lord Treasurer Cromwell built at his castle of Tattershall. Though the great plan was never fulfilled, workmen were constantly employed at the castle for it was kept more or less in good repair until the mid-16th century, whereafter the sojourns of the Percys in the Tower of London far exceeded the periods when they would have been at liberty to live on their own estates, and the buildings became ruinous.

In 1608 it was reported that the castle was being used as a cattle-fold, and that its gates were left open day and night. Shakespeare's description of Warkworth as 'this worm-eaten hold of ragged stone' was certainly not true of the castle of Harry Hotspur, but may have been an accurate account of what it was like in Shakespeare's own day. In 1617 when James I and his retinue passed by Warkworth on their way to Scotland, they were 'much moved to see it soe badly spoyled and soe badly kept.' The decay of this once proud stronghold continued relentlessly, though the heirs of the earls of Percy at the end of the 17th century were thought to be going to make it their home again. Today it is still a ruin, but a well-repaired one, with a small part of it even made habitable. It remains a picturesque hint of what might have been, had the dukes of Northumberland not rebuilt their other great castle at Alnwick.

The late 14th-century keep seen here from the southwest in a loop of the River Coquet is the most intact surviving part of this Percy stronghold

Warwick WARWICKSHIRE

Behind the Gothic windows of this fine façade, facing south-east and raised on a small escarpment above the river Avon, the earls of Warwick have enjoyed a sunny position of privilege since the early days of the Norman Conquest when Henry de Newburgh was created the 1st earl in 1088. Warwick was recorded in the Domesday Book as already being a prosperous borough established some 150 years before, when the Saxon princess Ethelfleda, daughter of Alfred the Great, set up a wooden fortress to resist the Danes. It may be that the mount still standing at the south-west end of the present castle, and known as Ethelfleda's, is from this period. But little survives today of the earliest stonework, a Norman shell keep, probably octagonal, which was largely destroyed during the Barons' Revolt in 1264. The fragmentary remains form an indentation into the circle of the castle walls, in shape rather like the setting of a ring with a stone missing. Most of the outer features of the present castle date from the mid-14th century when it had passed to the Beauchamp family. The view from over the river shows the wing containing the Great Hall, where it has been suggested the unfortunate Sir Piers Gaveston received a summary trial before his execution by the barons on Blacklow Hill. It is a fine room, though now mainly Victorian, raised on a beautifully vaulted

Above, *aerial view*. Right, *looking from the River Avon along the Jacobean wing containing the Great Hall. At the end is visible the unusual double parapet of the 14th-century Caesar's Tower*

substructure of kitchens and bakehouses; running underneath and below the surface of the rock are the cellars. At the east end is Caesar's Tower, its three splaying lobes rising to a magnificent six storeys and crowned with an unusual double parapet. This together with the gatehouse was built by Thomas Beauchamp, one of Edward III's most distinguished generals. The other main tower, Guy's, was built by his son, again Thomas, and completed in 1394. These great towers, providing almost extravagant protection for the already strongly defended three-storey gatehouse and barbican, are probably the two most extraordinary features of the castle.

After the Beauchamps Richard Neville succeeded to the huge estates and title. His dazzling political and military manoeuvres in the Wars of the Roses, together with his vast purchasing power, earned him the title of Kingmaker. His household was a brilliant one, but he made no interesting contribution to the architecture of the castle, unlike the dismally unsuccessful Duke of Clarence, who, in the seven years of his tenure of the castle before his supposed drowning in the Malmsey wine in 1478, managed to build a tower at the northern entrance.

The interior of the castle dates mostly from a later period than its outside masonry. When James I gave or sold it to the wealthy local member of Parliament, Sir Fulke Greville, the castle was in a dilapidated state and many internal repairs and alterations had to be made, which Sir Fulke energetically undertook, creating the pleasing Jacobean wing overlooking the river. In 1621 he received the title of Baron Brooke, but unfortunately was killed by one of his servants before he had time to enjoy the benefits of either his peerage or his new home at Warwick. Some 250 years later the ancient earldom was recreated for Sir Fulke's descendants, who still live in the castle.

As the 18th century progressed the owners of Warwick were prominent tourists on the Continent, and many of the treasures of the castle date from their grand excursions. The Armoury and State Rooms contain astonishing collections, which could in their early days have been destroyed by the only military action ever to involve the castle, when it was held in the Civil War for Parliament by Robert Lord Brooke. Fortunately the assaults made no impression and after three days the besiegers diverted elsewhere. Nor were the precious contents of the State Rooms touched by a very damaging fire in 1871, which destroyed much of the interior of the Great Hall. Thus a series of lucky accidents combined with a stability unusual for the times has led to an extensive collection of paintings and possessions being still housed in a splendidly maintained medieval and Jacobean context.

Windsor BERKSHIRE

Right, *the massive shell keep deriving from the original Norman foundation dominates the River Thames and the meadows of Eton.* Top, *Henry VIII's Gate, the main entrance to the castle;* above, *entrance to the Horseshoe Cloister built to house clerics of St George's Chapel seen behind.* See *Colour Plate IV*

Most of the early Norman castles in Britain consisted of wooden stockades perched on the top of artificial mounds of earth. At Windsor, however, it has recently been argued that William the Conqueror's great Round Tower was built of stone from the very beginning, as the vast base on which it stands, crowning his chosen site some 100 feet over the River Thames, is a natural chalk mound, and therefore quite suitable to take a great weight of stone on top of it. Obviously a stone keep was proof against fire, and was in every way a more durable proposition than wood. Thus at Windsor, where it was more important to build a permanent castle than a hasty one, local sandstone was chosen as the material for the keep. Though much repaired and refaced, it is probably still in its foundations the same early stone structure that was built in about 1075. Contemporary with the mound and tower were the two enormous baileys or wards, suitable as a protected camping ground for a garrison, which were laid out to east and west, giving a curious boomerang shape to the area enclosed.

Since then the castle has been continuously occupied, and like a mollusc the accretions of time have effected most interesting changes. A great many of the monarchs between the 12th and 19th centuries have modified or added to the original structure. The first extensive remodelling of the keep was done by Henry II in 1175. The buildings ranged round the inside of that first early shell of King William's must already have been suitably developed as a royal residence, for it was here that Henry I had held court and in 1121 celebrated his marriage, but Henry II decided to retain the original structure only as a base for his own new tower, again a shell keep which rose to a height of 34 feet. He also rebuilt the curtain wall round the bailey, fortifying it with towers, and constructed a house for himself of which a part still remains as the basement of the present royal apartments. Thus the castle began to develop, and a pattern of its growth might in general terms be related to the individual characters of its various royal owners. By the end of Henry III's reign a writer of the period describes Windsor as 'that very flourishing castle, than which at that time there was not another more splendid within the bounds of Europe.' King John had had the notorious distinction of causing the only two sieges in the castle's history, with considerable ensuing damage to the fabric, and Henry III inherited the task of repairs on a large scale. The three fine towers of Garter's, Belfry and Chancellor's still remain from this date. The earliest buildings in the Upper Ward today were built by Edward III, who had been born in the castle in 1312 and was known as

Edward Windsor. His reign saw for the first time the large-scale realization of quite unmilitary projects, and housing in the castle was provided for minor canons, choristers, the Poor Knights and the many officials involved in his new institution, the Order of the Garter.

A century later Edward III's Knights of the Garter were to claim as their traditional place of worship the most splendid of all the many buildings to grow up within the castle precincts, St George's Chapel. The massive task of building this beautiful church was begun by Edward IV in 1477. It occupied a great number of skilled craftsmen from all over the country for about fifty years until the spectacular stone vaulting was completed by Henry VII in 1528.

Almost the only other major contribution of the Tudors to the castle was the main entrance, built probably in 1510–11 by Henry VIII and named after him. This gatehouse, although no longer a self-contained military unit such as Edward I would have demanded, is nevertheless a very fine building,

perhaps the last of its kind to be erected in England.

With the exception of Charles II, who in 1685 made a conspicuous embellishment to the castle with the famous three-mile avenue from the Great Park, known as the Long Walk, and who commissioned Grinling Gibbons and Verrio to decorate a completely new set of buildings in the Upper Ward, there were few changes or even repairs to the structure until George IV employed Sir Jeffrey Wyatville in the 1820s to modernize the castle. With the stimulating sum of £1 million to spend on improvements, Wyatville applied himself to raising the standard of domestic comforts in the castle, and thereby too the number of storeys of the Upper Ward in order to house more servants. The Round Tower also was appropriately heightened to retain a dignified relationship to the surrounding buildings, and the flag turret was added. And so the money was spent, but the resulting improvements were so far-sighted that up to the present time little further work has been thought necessary.

Anglesey

Beaumaris ▲

Conway

Rhyl

Flint ▲

C L W Y D

Caernavon ●

G W Y N E D D

Portmadoc

Llangollen ●

Chirk ▲

▲ *Harlech*

Newtown ●

P O W Y S

Aberystwyth ●

Llandrindod
Wells ●

● Cardigan

D Y F E D

● Brecon

● St. David's

● Carmarthen

● Haverfordwest

▲ *Kidwelly*

G W E N T

▲ *Carew*
Pembroke ▲
Tenby

W. GLAMORGAN

MID
GLAMORGAN

Chepstow ▲

Swansea ●

Caerphilly ▲
Castell Coch ▲

Bridgend ●

Cardiff ●

S. GLAMORGAN

0   50 miles

WALES

THE CASTLES of Wales have a unique distinction. The greatest of them (Conway, Caernarvon, Harlech, Beaumaris) were built in one rapid sequence (they were all begun between 1283 and 1295) by a single architect (Master James of St George) and for one patron (Edward I)— and this at a time when the design of castles had reached its high point of sophistication. An unspoilt range of examples from a classic period; to the *aficionado* of the medieval castle north-western Wales is roughly what Bath is (or was?) to the lover of English town architecture.

This is not to say that Wales does not also have important and attractive castles of other periods. The Normans had reached Pembroke as early as 1093, and founded there a castle on the curve of the estuary which developed in about 1200 its present magnificent features. At the other extreme Castell Coch shows the fanciful delights of nineteenth-century medievalism as finely as its not-too-distant neighbour Eastnor —on the other side of that shifting and much disputed border between England and Wales. But it is those great Edwardian strongholds which remain the real British champions, standing along that northwestern coast like armoured giants, infinitely powerful but more than a little puzzled as to where the nimble enemy has vanished. Into the sea? Rescued by Merlin? The medieval English would win the day by brute force in Wales, but it remained a mysterious place.

Beaumaris ANGLESEY

The beautiful marsh covered with bulrushes on the Isle of Anglesey, which must have inspired the Norman name of this great castle of Edward I, has today more or less drained away and become instead a flat and gentle pastureland, in summertime profusely spread with buttercups. It is a placid landscape and one which fits the almost totally uneventful history of this simple symmetrical castle.

It was started by Edward I in 1295 as a last and final safeguard of his new principality of Wales, and as a convenient place to keep extra troops should they be needed on the mainland. The danger, however, from the native Welsh rebels had for the time being receded. Llewelyn, their last great prince, had died thirteen years before, and Madog, his kinsman, after one brilliant stab at the English in their new stronghold at Caernarvon, had been effectively squashed. Master James of St George, Edward's great French architect, was given the agreeable task of building a castle on a site uncluttered by earlier Norman fortifications such as he had had to contend with at Caernarvon, a flat and relatively pleasant terrain, without imminent danger of attack, and with enormous resources at his disposal. The records remaining give a detailed account of Master James's operation, in which 400 masons, 2,000 labourers,

Early 14th-century Norman chapel, lime-washed and vaulted ceiling in Gothic style. Right, *the Gate next the Sea and small dock.* See *Colour Plate X*

200 quarry-men and 30 smiths and carpenters were employed. The result is most interesting—a toy-like, concentric castle, its moat surrounding the octagonal outer walls which in turn contain the inner ward or courtyard, a simple rectangle. This inner ward is unusual in having two great gatehouses, both equally strong, one on the land side and the other facing out to sea, to deal with attack on whichever side it should fall. Inside the north gatehouse is the main room of the castle, the great hall on the first floor, with its five huge windows.

The outer ring of defence with its twelve towers and two minor gatehouses was built some 20 years after the inner ward. Its walls were lower and thinner than the massive 15-foot-thick inner ones, and its purpose was not just to keep the enemy at arm's length as he attacked, but to force him, should he have penetrated so far, to approach the inner gatehouse at an unfortunate angle, exposed on his flank. The main entrance to this outer ward is known as Gate next the Sea. Beside it, on the south side of the castle, stands a small dock into which ships could sail at high tide, a most useful device in time of siege.

The building of the extra defence round the castle proved a quite unnecessary precaution. There was no further danger from the Welsh princes, nor was it attacked by Owain Glyndwr; the only time it might have been put to the test was in 1646 when garrisoned for the king in the Civil War. Spanning the centuries an interesting relationship develops between Master James of St George and Cromwell's famous Commander, Major-General Mytton. They were the two figures in history perhaps most directly concerned with the fabric of the Welsh medieval castles. At the end of the 13th century Master James was commissioned by Edward I to build the eight Welsh strongholds of Flint, Rhuddlan, Aberystwyth, Builth, Conway, Caernarvon, Harlech and Beaumaris. Nearly 400 years later it was again one man commissioned by his superiors who effected a devastating change in the Welsh countryside. Major-General Mytton distinguished himself almost above all others in the Civil War by his famous repeated successes in demolishing Master James's castles: Rhuddlan, Conway, Caernarvon, Harlech—all seemingly impregnable strongholds—fell under his assault as he moved around the country as if in relentless pursuit of the very spirit of the master architect. Beaumaris escaped, and here his guns destroyed nothing, for in 1646 news of the successful siege of Caernarvon and the Royalist defeat in a nearby battle persuaded the garrison on Anglesey that discretion was better than valour. They promptly surrendered to Mytton, who could then proceed to deal with his next target—Conway.

Caernarvon GWYNEDD

To the south-west of the Menai Straits, where the River Seiont joins the sea, the Romans built their fortress of Segontium. It was over this same westerly area leading up to Snowdonia that Edward I realized he must mount guard. He chose Caernarvon as his administrative centre in his great bid to establish English influence and to pacify the conquered people of Wales, and within six months of the death in 1282 of Llewelyn, the last Welsh Prince of Wales, he had started work on his second chain of castles along the coast. First there had been Flint, Rhuddlan and Aberystwyth, and now Conway, Caernarvon, Harlech and Beaumaris. It was a massive and rapid expression of his new power.

At Caernarvon the castle stands at the water's edge, by the side of the Roman town, and on a site previously occupied by an 11th-century Norman castle. The existing township had been a place of importance to the native Welsh princes who sometimes resided here, but in spite of this long royal connection it was in fact Rhuddlan, some 40 miles to the east of Caernarvon, which had been their major stronghold; there is some evidence that Edward considered making his base there too, and it was there, in 1284, that he proclaimed his new Statute of Wales. But Caernarvon offered one practical advantage which must have swayed his decision—it was further into the heart of the troublesome Welsh territories. It also offered a better site for what was to be an ambitious and grandiose scheme. It would seem from the very start of work in 1283 that the great unit of castle, town and walls was seen as a future royal seat, and in 1286 it was put in the charge of the king's special adviser Otto de Grandson, as a kind of Viceroy of North Wales. Conveniently a son was born to Edward at Caernarvon in 1284, and tradition has it that he immediately presented the prince to the Welsh as their future king, blameless, born on Welsh soil, and speaking no word of English—a splendid piece of effrontery more likely to have been added to Edward's legend in later centuries than to have occurred at the time. In 1301 the young Prince Edward was formally invested at Caernarvon as Prince of Wales, and from this date the castle has been associated with the title, one traditionally but not automatically conferred on the monarch's eldest son.

The grandiose purpose for which the castle had been built was never realized. Towards the end of his life the king's financial difficulties became pressing—unprecedented sums of money had already been spent on his Welsh castles, and his presence was now needed in Scotland. Work continued at Caernarvon for some 40 years, but before the interior was even finished Wales had settled into a state of relative calm, and the castle became neglected. Edward II did little

Above, *aerial view*. Right, *the Eagle Tower, 124 feet high, one of the largest towers of the Middle Ages*

to glamorize the invested title of Prince of Wales, nor did he have much occasion to use his intended residence. It was not again visited by royalty until 1399, when it proved sadly unprepared and could only offer Richard II a bed of straw on the floor. With the Act of Union in 1536 the castle lost most of its earlier military and administrative significance, and there was no justification for future outlay of funds on its upkeep or even the completion of its interior. It was garrisoned in the Civil War for King Charles, but fell to Major-General Mytton in 1646. Fortunately an order to demolish it entirely was never carried out. Its present ruined form is that of a magnificent and perfectly surviving hollow shell, the exterior almost intact and the inside gone. The walls today, with their characteristic pattern of light and dark bands of stone, must still look much as they did when newly built in 1300. The all important purpose then would have been to complete the outer defences as quickly as possible, leaving the inside building to develop more gradually. The Queen's Gate, with its two backless polygonal towers, was never finished.

The great tower at the western extremity of the castle, known as the Eagle Tower, is 124 feet high and one of the largest single towers built in the Middle Ages. Except for this one, all the other twelve towers of the castle have been known by different names at different times—the eagle was perhaps derived from the eagles on the coat of arms of the castle's lieutenant, Otto de Grandson, Edward I's Justiciar of North Wales. On the first floor is a small room which is the traditional birthplace of Edward II. It seems, however, that the building of the Eagle Tower had not reached the height of the first floor by 1284, the date of the prince's birth, and that work continued until 1317. The notion therefore is most certainly a romantic fiction, but one probably put about from an early date. The birth more likely occurred in some more temporary royal residence within the town.

The castle's unusual design of irregularly angled walls—instead of the more usual arrangement of rounded towers and rectangular sides—and its alternating bands of light and dark stone were the work of Edward's chief architect, Master James of St George. He had already built a castle with many-angled towers for a patron near Lyons and may well have derived the idea from the walls of Constantinople, which those of Caernarvon resemble and which he would certainly have seen when accompanying Edward on Crusade. Windsor has towers with similar stonework, and it was Edward's intention to build himself not merely a castle at Caernarvon, but a royal residence. The gatehouse is characteristically Edwardian, but in its general layout Caernarvon does not follow his favourite concentric pattern. It is a long single enclosure, which was intended to be divided across the middle by the gatehouse but its internal details were never completed. Nor was any work done on the existing Norman mound, which it is thought Edward anticipated using as the great base for a splendid stone tower, seen and seeing for many miles around, again much like Windsor Castle with its famous Round Tower.

The castle's somewhat forlorn and unfulfilled history took a surprising turn at the beginning of this century, when David Lloyd George, as Constable of Caernarvon and Chancellor of the Exchequer, officiated at the Royal Investiture of the Prince of Wales in 1911—virtually the first recognition by England of the fact of Welsh national identity since the Act of Union some 400 years before. But it was not until 1963 that the Queen conferred on the town the long-overdue title and status of Royal Borough, presumably in anticipation of the Investiture of Prince Charles in 1969. This modern ceremony must have been a very different affair from that first investiture in 1301, and over the centuries English attitudes have changed too: Edward I, hoping to pacify the Welsh, built his great stone stronghold; Prince Charles, a more delicate tactician, set about mastering the intricacies of their difficult language.

Built 1283–1327 as part of Edward I's royal Welsh seat combining castle, town and walls on the site of the Roman fortress of Segontium

Caerphilly <small>MID GLAMORGAN</small>

Above, *southwest angle and lake. To the right can be seen the leaning southeast tower.* Right above, *the remarkable fortified dam, holding the artificial lake;* below, *aerial view of the castle, built in 1268, whose concentric design was much in advance of its time*

Caerphilly's famous south-eastern tower, which leans so boldly out of perpendicular as if frozen in mid-fall into the lake below, is one of those unexplained curiosities that give rise to legend. Most probably it was the Parliamentarians at the time of the Civil War who failed to demolish it, but there is a tradition also that links its Pisan character with Queen Isabella. It is said that while hunting down her unfortunate husband, Edward II, she arrived with her troops and captured this tower which contained the furnace for producing the molten lead, so necessary to a good siege. In an attempt to destroy the foundations, the enemy let the water of the moat come in contact with the furnace. The resulting explosion was such as to cause the tower its present dramatic 9-foot lean. Fortunately the late Marquess of Bute in his careful restoration of the castle left this strange, dramatic tower at its own eccentric tilt.

The castle has other more deliberate features which distinguish its structure. It is usual to associate the concentric castle with Edward I, who came back from the Levant with the idea that a castle consisting of fortified rings, each enclosed by another, must present the most efficient and logical arrangement. But at Caerphilly—long before Edward's Welsh expedition and while he was still away crusading in the Holy Land—a castle was being built in 1268 by his son-in-law, Gilbert de Clare, which was essentially concentric in design. After the Tower of London it is the greatest example of this type of castle in Britain.

How Gilbert de Clare came to build his castle to so advanced a design is not specifically known. Ideas were obviously filtering back from the East, and in any case such an arrangement of fortifications was perhaps a natural development in the history of defence. De Clare was one of the Marcher or Border Barons, living in constant warfare with the Welsh under their last great native prince, Llywelyn ap Gruffydd, and a new quite revolutionary concept to replace the Norman keeps and single enclosures was clearly necessary against the increasingly effective Welsh siege-engines.

The castle which rose on an open site at the edge of the marsh near the River Nant-y-Gledyr was to be the largest in Wales, covering some 30 acres, and was only exceeded elsewhere in Britain by Windsor. The low-lying land has little natural strategic authority, and the castle relies entirely on the sheer weight of its masonry and the ingenious combination of its water and land defences. The river valley in which it stands was turned into a great artificial lake, kept in by an extensive fortified dam spanning some 400 yards. This barrage with its great buttresses served both to hold in the huge volume of water and to provide extra points of defence for the castle. Even by modern standards it is a notable feat of engineering.

The castle was not involved in Edward I's Welsh wars at the end of the 13th century, but some years later it did play a part in the affairs of the nation in connection with the dismal fate of Edward II. Hugh le Despenser, a companion and favourite of Edward, married into the de Clare family and became the Lord of Caerphilly, and it was here that the harassed king, pursued by his powerful wife Isabella and other enemies, sought a refuge for himself and his possessions. He had moved elsewhere before he was finally captured, but Isabella continued to besiege the castle until it surrendered some months later. The king's wealth was handed over to her and Despenser was beheaded.

Apart from another brief military engagement at the beginning of the 15th century, when Owain Glyndwr captured and held it, the castle had little further importance in the history of Wales. Already by the end of the 13th century the country had been effectively subjugated and a fortress on the scale of Caerphilly was no longer necessary to withstand the later minor revolts. It remained useful as a permanent subduing presence in the Welsh Marches, and as a base for the collection of taxes and the holding of an occasional court. But this was not enough to prevent its decay into the present state of ruin.

Carew DYFED

The earliest part of the castle was constructed before 1116. The towers were built in the late 12th century, the two south ones are seen above; right, *the Elizabethan wing*

The ornately carved high cross on the way to Carew Castle is a graceful memorial to the native Celtic tradition which existed before the early Norman invaders established themselves in this part of Britain. Their legacy in Wales was the castle, hitherto unknown in the Welsh domestic context.

In 1095 a Norman knight, Gerald de Windsor, who already held Pembroke Castle in the name of Henry I, received the castle at Carew as part of his wife's dowry. This was Nesta, famous in her own time for her abduction by a Welsh prince but today more fondly thought of as the grandmother of Giraldus Cambrensis—the vigorous opponent of Anglo-Norman authority over the Church in Wales.

At Carew nothing remains of that original Norman stronghold, but the earliest surviving stonework, now incorporated into the east front, does probably date from the 12th century. The four towers and gatehouse surrounding the courtyard—the basic features of today's ruined castle—were the work of Sir Nicholas Carew, who died in 1311. The castle's most flamboyant owner was perhaps Sir Rhys ap Thomas, Henry VII's powerful Welsh ally, who energetically remodelled and improved the existing structure. The future Henry VII stayed at Carew on his way to victory at Bosworth Field in 1485, but the lavish new apartments with the great hall and the stairs were no doubt built later—in time for the great tournament of 1507, given by Rhys to celebrate the new dynasty of the Tudors.

The goodwill of each successive monarch was unpredictable and Rhys's grandson forfeited the estate to a new owner, Sir John Perrot, reputed to be a son of Henry VIII. He also made ambitious and spectacular alterations, in the form of the handsome Elizabethan wing, with spacious rooms and large quite unmilitary windows. But the wheel of fate might almost have been designed for the owners of castles. Sir John too, after an illustrious career, was condemned to death for treason against Elizabeth.

His new castle proved less flabby than it looked. It was made unnecessarily vulnerable by the fine Elizabethan wing which broke right through the original structure of the walls, but even in this civilian state it held out surprisingly well against the Roundheads in 1644, proving that the most decadent old thing can put up a tough fight if provoked. The Puritans won through in the end, and took some vengeance on the fabric. But even that stood up well, and continues to do so today.

VIII Harlech, Gwynedd

On its magnificent site once overlooking the sea, this castle, built by Edward I between 1283 and 1289, is a fine example of concentric design, and survived many sieges and attacks, including bombardment with massive stone cannon-balls in 1408. *See* p. 158.

IX Kidwelly, Dyfed

When Henry granted the lands of Kidwelly to his minister, Roger Bishop of Salisbury, the River Gwendraeth was navigable at high tide, giving the Normans access to the estuary even if they lost control of the surrounding land. In the event it proved only a precarious perch for the invaders, for the castle that Bishop Roger built was for long periods in the hands of the Welsh, whose own chronicles record that it was built in 1190 by Lord Rhys. This was just one of three major reconstructions that took place before Edward I virtually gave it to his nephew Henry of Lancaster by arranging his marriage with the Kidwelly heiress in 1291. Henry set about bringing the castle up to date, incorporating all the innovations of Edward's concentric system of fortification. Round the existing rectangular castle with its four drum towers he built an outer curtain wall with four more towers and two gatehouses, the main one being a massive structure of three storeys. The Welsh Wars, however, were almost over, and the new defences were not needed for another 100 years, when they proved as formidable as hoped. During the years 1403–5 Owain Glyndwr twice besieged the castle, but each time without success. Thereafter it declined in importance; it passed as part of an inheritance to Blanche, wife of John of Gaunt, then to the Crown, and although it was involved in the usual alarms of the Civil War, its useful life was clearly over.

The road to the castle still leads through the main gateway of the old walled town of Kidwelly. The medieval houses have all been replaced, and apart from the castle nothing remains of Bishop Roger's original Norman settlement except the Priory Church on the other side of the river—a much-altered memorial to him, but one for which even a warlike Norman bishop might prefer to be noticed in heaven.

X Beaumaris, Anglesey

Last of Edward I's great ring of castles built to protect his new principality of Wales, Beaumaris surrendered to the Parliamentarians in 1646 but escaped the usual slighting and is today the best preserved concentric castle in Britain. *See* p. 134.

Castell Coch MID GLAMORGAN

Above, *view from the southeast.* Right, *the delicately painted doors and walls within the keep*

The castle known as Castell Coch is so closely crowded by thick beech woods that only by descending down past them to the south-east can one see, rising up like three beaks from a nest, the conical towers of this fantasy creation. Perhaps this accounts for the old tradition that there are inside the castle three ravens guarding its secret treasure. A photograph of 1875 shows an ivy-covered ruin with only the vaguest suggestion of a tower at one end. This was all that remained of the original Castell Coch or Red Castle, about which little is known except that it was destroyed probably in the 15th century. It was on the base of these red crumbling walls overlooking a gorge of the River Taff that William Burges was commissioned by Lord Bute to fabricate a 13th-century castle. The Marquess of Bute was well steeped in all kinds of antiquarian knowledge and was fortunately energetic and rich enough to translate his interests into a wonderful antique building. William Burges treated the commission with fastidious academicism except when his personal fantasy took over, ruining the whole documentary effect but providing his patron with many delightful features—such as conical turrets instead of the more orthodox flat roofs with parapet and rampart, which were typical of an early Welsh castle. Otherwise the castle certainly has the look of a serious fortress. Its towers rise from their red sandstone base at a thickness of 10 feet, two of them buttressed out to a square base, the third standing in a dry moat crossed by a wooden bridge— to be set on fire at the moment of attack. A portcullis preceded by a drawbridge, each with its own wind-lass, was to provide further protection before any undesirable Victorian visitor could finally reach the heavy entrance door. A modification had to be made, however, when Lord Bute's need for a comfortable bedroom on the second storey, preferably without the draughty presence of a windlass coming through the floorboards, dictated that the windlass equipment should be sited on the first floor instead, dangerously near the fires which would-be attackers could start in the gatehouse. Burges compromised further and the system finally built was a simpler device operating drawbridge and portcullis together.

The castle inside is surprisingly small—the main rooms, grouped round the central courtyard, consisting only of banqueting hall, drawing room, two bedrooms, servants' hall, kitchen and discreet lavatories. The only items of furniture that remain, the strangely shaped beds, basins and carved oak benches and chairs, were clearly designed by Burges to inflict ruthlessly on his keen patron all the horrors of genuine medieval discomfort. Had there been any rooms for guests, it is doubtful whether they would have shared the 3rd marquess's enthusiasm for this kind of Gothic authenticity. Whether because it was not possible to entertain there or was just too dreadfully uncomfortable, the marquess, though delighted with the result, was seldom in residence.

The main rooms, which Burges called the Castellan Rooms, are decorated most elaborately with paintings and carvings; every panel is worked with wonderful patterns and figures, and the effect is much like the margin of a Book of Hours. Perhaps the high-vaulted room on the first and second floors of the keep is the most delightful and profusely decorated of all. The doors and walls round the lower part of this octagonal-shaped room have delicately painted flowers in panels, while at eye level and above are illustrations from Aesop's fables: Stork, Hare, Tortoise and others, all exquisitely painted amongst the bowers of dangling fruit and flowers. The three carved shields proclaiming the family pedigree under trefoiled arches intrude somewhat on this pastoral scene. Equally unwelcome are the Three Fates on the opposite side of the room over the mantelpiece, but from the gallery above, where it is possible to walk, the birds and butterflies seem to have escaped to join the stars in a distant sky. Other butterflies have stayed, carved wooden ones, each painted a different colour, and they sit clustered together on the golden ribs of the dome. Burges left very detailed note-books but did not say who were the artists responsible for the decoration of the rooms; presumably there were several working under his supervision.

The Lady's Room, reached only by a spiral staircase, is on the two floors above the Drawing Room. Here the decoration is more uniform and perhaps less successful, but there is an interesting double dome to make maximum use of the height of the conical turret. At the top of the castle already, the tour is surprisingly soon over, but it is easy to imagine with what pleasure Lord Bute must have conducted visiting friends round his creation.

Chepstow GWENT

In the first years after the Norman Conquest the whole of Britain south of Chester was controlled by a fairly even distribution of castles. The Norman lords were granted large holdings of land and each had as his principal seat a castle, usually sited if possible on a high bluff overlooking a river, and from which he would either maintain discipline over the new subjects or push forward the Norman frontiers of control. Chepstow Castle is recorded in Domesday Book as built by one of the Conqueror's chief lieutenants, William Fitz Osbern, newly created Earl of Hereford. It is most excellently placed on a long high cliff above a harbour on the Wye, defended from behind by a deep ravine known as the Dingle. Then, as now, this was where the main land route into South Wales crossed the river. Thus the castle was well placed as a centre for Norman penetration further westwards, and its significance in the overall strategic plan is implied in the uncommon use of stones rather than timber for the building. The walls of the large two-storeyed tower that William Fitz Osbern built, though altered and heightened at later dates and now totally gutted, are substantially those of about 1070. The tower occupied the central portion of the ridge, leaving room across the width of it for only a narrow easily defended passage connecting the enclosed spaces to either side. It was obviously most adequately built for its day, as only small sums are recorded as being spent on it in the 12th century when it belonged to first Gilbert then Richard 'Strongbow' of the de Clare family. In the early 13th century it passed by marriage into the hands of the great military figure, William Marshall, also of Pembroke Castle, who began at once to modernize the defences. This was a massive operation, to be continued after his death by each of the five sons who succeeded him. By 1246, when the last died, all the walled enclosures outside the keep had been greatly extended to increase the size of the main body of the castle. These new works were defended by great bulky walls, in places 18 feet thick, with a double-towered gatehouse and fine drum towers, which remain today as interesting examples of a very early use in England of round as opposed to square mural towers. The great original keep was remodelled, and embellished with large windows on the secure north side overlooking the Wye and an additional storey was added to provide more comfortable and spacious living accommodation.

The castle was by now formidably strong, and the only important alterations before Tudor times were made at the end of the 13th century by a great-nephew of the Marshals, Roger Bigod III. A three-storey gatehouse was built to guard the western approach and to provide (as at Conway) a back entrance, and an entirely new range of two great halls was completed to the north-east, probably by 1285, when the castle was visited by Edward I. At the south-eastern corner of the outer wall, where the site affords least protection, there was also built a round projecting tower containing a hall and chamber and adjoining it a chapel, in short a complete self-contained lodging for the lord. This is now known as Marten's Tower, and certainly of all its occupants Henry Marten, one of the judges to sign Charles I's death warrant, was the most famous. Imprisoned here at the Restoration by Charles II, he lived with his wife in what appears to have been considerable comfort and style, rather gentle treatment at the hands of the Royal Martyr's son. Marten's Tower remained roofed until the early 19th century, when the castle was finally abandoned as a dwelling.

By an accident of history the castle's superb fortifications never proved their worth in the times for which they were designed. Had the fighting reached Monmouthshire during the Welsh Wars of Edward I, the castle would no doubt have proved a useful stronghold, but the danger was never more than imminent. Likewise on a later occasion, when Edward II retreated there with Hugh Despenser to whom it belonged at the time, there was no siege as their supporters capitulated instantly. It was in the Civil War that the castle was for the first time put to the test in the only two recorded sieges of its history. Thus its first taste of military action was against weapons for which its defence had not been designed, in the form of heavy guns which destroyed the battlements and breached the walls, convincing the Royalist garrison that further resistance was useless. Unlike most other castles, however, it was not dismantled, but instead was repaired and garrisoned by Cromwell and later Charles II. The last major expense seems to have been in 1662 when an attempt was made to strengthen the castle against the new artillery. Strong parapets were built to replace the medieval battlements and the walls were enormously thickened, perhaps with stones from the domestic areas. Thereafter it was maintained as a prison rather than a dwelling, and finally as nothing more than a source of revenue for its owners, when it was let out as a general market area to the local townspeople. Its inherent strength and comparatively peaceful existence have meant that even today, though a roofless and empty shell, its walls still stand immensely solid and almost to their earlier height.

Dramatically sited over the River Wye by William Fitz Osbern in about 1070, Chepstow was enlarged in the 13th century and destroyed in the Civil War. Right, *an aerial view;* above, *the castle seen from across the river*

Chirk CLWYD

Top, *the north towers and main entrance to the courtyard from the Upper Park.* Above, *a detail of the superb wrought-iron gates of the entrance to the park, the work of the Davies brothers of Bersham, c. 1719.* Right, *the original 14th-century staircase leading to the watch tower*

By the time the Ceiriog river reaches the pleasant pasture around Chirk Castle it has lost the turbulence of its earlier passage through the Welsh mountains: in the Border Country, on the face of it so peaceful, it is man who has provided the turbulence. Two miles from here in 1165 Henry II's English forces were defeated at the famous Battle of Crogan, and until Edward I's intense and systematic drive against the Welsh princes these hills and wooded valleys were the base for habitual raiding and skirmishing. With the death in 1282 of Llewelyn, the acknowledged Prince of Wales, the heart went out of the Welsh resistance. A grant of confiscated lands was the surest reward for loyal service and Edward followed this obvious method of wooing the Marcher Lords. His favours were of course attendant on good behaviour and were easily reversed. Perhaps the need for a frontier fortress in this particular district had now passed, but Roger Mortimer, receiving from Edward the very satisfactory gift of the lands of Chirk, built himself a strong rectangular castle with round towers at the angles and half towers midway on the walls, similar in style to those other great Welsh castles of the day which stood in a chain further west.

Chirk was completed about 1310 and has been lived in ever since, its present-day shape and appearance gradually emerging as its successive owners extended and rebuilt to suit their needs. Much restoration had to be done after the Civil War, when, like the English castle of Old Wardour, it was most unusually subjected to siege by its owner, Sir Thomas Myddelton. This Sir Thomas, ancestor of the present owner, was the son of a splendid merchant adventurer, an associate of Sir Walter Raleigh and Lord Mayor of London. For his son, although a distinguished general in the Civil War, success at home was harder to come by. In the strange upheavals from which Cromwell emerged as Lord Protector, Sir Thomas failed once as a Parliamentarian to dislodge the occupying Royalists from Chirk and once as a Royalist to withstand the Parliamentarians. Luckily his alternating allegiance fixed finally on the monarch, and Charles II awarded him the handsome sum of £30,000. Thus Chirk, unlike so many of today's picturesque ruins, survived its military life and moreover collected a rich endowment which enabled its later owners to modify and embellish the structure. Gables were filled in, windows pushed through the great walls, an impressive Long Gallery was built, and in the mid-19th century Augustus Welby Pugin was engaged to introduce the Gothic. Yet much of the early stonework remains, including a large deep dungeon and two early staircases dating back to Mortimer's construction at the beginning of the 14th century.

Conway GWYNEDD

Begun by Edward I in 1283 and completed within five years. The twin 19th-century bridges of Telford and Stephenson pass alongside the castle. Right, *seen from the estuary*

In 1283 Edward I started the building of Conway as part of a network of large castles to hold down the newly-conquered territory of Wales. Its magnificent array of high walls and eight strong drum towers, designed by the Master of the King's Works in Wales, the great James of St George, was substantially completed within five years, the result of a concentration of labour and outlay of public funds such as had previously only been seen in Britain with the works of the Romans.

Externally the castle remains almost intact. It is not one of the concentric castles typical of Edward's reign, but its massive grey walls, 15 feet thick in places, follow instead the oblong contour of the rock on which it stands, dominating the shore from its east barbican and from the tower built out into the estuary. The adjacent hamlet was to become a strongly fortified town with 1,400 yards of stout wall, three gates and 21 towers, forming with the castle a most complete and daunting defensive unit.

It is approached today along a path leading up the north-west rock face through a modern entrance in the wall. Unusually, there is no gatehouse. Instead the enemy attacking from the town side would have had to climb a steep flight of stairs, winding unseen ahead of him, cross a drawbridge, and pass through two gateways, to find himself no further than inside the barbican. The forecourt was strongly defended by two of the massive towers, and was as likely a place for an ambush as any narrow gorge or valley. From the barbican a gate led through the walls into the outer ward of the castle, where the garrison was accommodated. At the east end of the ramparts there were similar hazards to deter any would-be attackers from the river.

Before the use of heavy artillery in warfare, a castle as strong as Conway was unlikely to be forced to capitulate by a mere show of strength, but a very real threat lay in the continuing shortage or even total severance of supplies, inevitable in a long siege. Ironically it was this that brought Edward himself near to capture by Welsh rebels in his own magnificent fortress. In 1294 he had arrived at the castle accompanied by only a small force, and found himself cut off from the main army and from supplies by an exceptionally full river. The stalwart defences may not altogether have compensated for such unpalatable

food as could be mustered, till the river subsided.

Later on, in 1399, it was again visited by a king, but for Richard II, the consequences were more grave. It was at Conway that he received Henry Percy, Earl of Northumberland, as Bolingbroke's ambassador, and accepted a false promise of safe conduct to meet Bolingbroke, which resulted in an ambush on the road, imprisonment for the king, and his death within a year.

From this time on the fabric of the castle slowly deteriorated. Even before the Civil War it was pronounced in a State Paper dated 1609 'Utterlie decayed,' and in 1628 it was sold for only £100 to Viscount Conway. With the outbreak of the Civil War many dilapidated castles were repaired and put into working order. Conway aroused the interest of the Archbishop of York, John Williams, a local-born man. An ardent Royalist, he repaired the castle at his own expense, but in 1646 it was taken without much difficulty by the Parliamentarians under Major-General Mytton. After the Restoration it was clearly in a bad state of repair, for by 1665 a demolition

contractor was at work there for the 3rd Earl of Conway, shipping all moveables to Ireland. Thus it came to be the ruin we now see. Recently it came under the care of the Government, and much useful restoration has been carried out.

The interest of the castle is today enhanced by two attractions dating from many years after the castle's own destruction. The tourist route of the late 18th and early 19th centuries along the coast of North Wales to Anglesey led to the splendid addition of two pairs of bridges by two of the greatest of British engineers standing side by side near two of Edward I's castles. At Conway Telford's delightfully delicate suspension bridge had carried a road across the river for some 20 years before being joined by Robert Stephenson's tubular railway bridge in 1848. Twenty-two miles along the same line a similar pair of bridges lead over the Menai Strait to Beaumaris Castle. Both of Telford's bridges were among the first great experiments in the structural use of cast-iron, just as Stephenson's tubular-girder bridges were the most extraordinary engineering feats of their day.

Harlech GWYNEDD

Half a mile from Tremadoc Bay over an undistinguished strip of gorse and dunes there soars the spectacular rock of Harlech Castle. When Edward I built the great fortress in the 13th century, the sea filled this sandy no-man's land beneath the 200-foot rock and a busy harbour here was part of the sea-going life of the Welsh coast. Although now dry as well as high, the castle remains one of the great landmarks of Britain, with long views across to Snowdonia.

The castle, virtually complete by 1290, was one of Master James of St George's major achievements as Edward's chief architect. It is an immensely strong and fine example of the concentric castle, with its system of separate encircling defences and tall twin-towered gatehouse. In castles of the 13th and 14th centuries the gateway was no longer the weak point, but had become instead a mighty defence unit. The gatehouses of the period therefore take over in many ways the function of the earlier keep and contain the main residential apartments. Such pleasantly large windows as those facing the inner ward at Harlech would not be found on the other side, where they are much narrower and heavily barred. A small discomfort attendant on gatehouse life was the machinery of the portcullis which moved up and down through the chamber above the entrance passage, in this case the chapel. Master James of St George was himself appointed Constable of Harlech from 1290–93, and lived and worshipped safely in this gatehouse. It still stands in a good state of preservation (fortunately Cromwell's guns proved too unwieldy to negotiate the bad roads to Harlech) and it remains the chief feature of the castle, dominating the simple quadrangle of the inner ward. The entrance is a narrow passage protected by two portcullises and seven sets of 'murder holes', useful for dropping missiles or water should there be a fire.

One inherent weakness in Master James's plan lay, paradoxically, in the splendid site itself. Being accessible on only the land side, it was a relatively simple matter for the attackers to cut off help that might have come from the other English strongholds. When it was built Edward I had control of the sea and it was safe to assume that help and provisions could always reach a beleaguered garrison—Criccieth Castle was within sight across the bay. In 1294 the Welsh rebel Madog had achieved nothing in his siege against Harlech, for help duly arrived for the English from Conway and Caernarvon. But the three great sieges for which the castle is famous demonstrate the special danger to which it was so often subject. In 1401 Owain Glyndwr blocked the land route while the fleet of his French allies patrolled the water below. With no remaining access to the castle, the garrison could hope for no relief and inevitably, after a long and bitter siege, was forced to surrender. Owain Glyndwr in turn, having made this splendid fortress the main base from which to conduct his rebellion and hold his parliament, found himself finally in a situation as hard to get out of as into, and with his surrender in 1409 the English again took possession.

The next 50 years were to be the short respite before Harlech's finest—or more accurately its grimmest—moment in history. In the Wars of the Roses it was strongly Lancastrian under the charge of Dafydd ap Ieuan, and his men were the Men of Harlech who inspired the famous marching song. Victory, however, was not 'hovering o'er them' and they suffered great hardships before surrendering to the Yorkists under Lord Herbert, Earl of Pembroke. Dafydd had once held a castle in France for so long that all the old women of Wales had talked of it, and his rallying cry at Harlech was that he would do the same in Wales, until all the old women of France should get to hear of it. He was the last of the Lancastrian commanders in England and Wales to surrender to the Yorkists, and did so on favourable terms in 1468.

Thereafter the castle decayed, except for the Prison Tower which was useful for housing debtors and so remained as the only part where the roof was kept in repair. Astonishingly, even in this ramshackle state the castle withstood Cromwell's army under the indomitable Major-General Mytton, and in 1647 was again the last garrison to surrender, this time to the Cromwellians, but the demolition order after the Civil War was never carried out.

Above, *an aerial view*; right, *the gatehouse from the wall walk*. See *Colour Plate VIII*

Pembroke DYFED

Above, *view along the battlements to the room in which Henry VII was born;* right, *a reconstruction of the original steps leading to the entrance on the second storey*

At low tide the mud flats of the Pembroke river join with the marsh of Monkton Pill and stretch out of sight of the town into the larger inlet of Milford Haven. The castle, on its wooded rock at the head of the creek, then looks deceptively vulnerable, an insignificant feature of the wide landscape of shining mud and stranded fishing boats, with its great moat reduced to a narrow rivulet. But the enormous cylindrical keep and the outer curtain wall, following the rugged contours of the rock and protected by large round towers and gatehouse, were formidable enough defences in themselves to establish Pembroke's position as the strongest castle in South Wales, even without the added protection of the water.

More than the river it was the mountains isolating this remote Celtic corner of Britain that proved the greater obstacle to the Norman invaders, and it was by sea that Arnulph de Montgomery came here to fight the Welsh in 1093. The castle he built was recorded to be 'a slender fortress with stakes and turf', presumably relying on the natural advantages of the site; this was hardly a description to fit the immensely strong ruins of the castle as it is today.

The keep was in fact built around 1200 by the family of Marshall, earls of Pembroke, who took their name from their office—Marshals of England. The outer bailey, towers and gatehouse are all the work of this family. It was a little later, towards the end of the 13th century, that the town walls were built, with their bastions and gates.

The castle became incomparably powerful in the hands of this important family and its subsequent owners, who were constantly modifying and refortifying the structure. Already in 1172 it could offer Henry II accommodation suitable for him to spend Easter there on his way to Ireland. King John also visited the castle, but the most significant royal event of its history was the birth there in 1456 of Henry Richmond, later to become Henry VII and founder of the Tudor Dynasty. He was to spend about 15 quiet years here until the castle was besieged by Yorkists and he fled to Brittany, but it was again to Milford Haven that he returned in 1485 to claim the crown at Bosworth Field. He made his son Henry VIII Earl of Pembroke, and with this gift the whole nature of the castle changed. It was no longer an enclave of strong, semi-autonomous baronial rule, where the King's Writ was unknown, but became instead a strongpoint in the king's armoury.

However, in the Civil War the authority of the Crown was unable to compete with the popularity in the district of a local resident, the Earl of Essex, whose quarrel with Charles I roused the enthusiastic support of the town to such an extent that the Mayor,

The castle showing the huge cylindrical keep; right a room in the great gatehouse providing spacious accommodation in one of the most strongly defended parts of the castle

John Poyer, garrisoned the castle for the Parliamentarians and equipped at his own expense a small fleet of vessels to help defend it. Thus Pembroke, alone of all Welsh towns, had declared for Cromwell.

In spite of the hostility of the surrounding Royalist countryside, the castle and town held out against repeated attacks, although in 1644 it was particularly close to capture before the timely arrival of a Parliamentary fleet. This courageous example was no doubt an inspiration to the Roundhead cause in South Wales. But the people of Pembroke, perverse once already, had a second surprise up their sleeves. By 1648, when the war was virtually over and the

country was as entirely subdued by Parliament as it had previously been Royalist, John Poyer had perhaps become disillusioned by the realities of Cromwell's dictatorship or merely had acquired a taste for the military life. He declared for the king, and told his previously Roundhead townsmen to take up arms and fortify once again. Suddenly the Royalist cause was rekindled in South Wales, and an army gathered in the castle under Major-General Laugharne on behalf of the king. The rising was of so serious a nature that Cromwell himself arrived to conduct the siege of the castle. He described the rebels of Pembroke as 'a very desperate enemy, very many of them gentlemen of quality and thoroughly resolved, and one of the strongest places in the country'.

Royalist support, however, was less forthcoming in the hour of need, and after seven weeks of siege a shipment of heavy guns for Cromwell arrived at Milford Haven by sea from Gloucester. The castle's

water supply was situated in a large cavern called Wogan, to the north-east and under the outer hall. This was where Cromwell directed his fire. The castle surrendered and the eccentric mayor was shot.

As was customary, the castle was then slighted, the outer walls and towers being partly blown-up, likewise the walls of the town. Curiously, the massive keep was left to stand and remains today the finest cylindrical keep of its period in Britain. Possibly the enormously thick walls would have been too troublesome to destroy, but it was also already obsolescent in the current military context. Perhaps Cromwell had no need to demolish more than the outer walls of the castle and some of the lesser but more strategically placed towers. So today the keep's masonry can still be seen splaying out on its great plinth of grey limestone, and views round its base provide abstract patterns of massive elegance reminiscent of the famous turn-of-the-century stage designs of Adolphe

Appia. It rises to a height of some 75 feet quite unsupported by anything except the solidity of its walls, at base over 19 feet thick. The entrance was originally at the second storey and was reached by a flight of steps and a drawbridge. The present stairs are a modern reconstruction in accordance with the original measurements, and they still present a dramatic appearance. Inside there were four storeys, but the floors have long since disappeared so that there is an unimpeded view upwards to the great stone dome of the roof. The circular staircase in the thickness of the walls was restored in 1928. This leads up to the roof, where from its great height, well above the rest of the ramparts, the keep becomes an impressive watch-tower with commanding views in all directions over the surrounding countryside, no matter whether the look-out in that particular year was on the *qui vive* for Cavalier or Roundhead, Yorkist or Lancastrian.

Thurso

Wick

CAITHNESS

SUTHERLAND

Lochinver

Outer
Hebrides

ROSS and CROMARTY

Coxton Tower

MORAY

NAIRN

Inverness

Dunvegan

Portree

14

Kyle of Lochalsh

Eilean Donan

Huntly

BANFF

ABERDEEN

Corgarff

Ballater

Craigievar

Aberdeen

Kisimul

INVERNESS

Balmoral

Crathes

Stonehaven

Braemar

1

Dunnottar

Blair

Pitlochry

Edzell

ANGUS

Glamis

Arbroath

15

Duart

ARGYLL

PERTH

Oban

Perth

Claypotts

FIFE

Inveraray

2

Doune

3

Castle Campbell

Stirling

Blackness

9

Tantallon

5

Newark

Linlithgow Palace

Edinburgh

Rothesay

16

6

7

Glasgow

8

Crichton

BERWICK

17

Brodick

Kilmarnock

LANARK

Lanark

10

Lauder

Ayr

Melrose

Kelso

11

AYR

Jedburgh

ROXBURGH

Culzean

DUMFRIES

Hermitage

Newcastleton

Dumfries

Caerlaverock

13

12

Stranraer

Threave

Kirkcudbright

1 Kincardine
2 Kinross
3 Clackmannan
4 Dumbarton
5 Stirling
6 Renfrew
7 W. Lothian
8 Mid Lothian
9 E. Lothian
10 Peebles
11 Selkirk   14 Skye
12 Kirkcudbright   15 Mull
13 Wigtown   16 Bute
    17 Arran

0   50miles

SCOTLAND

THE FIRST castles in England were built by Normans to control the English. The greatest castles in Wales were built by the English crown to suppress the Welsh. Only the Scots can truly say that they built their own castles for their own benefit.

The best of them fall into two broad historical groups. First there are the royal and baronial strongholds from the earlier period. Edinburgh and Stirling must yield for sheer size to their royal sister at Windsor, but nothing in England can match the impression of those two sheer rocks rising from the plain. Nor could English barons find such dramatic sites as their Scottish rivals. Dunnottar is the best example of all, lying like a clenched fist off the coast of Kincardineshire. Tantallon, home of the Black Douglas, is a good second—with a marked danger for the incautious tourist of falling hundreds of feet off the lawn. And does any building in Britain give such a brooding impression as Hermitage of the realities of border warfare? Not for nothing was Scott a Scot.

Then there is the next enchanting wave of Scottish castles—the tower-houses of Aberdeenshire, such as Crathes or Craigievar, stalagmites of stone rising into the sky to delight one at first by their outline (the nearest that anything in Britain comes to the castle of fairy tales) and then to amaze by revealing within a series of rooms, stacked ingeniously above each other as if in a chimney and yet with all the elegance of delicate plasterwork or painted ceilings. Blair, too, springs the same surprise on an earlier and grander scale, with its lovely baroque rooms hollowed out, almost like rock-temples, from the massive walls of the castle.

These two great groups still fail to do justice to the riches of Scottish castles, for they leave out the treasures set among the creeks and bays of the west: stark Dunvegan, Eilean Donan unashamedly picturesque, and most remote of all, little Kisimul at the extreme outer edge of the Hebrides, on an island off an island, requiring a boat trip after a boat trip, and with no space outside the castle walls for even a dustbin. The ultimate in defence, but less good than Windsor or Stirling for wielding power.

Even then there is another whole range. 'Scottish baronial'—the very phrase seems to sum up the nineteenth-century castle, and the royal creation of Balmoral set a seal of approval on the fashion. When it comes to castles one can turn the tables on that arch-Englishman Samuel Johnson. Here at least the noblest prospect is the high road that leads to Scotland.

Balmoral ABERDEENSHIRE

About 100 yards to the south-east of the castle of Balmoral a stone marks the site of an earlier building demolished in 1856. This former castle is shown here as it was in 1848, the year that Queen Victoria and Prince Albert paid their first visit to Balmoral, arriving somewhat tentatively to take possession of a property they had bought but never seen. The queen described the house as a 'pretty little castle in the old Scotch style', and was evidently delighted with the new purchase and its surroundings. The

extremely pleasant wooded countryside of the river Dee has a more gentle and mellow aspect here where the valley widens out than either in its higher or lower reaches, and it offered the perfect environment for a royal holiday home. Moreover, Queen Victoria's physician had recommended the climate above all other in Scotland for its dryness and purity, and as being greatly preferable to the never-ending rain of the west coast.

The estate had belonged at the end of the 18th century to the Earl of Fife, and in the 17th century to the Farquharsons. It was first mentioned in records in 1484, when Alexander Gordon, son of the 1st Earl of Huntly, paid an annual rent of £6. 8s. 6d., for what was probably a small tower house in the Scottish style of the 15th century. The 19th-century mansion, which Prince Albert demolished in 1852, had been built less than 20 years previously by John Smith, an Aberdeen architect.

By the 18th century the architecture of the classical world, that had fired people's imagination for some 300 years, was yielding to another source of inspiration, and it was not long before a consensus of taste had concluded that what it wanted was to be found in the heritage of the Middle Ages. Castellated mansions were being built by Nash, Sir George Gilbert Scott and others. Sir Walter Scott had spent the money earned by medieval novels by building himself a medieval home at Abbotsford. Bridges, gaols and even railway stations were built to look like fake castles. Whether or not the initiative for the new style was entirely in the hands of the leading architects of the day, they were followed in close and devoted collaboration by their happy patrons. Smith father and son were both deeply committed to the modern fashion, (though by the 19th century it was hardly correct to call the style of architecture new), and they could hardly have found a more sympathetic patron than Prince Albert for a neo-Gothic undertaking. The result of this collaboration was a picturesque mansion of the castellated sort, its theme the Middle Ages, but with the real medieval elements quite submerged in a fanfare of turrets and towers, round and square, and rippling crenellations.

Although using the same structural vocabulary as other buildings of the day, Balmoral is awkward in proportion. The great square tower, rising to 80 feet and capped with pepper-box turrets, is disturbingly top-heavy. And yet the building is not undistinguished: the stonework is considered the finest of its kind in Scotland, and the granite from the estate quarry is pleasantly pale in colour. Certainly the whole imposes its climactic features on the landscape in a way that must have interpreted to perfection the wishes of the delighted young queen.

This immense castellated mansion was commissioned in the mid-19th century by Prince Albert for the Royal Family's private residence. Top, *19th-century engraving;* above, *the castle today;* right, *the tower from the north-east*

Blackness WEST LOTHIAN

Blackness is often known as the Ship Castle, as once it was probably totally isolated from the mainland by an area of marsh. Today its strong shape at the end of a rocky promontory is more like a great lobster claw stretching out into the Firth of Forth. Blackness is quite unlike other castles of its period. It has never been lived in on a regular basis except as a prison or garrison, nor has it ever been domesticated, and there have been no long generations of ownership to foster it to a picturesque maturity. Its tiny windows do little to relieve the severity of its sheer walls, and no overlay of turf covers the jagged floor of the courtyard; only small worn patches of pebble and paving remain as ill-received guests on the unfriendly bedrock. The fort was built because of its obvious strategic position in the Firth of Forth. In medieval times Blackness was an important port, near to the royal burgh of Linlithgow, as well as to Edinburgh and even Berwick-on-Tweed. But, without any of the usual resources from the immediate surroundings which would be available to a land castle, set among rich pastures, it could never be more than a stronghold, a useful security. Its owners would always live somewhere more amenable.

In the 15th century Blackness was part of the estate of Sir George Crichton. In the course of a family struggle it was seized by his son who imprisoned him in his own castle. This rash act not surprisingly attracted the attention of the king who besieged and stormed it. Thereafter it remained as royal property under the captaincy of various families and was used to hold State prisoners, including distinguished Covenanters during the 17th century. The less influential prisoners were probably put in a prison to the north and kept in order by the daily visits of the tide through the drain.

The picture shows the main west tower, which dates from the 15th century and is the oldest part of the castle. The round staircase tower is a later addition, probably of the 17th century. A well cut through the rock is immediately outside. The barmkin walls, enclosing the courtyard, were built in the 16th century and widened internally in the 17th to accommodate a gun platform. Because of the varying practical uses to which the castle was put, all manner of temporary structures were quite naturally erected over the years within the walls, a barracks was built, horses were accommodated, even a brewery was set up. The castle as seen today, however, must resemble closely the building in its 17th-century form, for its modern guardians, formerly the Commissioners of H.M. Works and now the Department of the Environment, have removed the more recent masonry and restored it to its former state.

A dramatic iron yett guards the doorway to the courtyard. Methods of defending the entrance to a castle varied regionally. Yetts are associated with the north of England and Scotland, 'yett' being the old Scottish version of the word 'gate'. The gateway, the focal point of an attack, was the centre at which to assemble the best of the castle's range of gadgets for defence. The common device of the drawbridge, so simple once thought of, was further protected by portcullis, machicolations and arrow-loops. In Scotland many of the tower houses were without moat and drawbridge and relied purely on the strength of their yett, which hinged and bolted to the wall. The yett could stand alone, as does this one at Blackness; alternatively it could combine with a heavy wooden door for added protection. The Blackness yett is constructed in Scottish fashion, the bars being forged so as to slot together without rivets, each joint consisting of one metal bar threaded through another. The English method, by contrast, was to rivet two flat bars together to form each join, and often to fill the spaces with wood.

Above, *an iron yett or gate protecting the main doorway.* Right, *the oldest part of the castle dating from the 15th century and used as a prison for distinguished Covenanters*

Blair PERTHSHIRE

The great stronghold of the earls and dukes of Atholl since the 13th century. Much restoration was carried out in the late 18th century. Right, *the Picture Staircase built in 1756. Seen here is the portrait by Jacob de Witt of John, 1st Marquess of Atholl, as Julius Caesar*

One of the largest of Scotland's great houses, Blair Castle today is an elegant and stately home, its turrets, towers and restored medieval appearance proclaiming the tastes of the Victorian era rather than the crucial needs of defence for which it was built, and indeed put to the test as late as 1746, when it was attacked by a Jacobite army, the last castle in Britain to endure a siege. The garrison-like building set up by its earliest owners and now forming part of the north-west corner is known as Cumming's Tower with foundations dating to about 1270. By the time Mary Queen of Scots stayed there in 1540 this early tower had belonged to the Atholl family for more than 250 years, and had been extended southwards to include a great hall. Since then the castle has undergone many changes, expanding and improving with the fortunes of the Atholl family as they prospered from earl to marquess and finally to duke.

During the Civil War the castle with its Royalist earl suffered siege and was captured by Cromwell's troops, who held it for ten years until the Restoration, when the son was created marquess by a grateful monarch. This kind of adventure may have improved the family's dignity but hardly provided an incentive to do more than patch the fabric against further alarm. Continuing loyalty was rewarded once more in 1703 when Queen Anne created the 2nd marquess Duke of Atholl, but little alteration was made to the castle until the duke was succeeded by his youngest son. The other sons had dropped out of the inheritance by supporting the Jacobites, and indeed one of them, Lord George Murray, arrived with an army and laid siege to his own former home. So the last siege in Britain was a family affair, and remained, as it happened, ineffectual, more impertinence than outrage. With the prospect of peaceful times to follow, the 2nd duke resumed his work on the castle, remodelling it as a Georgian mansion. Turrets and castellations were removed, and chimney stacks, low roofs and elegant sash windows appeared. Cumming's Tower was suitably lowered.

Already in England the staircase had for two centuries been used as a splendid gallery for all the family portraits. Almost every rich family had long been in the habit of commissioning Holbein, Lely, or their imitators, to perpetuate and no doubt improve their images. Where better to show off their results than that great area of wall space stretching the full height of the house, with a perfect viewing of every part?

In Blair many of the earlier portraits are in the earlier part of the castle, and those shown on the Picture Staircase date from the 17th and 18th centuries. It was designed and built in 1756 by the architect Winter as part of the improvements made by the 2nd duke, and has a magnificent domed ceiling, decorated in elaborate stucco by Clayton. The exhibition is dominated by the full-length portrait of the 1st marquess, painted by Jacob de Witt. He is depicted as an 18th-century Julius Caesar, profusely bewigged, but elsewhere the great torso is scantily clad—bare feet and shoulders emerging from swirling yards of silken brocade. Behind him there rages the battle of Bothwell Brig, where the enemy would certainly have stopped in their tracks at such a godly apparition. Around the glorious marquess, as if filling in on a gigantic scale the pages of an expensive stamp album, hang the more peaceable members of the family in special spaces outlined by delicate ribbons of plaster, in pointed contrast to the martial trophies which provide an apt setting for him.

The next member of the family to undertake radical alterations was a purposeful Victorian, the 7th duke. In 1869 Bryce was commissioned to smarten the old place up in contemporary style by restoring its medieval appearance. Turrets, corbels, castellations and other frills came trooping back. A new entrance hall was provided, panelled high to its ornately moulded ceiling to receive the generations of arms, rifles, swords, cross-bows and powder-horns thought suitable to greet visitors as they entered. Cumming's Tower resumed its former splendid height with turret, parapet, and corbel all restored. In modern times Blair still retains a unique military distinction. The last castle to have sustained a private siege is also the last to maintain a private army. The present duke is still at the head of his famous Atholl Highlanders.

Braemar ABERDEENSHIRE

Defending the ancient mountain passes of the Cairnwell and Tolmouth and thus controlling the route between the southern and northern parts of the kingdom of Robert I, there lie today in the village of Braemar the ruins of the 13th-century royal castle of Kindrochit. Fearful legends of plague and atrocities aided the decline in the 16th century of this once important fortified residence, and probably accounted for the building during the 17th century of a new castle at a slight remove from the old site.

Standing at a commanding height above the River Dee, the castle of Braemar recalls the early rivalries of the historic kingdom of Mar. Though building started at the comparatively late date of 1628, the clan feuds and tradition of local war harked back to medieval times when the earls of Mar were asserting themselves as the rulers of this northerly province. These early leaders, in turn the inheritors of the ancient and even more shadowy Pictish rulers, found at all times their authority challenged by other families, and it was mainly to curb the growing power of the Farquharsons that the castle was built. However, the violence and uncertainty of daily life inevitably attendant on this kind of guerilla warfare served in no way to distract from the important business of sport in the great forests of Deeside; thus Braemar Castle was ostensibly built as a hunting-lodge, though its fortifications and dungeon pit were conspicuously designed more for Farquharsons than for deer or even wolves.

In the wider context of who should rule Scotland these family feuds were overshadowed but by no means forgotten, and both the Jacobite cause and that of William of Orange relied heavily on clan support. The Earl of Mar declared for William and Mary, and Braemar Castle was occupied by government troops. The Farquharsons under the leadership of the clan's most glamorous and legendary hero, John Farquharson, the 'Black Colonel', were staunch in their support of the Jacobites, and in 1689 during the Claverhouse rising, not only was a strong blow struck for King James when the Black Colonel captured and burnt Braemar Castle, but also the traditional feudal superiority of the earls of Mar was to suffer a lasting wound—for 60 years the castle stood as a burnt-out shell. The earls of Mar were never to live there again, and—final indignity—in 1732 it was none other than John Farquharson, 9th Laird of Invercauld, who bought the ruin and surrounding lands.

The Farquharsons, however, were not to rebuild the castle. Dissociating himself in 1745 from the by now hopeless Jacobite cause, John Farquharson leased Braemar to the Hanoverian Government for the sum of £14 annually. Restoration was started in 1748 by the young architect John Adam, the eldest but not the most distinguished of the four famous brothers, who was working at the time for the Board of Ordnance in Scotland.

Apart from the roofline, where the original conical turrets were heightened into small crenellated towers, the walls of Braemar have remained little changed from the 17th century. The castle's outline, however, was altered entirely with the addition of a zig-zag encircling rampart, from the gunloops of which the garrison could cover all angles with their cross-fire. Thus Braemar, like nearby Corgarff, was manned by Hanoverian troops as a vigorous measure to control the disaffected clansmen. It was not until the 19th century that the castle was finally lived in by the Farquharsons, who adapted it from a garrison to a family residence. The ramparts have been kept and externally it remains a strong and impressive fortress, though today in Braemar when the clans gather from far and near nothing more dangerous occurs than much piping and tossing of the caber at the famous annual event attended by the reigning monarch.

Tower house built by the Earl of Mar in 1628. An unusual star-shaped curtain wall was added by English troops in the 18th century

Caerlaverock DUMFRIESSHIRE

When Edward I was moving northwards in one of his drives against the Scots, Caerlaverock was a magnificent new stronghold, a great triangular red stone castle built only about ten years before. Edward's chronicler wrote a glowing account of its structure and shape—'like a shield', he says 'surrounded by an arm of the sea'. It was indeed a very strongly sited fortress, built where the land curves down into the Solway Firth, with nothing between it and the estuary but woods and marshes. Thus its great double-towered gatehouse is approached only from the north. Of its two moats today the outer one is dry, and an early form of drawbridge has long since been replaced. To the south the remains of an earlier castle, dating to about 1230 and built on a rectangular base, have been found, and before that there were both Iron Age and Roman forts nearby, all of them set up presumably to guard the landing places of this important sea route into Scotland.

The castle fell to Edward I quite quickly in the famous siege of 1300. It must have struck the king and his army as strange to be besieging what clearly had the look of one of Edward's own English castles. The high twin towers of the keep-gatehouse, with the rock foundations just visible over the surface of the moat, flank the castle's main defensive stronghold. This was the self-contained and massively protected focal point in which were the lord's quarters, and from here he could personally supervise the gate and direct the proceedings. A special feature of

Famous for its siege in 1300, Caerlaverock remains one of the most impressive 13th-century castles in Scotland. Above, the gatehouse; right, Murdoch's Tower showing the ruined south wall which reveals the Renaissance courtyard range

Edward's castles was in the forward positioning of the keep to command the entrance, as seen at Caerlaverock but not found elsewhere in Scotland for another 50 years. Perhaps this was pure coincidence, arising from the shape of the site, or perhaps it was indeed an English Edwardian castle built a few years earlier as part of Edward's drive northwards and more recently lost to the Scots. Or again it could be that it had originally been built by the Scots, who, anticipating Edward's arrival, decided to confront him with just such a castle as he himself would have constructed for maximum defence. Whatever the facts may have been, it remained as a valuable and coveted possession throughout the rivalries of the Scots and the English, and the allegiance of its owners was often precariously balanced between the two sides in a mood of ambiguity which characterizes the castle right the way back to its origin.

Caerlaverock was besieged altogether five times and was at least once almost totally destroyed. Curiously it was the family associated with it from the early 14th century who themselves were responsible for one major act of demolition. In 1312 Sir Eustace Maxwell, no doubt sizing up the relative characters of the new English king, Edward II, and of the mighty Robert Bruce, decided to declare for the latter; and in keeping with the Scots policy of rendering useless any castle that might in the future be of help to the English, he set about dismantling it. Some of the present castle dates to the subsequent rebuilding in the 14th century, and there are other 15th century additions such as the fine machicolated parapets, but the most interesting work in the castle is of the 17th century, when Robert Maxwell, the 1st Earl of Nithsdale, created an elegant new block against the east wall. This building, with its extremely fine Renaissance façade of about 1634, was to provide rooms for guests, who until then had been offered quarters in the keep-gatehouse. Their new accommodation must have been more like that of an English country house of the period than of a typical castle. The building consisted of three floors with a pair of rooms on each, and underneath was a service area of kitchen, bakery and servery. The rooms would have been spacious and well lit by the large ornate windows, but their shape may have been slightly spoilt by an awkward central chimney system, round which they all had to be fitted. Unfortunately Maxwell and his guests had little more than a decade in which to enjoy their unusual comforts, for in 1640 the castle fell to the Covenanters and was destroyed beyond repair.

Corgarff ABERDEENSHIRE

When in about 1537 Thomas Erskine, Earl of Mar, built himself a hunting lodge by Cock Bridge, he can have had little idea of what a dolorous and eventful history this tiny oblong tower was to have. Looking out over the top of its curtain wall at the bleak Aberdeenshire landscape, the small castle of Corgarff happens to be most strategically placed to command the important routes through the passes of the Dee, the Avon and the Don. Its history has been a troubled one. Twice burnt by attackers, it was left a stone shell, roofless and without floors, but nevertheless it somehow survived to be later repaired. The first of these fires in 1571 was a horrendous affair, celebrated still in a mournful ballad of many verses. Adam Gordon of Auchindonn Castle lives on as Edom o' Gordon, the villainous leader of a small band of marauders, who, arriving at Corgarff in the laird's absence and angered by his wife's refusal to descend from her tower into his arms, set fire to the place, supposedly through a flue in the privy, burning to death the wife, Margaret Campbell, together with her family and servants—a household of 27.

The castle was repaired some years later, and was used by Montrose in 1645 as the modest headquarters from which he rallied the clans to his cause before the Battle of Alford. Again, during the Jacobite risings, Corgarff figured as a rallying point, this time for the Earl of Mar on his journey from Kildrummy to Braemar to declare for his James VIII in 1715. Later it was to prove equally useful for the Government troops after they had dislodged the Jacobites finally in 1746.

Instead of being dismantled and falling into complete ruin, as did many others, the castle's practical life was prolonged well into the 19th century, and its architecture reflects most interestingly the changing military developments during those 100 years. The latest type of defence for a garrisoned post was introduced by the Hanoverians in 1745. The original tower, with its basement cellars, two upper storeys and garret, were kept unaltered, but at each end were built low wings as additional accommodation. The whole was enclosed by an unusual star-shaped rampart or curtain wall, an interesting device developed by Vauban, the French military engineer, giving the garrison within both lateral and diagonal fire through the gunloops.

Nearby Braemar was similarly modernized and together they provided ideal bases from which the government could maintain discipline in this wild and disaffected area. Order in the district was eventually established, and by the early 19th century there would have been little need of such a force had not a sudden revival of smuggling in 1827 called for the return of a garrison. Thereafter Corgarff became derelict, until recently in the hands of the Department of the Environment a splendid refurbishing occurred: the moss has been removed from roof and ramparts, and white paint transforms the walls, restoring to this small lovely fort its earlier interesting character.

Built in the mid-15th century as a fortified hunting lodge, Corgarff was remodelled as a garrison post in 1748 after the suppression of the last Jacobite rising

Craigievar ABERDEENSHIRE

Erected by the Forbes family in the 1620s, this six-storeyed tower house has remained virtually intact as a superbly representative building of its period. Above, a medallion portrait of Alexander the Great worked into the plaster of the hall ceiling

In a county famous for its fine castles, Craigievar is perhaps the most romantic of all, the most spectacular. Its six storeys of delicate pink-harled granite crowd upwards in a tightly-packed combination of turrets, gables and an ingeniously placed square tower topped with a classical balustrade, and from its upper storeys there are long views over the rolling Aberdeenshire landscape.

Craigievar was built in the brief respite between the Union of the Crowns in 1603 and the outbreak of the Civil War in 1638. It was a time when the small landowners of Scotland, previously busy with military matters, found themselves without much to do and prosperous with land and wealth that had hitherto been the property of the Church. Many travelled abroad and took up commerce. Master William Forbes, known as Willie the Merchant, who is recorded as having completed the building and decoration of Craigievar in 1626, must have been of this new breed of laird. He bought the estate in 1610 from the impoverished family of Mortimer, and with it the castle, still only half-built. Having made a lot of money in Danzig, he could afford to complete it most lavishly—the ornate and exotic effects of the roofline are only a hint at the fine decorative work inside. There is no record of the architect's name, but it is thought that William Forbes would surely have employed John Bell, one of the great Aberdeenshire stonemasons, known today only by the signature with which he sometimes signed his work.

Perhaps the only feature to have changed since the castle's completion in 1626 is the barmkin or walled courtyard necessary to every Scottish castle, if only as a kind of farmyard. In Craigievar it was a paved area containing stables, dairy and other useful outhouses. Only a portion of the curtain-wall and one corner tower remain together with an arched entrance and wooden door bearing the initials of William Forbes's grandson, Sir John Forbes, popularly known from his complexion as Red Sir John, though he was in other respects much less colourful than his grandfather. William Forbes died unfortunately only a year after completing his castle, but it continued in his family, who, as the result of a marriage, combined their name with the Sempill family, until 1963 when the National Trust for Scotland bought the estate.

During the Civil War the building of this kind of castle came to an end. Thus Craigievar is not only the most beautiful of its kind, it is also almost the last—for the next generations of stonemasons were to start building the great palaces and town houses of the 18th century in the new classical style.

XI Linlithgow Palace, West Lothian

In the 12th century King David I built a wooden manor house on a promontory in the centre of Linlithgow Loch, but it was the English King Edward I who first enclosed the complex with a ditch and wooden palisade and thus established for himself a fort on the important route between Edinburgh and Stirling. He spent here the winter of 1301. In the late summer of 1313 a local farmer, William Bunnock, concealed a small party of men in loads of hay being delivered to the castle, ambushed the guard, quickly captured the fort and handed it over to King Robert the Bruce, who demolished Edward's military works —thus bringing to an end Linlithgow's brief spell as an effective castle.

It became nevertheless a favourite residence of many Scottish kings after James I had built a magnificent stone palace on the site in about 1430. Both James V and Mary Queen of Scots, his daughter, were born there. Charles I was the last to stay in the palace. Cromwell spent some weeks refortifying it, this time with a stone wall.

Today it is an empty ruin. The stonework remains in good condition, but the floors and roofs were burnt in a great fire in 1746. Hanoverian dragoons quartered in the palace left open fires burning, which set light to the straw of their bedding, and soon flames swept through the building. The royal patronage was never revived.

XII Brodick, Isle of Arran

The gigantic rhododendrons that crowd and cluster their many heavy flowers among the shrubs surrounding the castle are not for the most part native to the Ayrshire coast. Brodick's last private owners, the Duke and Duchess of Montrose, began in the early 1920s to remove the complicated tangle of growth that for hundreds of years had covered the area, and to create in its stead an informal garden of exotic plants from various parts of the world.

The appearance of the castle too has much changed since its early days. Nothing remains of the fortress visited by King Robert the Bruce after his defeat at Methven in 1306, but it was here at Brodick that he waited for the kindling of a great beacon on the mainland—the signal that was to summon him to begin his re-conquest of Scotland.

The earliest surviving fabric is in the north wing, which incorporates some 14th- to 16th-century work. In the early 1650s Cromwell's men installed themselves in this staunch Royalist stronghold—one of the last four in Scotland to hold out for the Stuarts— and added a new section to improve their living quarters.

Much of Brodick today is the creation of James Gillespie Graham in 1844, but he showed great affinity for the severe temper of the early work. The somewhat austere mass of the red sandstone castle blends informally both with the lush gardens and with the quiet luxury of an old house

XIII Castle Campbell, Clackmannanshire

To judge from the local names, Castle Campbell would seem to be some fortress of Gothic legend, or at the very least one would assume that that most famous of tinkers, John Bunyan, had passed this way, for its other name is Castle Gloom, and it stands firmly on the promontory between the rushing waters of the Burn of Care and the Burn of Sorrow. A great Puritan, who did indeed come here in about 1556 was John Knox. He records that he visited the Earl of Argyll in the castle and 'tawght certaine dayis'. Local tradition has it that he preached sermons to a great multitude before leaving Scotland for France and Geneva, standing perched on a rocky eminence in the immediate vicinity of the castle. John Knox's Pulpit is still pointed out in the rock at the south-west corner of the garden.

The Lord Argyll whom Knox was visiting was Archibald, 4th Earl, an active adherent to the reformed faith, and a member of an energetic family of great political influence. His ancestor Colin Campbell, the 1st earl, had been one of the great statesmen of his day, and was appointed to many high offices including Master of the King's Household and Lord High Chancellor of Scotland. He came into the inheritance of the 'Lands of Dollar and Glume' in 1481, and it is assumed that it was he who was responsible for replacing the existing buildings with the solid grey tower that forms the nucleus of today's castle. He also managed to have its name changed by Act of Parliament to the less mournful title of Castle Campbell. Thereafter the castle expanded piecemeal, as and how it could, on the rather restrictive site, when successive generations of Campbells needed to extend their accommodation. By the time of the National Covenant in the 1640s, when Archibald, the 8th earl and 1st marquess, was mustering all the men he could to uphold the Parliamentary cause, the castle must have been a handsome building, with its once solitary and isolated tower now giving on to a courtyard with additional ranges round the walls. Argyll fought relentlessly against the Royalist cause and in particular against his personal enemy, Montrose. Both of these young earls were to suffer the same fate of execution within a span of eleven years, but before his death in 1661 Argyll had probably seen the burning and destruction of his great lowland stronghold. In a letter to Cromwell dated 1654 General Monck wrote 'some small parties of the Enemy are abroad in the country and on Monday and Tuesday nights last burn't Castle Campbell an House belonging to the Marquesse of Argyll.' Thereafter only the east range could continue in use, while much of the rest was in ruins. The Argylls finally severed their connection with the property when George, 6th Duke, sold it in the early 19th century. Its present well cared-for condition as a pensioner of the Department of the Environment is a fitting conclusion to its brave and determined contribution in earlier days to the republican cause.

XIV Crathes, Kincardineshire

The Muses Room with its superb painted ceiling, completed 1602, now pleasantly set off with appropriate furnishings of the period, was one of the parts of the castle built by Alexander Burnett, great-grandson of the founder who began it in 1553. *See* p. 186.

Crathes KINCARDINESHIRE

The castle was built slowly during the turbulent latter years of the 16th century. Right, *ceiling of Room of the Nine Nobles.* See *Colour Plate XIV*

In the 16th century it was difficult to remain aloof from the political commitments that kept Britain in perpetual turmoil. The Burnett family, however, who built Crathes Castle and lived there continuously until 1966, do not seem to have involved themselves in any ambitious way in the affairs of Scotland until the early 17th century. They supported Robert I at Bannockburn, receiving a reward of lands and—tradition has it—the famous Horn of Leys, now on view in the High Hall, as a symbol of authority and ownership of those lands. They spent the next 230 years consolidating their tenure.

The building of Crathes was an extraordinary enterprise, rather like a family business handed from father to son. Alexander Burnard or Burnett started to build it in 1553, but it was not habitable until 1594 when his great-grandson, another Alexander Burnett, could move in. There was much flexibility in the spelling of the family surname, and the original design of the castle must also have veered about in the 40 years of its construction. The parts of the castle built to the direction of the younger Alexander Burnett and the beautiful painted ceilings, which were completed in 1602, are very much in keeping with the character of this civilized and erudite man. He must also have been extraordinarily energetic; not only did he settle the long drawn-out business of finishing the castle, but he also set himself the task of building another—Muchalls at Stonehaven, which was to be very modern and entirely his own creation. Unfortunately he died before this ambition could be fulfilled.

The one major alteration to Crathes was made at the beginning of the 18th century by his great-great-grandson, Thomas Burnett, who apart from his pressing need to find accommodation for his twenty-one children, wanted a more elegant and spacious style of life. He removed the surrounding wall or barmkin, planted yew hedges and an avenue of limes—the beginning of today's extraordinary garden—and spent the family fortune on reconstructing what is now known as the Queen Anne wing. His heirs, however, were forced to sell Muchalls Castle to meet his debts.

Crathes is built as a massive granite tower with a side wing adjoining. From the point of view of security the solitary tower would have been a more defendable unit, but by the mid-16th century danger came more from small-time marauders than from the attack of a full army, and the extra wing improved the quality of life immeasurably. Granite is the typical material for the Scottish tower house. Inside a certain amount of timber was obviously used, but the basic shortage of wood in Scotland even until the 19th century dictated a much wider use of stone than was normal elsewhere. Scarcity of wood leads to the same result as the scarcity of land—the evolution of the skyscraper. Wood was essential for roofing, so the particular tall thin shape of the tower house, where the roof area is minimized, was as much a natural shape for Scotland as the long low timber-framed buildings for Tudor England. Today the floor of the High Hall has modern timber laid, but originally there were stone flags. In fact the entire first floor is carried on stone vaulting, likewise most of the second; the need to avoid weight in the upper storeys led to the use of timber which would have been imported or bought regardless of cost.

In spite of the immense strength and severity suggested by the high granite walls, the castle is extraordinarily graceful. The walls do in fact taper to a slightly narrower top, but perhaps their elegance lies in the sheer plainness of the lower storeys, interrupted only slightly by the 19th-century window on the first floor, breaking out into a wonderful crowded skyline of turrets, gabling, corbels and heraldic decoration. The tower was fortunately not damaged in a fire in 1966 which destroyed the Queen Anne wing. The National Trust for Scotland, to whom the Burnett family gave the castle in 1952, undertook the rebuilding of this wing, and instead of reconstructing the three-storeyed Queen Anne building as it was, they have instead restored it to a very pleasing earlier form consisting of only two storeys.

The remarkable gardens were made at the beginning of the century by Sir James and Lady Burnett within the formal framework of the original 18th-century yew hedges, and they mingle many rare shrubs and trees with a profusion of herbaceous plants in bold combinations of colour and design.

no constancie of things spoken and promised be god or men. The gift of god which onely S...

Loue god aboue all thing

Loue thy nyghbour as thy selfe

Ag Boetius in his boke rehersi... in his temple of trauayling of musis of lippll... our temple

K G

heir is Clio

first of ... ... musis

Crichton MIDLOTHIAN

Late 14th-century tower house with additions by the Earl of Bothwell in the 16th century. Seen here from its northeast approach. Right, *the faceted stonework of the Italianate façade built 1581–91*

Leaving the road by the 15th-century parish church, the path to Crichton follows a winding crescent through a small copse, then comes out to a wide prospect of hillside dipping and rolling down to the river at the bottom of the valley. In the distance the castle sits on a breezy platform of rough grazing, its doorway protected from the sheep by a neat fence and green sward. Some 40 yards to the south is the stable-block looking, except for the horse-shoe window above the door, more like a ruined chapel with its high roof and great buttresses. This is the countryside of Sir Walter Scott's *Marmion*. After he published it in 1808, the ruined castle, hitherto only visited by wandering sheep, suddenly became the subject of great tourist interest, and it is now in the care of the Department of the Environment.

There were two main additions to the simple 14th-century tower-house—one in the 15th century and the other in the 16th. In 1440 Sir William Crichton, the Chancellor of Scotland, a powerful but unsavoury character, was responsible for the elimination in rather murky circumstances of two young sons of a rival family. Five years later, in retaliation, the castle at Crichton was besieged and considerable damage done. This, however, caused less sorrow than might have been expected since the early tower-house was obviously primitive and uncomfortable and altogether too modest a residence for the times. Sir William therefore built a magnificent new keep-gatehouse, strategically useful but also quite advanced in its internal arrangements and richly embellished with fine stonework.

Much more dramatic rebuilding was the result of the avant-garde passion for the Italian Renaissance, developed on his travels by Francis, the 5th Earl of Bothwell (his uncle, the 4th earl and husband of Mary Queen of Scots, had also owned the castle until his downfall in 1567). Referred to by a near contemporary as 'a terror to the most desperate duellists of Europe', Bothwell came back from Italy in about 1580 with an urge to build a palazzo comparable to those he must have seen abroad. He and his wife, Margaret, built up the north wing to contain a large dining-room with elegant fireplace and windows, two kitchens and pantries and an adjoining drawing-room —all in rather more flamboyant and ornate style than was standard at the time. His magnificent sculptured façade and arcade of stone pillars comes as a considerable surprise inside his essentially Scottish castle on its hillside, though a little later in 1604, Lord Edzell was to do something comparably exciting in his castle in Perthshire. Whether or not Lord Bothwell specifically chose as his model the Palazzo dei Diamanti in Ferrara, which he may have been one of the first foreigners to see as it neared completion, it would seem from the consistency of style and attention to detail in the stonework that he brought back with him an Italian architect to direct the Scottish stonemasons. In the picture it is possible to see on two of the capitals the monogram of Francis Stewart, Earl of Bothwell, and his wife Margaret Douglas. Underneath the lettering is a camel and anchor symbolizing the earl's nautical rank as Lord High Admiral of Scotland. Through the windows of the façade out across the fields, still looking exactly as it would have to anyone resting on the windowseat in the castle's youth, is the 15th-century parish church.

The new building may just have been completed in time to entertain King James VI, who stayed there in March 1586. After that there were few years left to enjoy it, for already by 1592 Bothwell and the king had fallen foul of each other over that most dangerous of 16th-century topics, religion. Bothwell had lent his support to the Catholic plot against James—an involvement which very nearly spelt the end of his lavish new castle, for the king ordered it razed to the ground. Fortunately the order was never carried out (its present degree of dilapidation is due only to the weather and to local builders short of stone), but the result was much the same for Bothwell. His castle had been forfeited, together with his other dramatic stronghold at Hermitage, and he himself was no longer safe in Scotland. He died in exile in Naples.

Culzean AYRSHIRE

*Built by Robert Adam in the 1780s round an ancient
fortified tower of the Kennedy family, the castle
stands above a sheer rock face over the Firth of Clyde.
Above, the sheltered southeast aspect of the castle*

Culzean is seen at its best at very low tide. Slippery
rocks and the necessity for careful timing make this
a hazardous business. The castle stands on a high
cliff, precipitous and sheer down to the waters of
the Firth of Clyde, where far out to sea on the horizon
there stands the famous rock of Ailsa Craig, a steep
volcanic island crowded with gannets and puffins and
owned since the Reformation by the Kennedy
family, who took their title from this rock when
created marquesses in 1831.

The long history of this famous clan traces back to
the earls of Carrick, but documentary history begins
with John Kennedy of Dunnure, who was confirmed
as clan chief by Robert II in 1372. Later James IV
created his descendant 1st Earl of Cassilis. It is hard to
imagine, from the fragmentary ruins that still stand
on the shore a little to the north of Culzean, what an
important stronghold Dunnure castle must have been
in the province of Carrick. The Black Vault of Dunnure
was the scene of a gruesome atrocity, when in 1570
the 4th Earl of Cassilis roasted to death his rival
Bargany kinsman. Meanwhile at this time Culzean
and its original tower house were part of the great
Kennedy estates, but remained only of secondary
stature until 1759 when the senior branch died out
and the Cassilis title came, after much litigation, to
Sir Thomas Kennedy of Culzean.

Finding himself in possession of the greater part of
the Kennedy estates, the 4th baronet declined to live
in Dunnure; perhaps the disrepair into which it had
collapsed during the many years of squandering and
venomous family feuds was even greater than its
unsavoury reputation. Little is known about the
castle at Culzean prior to this except that it stood,
probably a three-storeyed tower surrounded by a

courtyard, exactly on the site of what was to be the
later castle. In deciding to take Culzean as his
principal seat, the 4th baronet, by then the 9th Earl of
Cassilis, chose well. He was a true and splendid
gentleman of the 18th century, managing his estates,
introducing new methods of agriculture, and ac-
quainting himself with the Arts. He was succeeded
in the title by his younger brother, who, true to type,
had undertaken the Grand Tour, and it was he who
commissioned Robert Adam in 1775 to embark on a
complete reconstruction of the old building. The
inherent qualities of the site of this early tower, the
height and drama of the bluff on which it stood,
must have made this an exciting commission for
Scotland's leading architect.

The immediate result, however, was a large, elegant
Georgian mansion, almost entirely in the classical
style—but with certain medieval embellishments.
Turrets, towers and crenellations are neatly incorporated on the sheltered southern side, all the insignia
of the traditional castle are there, but the effect—
especially in combination with the palm trees and
balmy air—is bland to the point of inertia. Most
fortunately, though, the 10th earl was so delighted
with these effects that in 1785 Adam was requested to
continue with a remodelling of the other side, the
bleaker northern prospect. This time he responded,
once again to his patron's immense satisfaction, with
a bold and most dramatic façade, its huge round
tower splaying out to the very edge of the cliff and
creating inside the house the possibility of splendid
circular rooms. Culzean's round drawing-room—
together with the magnificent oval staircase right in
the centre of the castle, which was the last stage of
Adam's reconstruction—is considered among his
finest and most interesting work. In the castle's
new and military form real warfare seemed a
far cry, but in 1804 there came what was later to be
known as the False Alarm. At the time it must have
seemed far from false, such was the dread of Napo-
lean's might. A sea bastion was built on the north side
of the east forecourt, and gun emplacements were dug
on the cliff, but fortunately the great comfortable round
tower of the castle was never put to the ultimate test.

The only involvement of the castle with military
affairs in its present unwarlike form has been its
unexpected but now famous connection with Dwight
D. Eisenhower. In 1946, by which time the castle
belonged to the National Trust for Scotland, a separate
flat was created on the top floor. In recognition of his
services in World War II, it was offered to Eisenhower
for his lifetime. Courting a great soldier, Culzean
discovered—six years later—that it had caught a
president as well. The rooms are kept now in his
memory.

Doune PERTHSHIRE

In 1878 a strong wind blew down the old gallows tree which had grown since medieval times in front of Doune Castle—as much part of the scene as the great fireplaces or the well inside the castle. This was during the tenancy of the 14th Earl of Moray, who began the enormous task of restoring what had become a roofless ruined shell, last used a century and a half ago by Prince Charles Edward Stuart to house prisoners after the Battle of Falkirk in 1746.

The first of the long line of the earls of Moray, an illegitimate son of King James V, was assassinated at Linlithgow, leaving only a daughter, who married the Stewart Lord of Doune, and inherited one of the great traditional strongholds of the Stewarts. Today, thanks to the 14th earl, Doune remains one of the best preserved medieval castles in Scotland, and in essentials looks much as it must have done when Robert Stewart, Duke of Albany and Regent of Scotland, built it at the end of the 14th century.

The castle stands on a carefully chosen site controlling the intersection of routes from both Glasgow and Edinburgh and dominating the River Teith at its junction with the Ardroch water. The Duke of Albany was a man with spectacular powers in the Scotland of his day. As regent in the last years of the reign of Robert III and during the captivity of James I in England (from 1405–24), he was without doubt the single most formidable man in the country, and it was perhaps this strict personal control of Scotland that he translated into architectural terms. The most unusual feature at Doune is its striking keep-gatehouse. There were other castles in Scotland at this time which followed a similar pattern of placing the Lord's quarters over the entrance, such as Caerlaverock or Tantallon, but in those cases it seems to have been as much the shape of the site as any deliberate strategy which dictated the arrangement. At Doune the design seems so perfectly to express the nature of the Duke of Albany that it is hard to believe it was not his own personal arrangement, for he sat self-sufficient and apparently unshakable astride his gatehouse, much as he bestrode the kingdom at large. From his magnificent hall he could control the portcullis and supervise personally all admission to the castle, and could himself only be approached by a separate stairway from the courtyard. Water from the well and provisions were both drawn up through trapdoors, thus he could isolate himself from the enemy within as well as without. The door joining the Lord's Hall to the adjacent retainers' Hall is a modern one, for to allow such incautious access to a garrison of professional soldiers would have been a disastrous breach of security.

The duke was in the event never besieged in his stronghold, but his son who inherited was less fortunate, and was executed by the king within sight of his castle at Doune. Its only siege took place without any loss of life, when during the upheavals that followed Mary Queen of Scots, flight into England the Regent Lennox captured it on behalf of the young King James. Although the castle was not very much involved in the Civil War, it was roofless by the end of the 18th century—the result of disuse and neglect. Although now roofed again, it is still uninhabited, but maintained in an excellent state of repair with the Moray flag flying from the battlements. When the great gallows tree fell in front of the castle, the 14th earl, with the same carefulness characteristic of his restoration, used its wood for the magnificent oak furniture to be seen still in the Lord's Hall.

One of the best preserved castles in Scotland, Doune has remained largely intact since the 14th century

Duart ISLAND OF MULL

In the deeply indented coast of the Inner Hebrides the Bay of Tobermory offers excellent anchorage at the entrance to the Sound of Mull. It was here in 1588 that the Spanish galleon *Florencion* sought shelter, but was instead blown up by a young Maclean clansman, an act of sabotage in which he died. Duart Castle had been built by his Maclean chieftains probably in the 13th century, and it became once again the home of the present Chief of the Clan when Sir Fitzroy Maclean bought and restored it in 1912. The memory of the Spaniards also lives on, for through the great doors of the castle's entrance there is a dungeon containing the models of two of the galleon's officers, and upstairs there is a small Spanish cannon. In fact the whole castle has become a repository for all kinds of strange things; over the years many small and interesting objects have found their way into this crusty mollusc on its rocky edge, and become lodged there. A permanent Scout Exhibition is one of the most surprising items, likewise a display of the

Built in the 13th century to command the entrance to the Sound of Mull, Duart is still the ancestral home of the Maclean family

Regimental Colours of the 236th Canadian Expeditionary Force—a little of everything, all accumulated through the network of the great clan.

The present castle was entirely recovered by Sir Fitzroy Maclean from an uninhabitable ruin, for the family left the castle at the end of the 17th century, retreating to the Treshnish Islands to hold out as a garrison for James VII. The Government troops then moved in to this commanding fortress and remained there until 1751. Like Kisimul on another Western Isle the castle remained empty, but it was a modern interest in clan history that brought the family back and restored the castle to something of its former splendour.

Dunnottar KINCARDINESHIRE

Dunnottar occupies the flat grassy surface of a great red sandstone rock, an extraordinary geological formation which thrusts out into the North Sea like a huge mailed fist. A narrow spine, known as the Fiddlehead, once connected it with the mainland, but this link has been ingeniously cut away to a vertical plunging point to prevent access. The castle is instead approached along a narrow path of rock and turf winding and dipping almost to sea level, which then leads upwards to the gatehouse. Thus anyone approaching would be in full view and range of fire, and extremely unlikely to be able to take the castle by storm. Yet, in spite of all the advantages of its natural site, it was captured more than once.

It had from earliest times been a useful stronghold, but little is known about it until St Ninian arrived there amongst the Picts in the 5th century and founded a chapel. William Wallace captured it in 1297 and burned alive the English garrison in the castle church; and in 1336 Edward III also managed to seize and hold it for a few months. Montrose failed to capture it in 1645 but caused much distress on the mainland among the tenant farmers. Its longest and most dramatic siege, however, involves one of the best known episodes of Scottish patriotic history—the defence of the Regalia in 1651–52. By then Dunnottar was the only place still flying the royal flag in Scotland, and it was here that the crown jewels had been deposited for safety, together with other treasures observed by a contemporary to be so valuable that if all were in Amsterdam they would yield £20,000 sterling. Unfortunately the garrison was only 69 men in all, with 42 guns, and when after eight months Cromwell's men under General Overton finally got their heaviest battering artillery into position and bombarded the castle with shells, the Governor of Dunnottar, George Ogilvy, was forced to surrender. The prizes so coveted by the Parliamentarians, however, were safely out of reach. During the long siege the Scottish Regalia had been lowered down the walls of the cliff and taken by a woman servant in her basket to await the Restoration in a hiding-place under the floor of a church. Likewise the private papers of Charles II had been smuggled through the enemy lines by another woman, who had stitched them into her clothes. The Parliamentarians gave vent to their anger in their later plunder of the castle.

Another event of particular national significance for Scotland was the castle's association with the imprisonment of Covenanters in 1685. As a result of Monmouth's and Argyll's rebellion, 122 prisoners were crowded into the castle cellar known today as Whig's Vault. At the end of two months many were dead and others who had tried to escape had been tortured. It continued to be used as a prison or as a

garrison under William and Mary until the Jacobite rising in 1715. For his prominent commitment to this cause George, 10th Earl Marischal, forfeited the castle and all his other possessions. Later in the century it was acquired by the York Buildings Company, notorious for their removal of floors and ceilings from deserted buildings.

The rock on which the castle sits occupies an area of nearly four acres, thus offering a spacious setting for the various domestic buildings which in other castles pack tightly where they can behind the curtain wall. The oldest part of the castle to survive is the 14th-century keep, a weather-beaten L-shaped

Perched at the extreme end of the great rock of Dunnottar, the keep was built in the early 14th century but additions were made until the 17th century

tower with rubble-built walls, perched on the south-west corner of the rock. The gatehouse is 16th-century and is a most thoroughly fortified building, perhaps the strongest of its kind in Scotland. These two together dominate the entrance to the castle which then spreads out eastwards to other buildings of the 16th and 17th centuries. Since the 14th century the powerful Marischals of Scotland have lived here. It became their chief seat, and it is they who erected the various other buildings. The great quadrangle was a splendid range of two storey buildings with good views up the coast, and it was probably the work of the 5th Earl Marischal, a distinguished scholar and founder of the Marischal College in Aberdeen. The chapel is almost entirely of the 16th century, but it may well have been built on the site of the 13th-century parish church consecrated by the Bishop of St Andrew's, which in its turn perhaps used the site of St Ninian's earliest holy place, for ground once hallowed tends to remain so.

Dunvegan ISLE OF SKYE

Dunvegan is not the oldest of the many castles still standing in Scotland, but it has been occupied continuously by the same family for longer than any other. Boswell was well aware of this when, in 1773, he accompanied Dr Johnson to this ancient stronghold of the Macleods on its rocky site, and got into warm dispute with his hostess. 'The lady insisted that the rock was very inconvenient; that there was no place near it where a good garden could be made; that it must always be a rude place; that it was a Herculean labour to make a dinner here.' Boswell was vexed to find 'the alloy of modern refinement in a lady who had so much old family spirit'.

The old family spirit he had hoped to encounter was perhaps that of the early pioneer Macleods, descendants of King Harald Haardraade, who came to Dunvegan in the 13th century and set up their castle on the rock overlooking the small seaweed-covered harbour. It was Leod, the progenitor from whom the clan takes its name, who first enclosed its summit with a stone fortification. Then, towards the end of the 14th century, Malcolm, the 3rd Chief, built a stone keep at the north-east end of the rock. To this nucleus was added at the beginning of the 16th century the Fairy Tower, and it was here that when visiting the castle in 1773 Dr Johnson was accommodated, and some 40 years later Sir Walter Scott. Externally it preserves its original appearance, and is perhaps the single most picturesque feature of the castle.

Fairies have occurred as a recurrent theme in the associations and legends of Dunvegan. Not far away lies the Fairy Bridge, and of all the castle's treasures the Fairy Flag is the most famous, though its origins may be even more interesting than its long popular derivation from the local sprites. This ancient fragmentary piece of cloth has recently been suggested as the famous banner Landoda, that Leod's ancestor, Harald Haardraade, brought from Palestine.

The castle was never much damaged by warfare; it was besieged in the early 15th century by the traditional enemies of the Macleods, the Macdonalds of Sleat, and again in 1557 when it was captured by Iain Dubh, a jealous uncle who aspired to become the legitimate chief. Its present rather modern appearance results from the many additions made by successive generations of Macleods. Had Johnson and Boswell arrived some 25 years earlier they would have had to approach the castle through the Sea Gate, at that time its only entrance, up a rough flight of steps through two heavy doors and a portcullis, but the most significant change to the castle occurred in the 19th century when it was entirely modernized. During the years 1938–40 it was substantially rebuilt in its present form after a major fire which completely destroyed the floors and roof of the south wing.

Today the garden, of which Boswell's Lady Macleod lamented the lack, thrives and flourishes around the castle. In the late 18th century, a few years after the visit of the 'great Cham of literature' and his young friend, General Macleod began to plant a variety of trees which have provided shelter for a profusion of vegetation, replacing the stark moorland of earlier centuries.

Occupied continuously by the Macleods since the beginning of the 13th century the castle has undergone many structural changes, the early features now being largely absorbed within the 19th-century additions

Edinburgh MIDLOTHIAN

Overlooking the wide bustling square of the Grassmarket, where even until the last century public hangings were conducted, is the sharply-angled south-east corner of Edinburgh Castle, from which, according to local tradition, the infant King James I was lowered in a basket to be smuggled away to baptism in the Old Faith. Above Mary Stuart's room is the Crown Chamber, containing the Honours of Scotland, the ancient insignia of Scottish royalty. Such are the traditions and associations which make this great grey fortress perched on its volcanic rock the natural focus for Scottish patriotic feeling, and account for the constant battering, bruising and patching of its structure over the centuries. The first reliable information about the castle dates from the 11th century, but such a culminating feature of the landscape as the rock must always have drawn eagerly to its summit those in search of a stronghold; moreover it had fresh-water springs and sufficient pasture for cattle.

Of the earliest stone buildings nothing remains except St Margaret's Chapel, built in 1076 on the highest part of the rock by Margaret, the Saxon wife of King Malcolm Canmore. It was once a fine Norman chapel, but has been much altered by well-meaning embellishments. This is the first trace of the castle being used as a royal residence, but from then on it was frequently lived in by the Scottish kings, especially as a place of refuge against the English. And even the inhabitants of Edinburgh have sought sanctuary there. Once when Richard II threatened a devastating attack on the town itself, which huddled unprotected on the ridge to the east of the castle, a charter was drawn up granting to the burghers of Edinburgh the right to withdraw into the castle and build houses there for themselves.

This increasingly important role of the castle, so well sited and strategically placed near the mouth of the Forth, contributed to the emergence of Edinburgh as capital of Scotland. It had long been used as an obvious place for Councils and Assemblies, but it was James II who began holding his Parliament in Edinburgh. For the same reasons there were few interludes in Scottish history when the castle was not the centre of preparations for war against the English. After a relatively calm period of stability under King Malcolm III and his Queen Margaret and their successors in the 12th century, the castle was handed over to the English in 1174 after the defeat of William the Lion. This was the first recorded occupation by the English and lasted only a short while. Later in 1291 Edward I's visit to Edinburgh to receive the homage of the Scots turned out to be only a prelude to a much longer and more humiliating surrender of sovereignty when he returned in 1296 with a devastating new war-engine to lob great stones into the castle, in the face of which punishing treatment the Scots surrendered after eight days. The English installed an elaborate company of 347 soldiers and household attendants (hopefully as permanent occupants), but 16 years later a party of 30 men under the Earl of Moray seized the castle after a heroic climb up the west face of the rock. King Robert the Bruce then ordered the destruction of the entire fortifications except for St Margaret's Chapel, to prevent the castle from being of further use to the English. Unfortunately his scheme backfired, for a few years later, during the minority of David II, the English once more moved a garrison into the defenceless castle and repaired the damage. Again they seemed set for a long stay and started restoring the orchards and gardens, building magnificent stables and even a tilting ground for the entertainment of the knights. But again they had discounted the tenacity of the Scottish character: the inevitable retaliation, perhaps the most celebrated in the castle's history, came in 1341. Froissart in his *Chronicle* gives a lively account of Scottish soldiers disguised as merchants unloading their wares in the gateway of the castle and blocking its closure, while their friends leapt from an ambush to rush the surprised garrison.

The castle was never once in fact taken by open assault. There were various ruses, and betrayals, otherwise it was bombarded into submission. When Cromwell arrived in 1650 he attacked it with heavy guns for three months, and had he carried out his further intention of detonating a large mine under the walls, there would have been little of the castle left to surrender. Its last great siege, again a protracted one, was in 1689 when the castle held out for James VII (II of England) against the forces of William of Orange.

The damage sustained in these many exchanges was massive, and the repairs inevitably expensive. So many tons of stone and metal hurled at the castle by successive generations have ensured that most of the early building has entirely vanished, and that the castle's interest is now more historical than architectural. Charles I visited it the night before his Scottish coronation in 1633, likewise Charles II very briefly, but thereafter no monarch until George IV set foot inside its walls.

Following the rugged contour of its great rock, Edinburgh Castle still stands on its 7th-century site. Right, *the Half Moon bastion and the façade of the Great Hall from just above the Grassmarket*

Edzell ANGUS

Early 16th-century tower house to which was added in 1680 a quadrangular mansion and a remarkable garden or pleasance which is seen, right above, *from the east.* Above, *the figure of Arithmetica;* right below, *the figures of Fortitude and Prudence, two of four Moral Virtues on the west wall*

In the early 16th century an enterprising family, the Crawford Lindsays, abandoned their early Norman hill-top castle, and set up a fine deep-red freestone tower in a sheltered spot at the bottom of a nearby hill. The following years were encouragingly uneventful, and in about 1580 Sir David Lindsay, Lord Edzell, added a large quadrangular courtyard mansion and then later on in 1604 a most spectacular pleasance, a summer-house and bath-house.

Unlike many nobles of the time, whose lives read as though they sank early into a deep slumber, Lord Edzell was obviously a gifted, interesting and most extravagant man. He travelled extensively on the Continent as a young man and came back with an enthusiastic taste for the new cultural experiments,

an affinity generally for all things German, and a particular fondness for two eminent mining engineers from Nuremberg, whom he invited to prospect for copper, lead and alabaster.

The pleasance was built in 1604 as a walled garden for pleasant recreation or dalliance—an agreeable venue for all the elegant things that the baron and his family might want to do with the new leisure that followed in the wake of peace in Scotland. The walls, built of the same glowing red sandstone as the castle, have been indented with compartments, niches and recesses to receive all the various sculptures, carved panels, birds' nests and flowers in heraldic shapes essential to the composition of this formally pleasing and above all symbolic Renaissance garden. The theme of the garden is of course an uplifting one. The seven virtues are all there on the west side, but not the equivalent sins. On the south wall there are the Liberal Arts, each with its name carved in relief, and on the east side the Planetary Deities, the currently fashioned representatives of Heavenly Guidance. As the Planetary Deities are copied from the engravings of a Nuremberg master signed I.B., initials which the stonemason of Edzell decided to include in his own sculptural rendering as a serious part of the design, it is probable that the inspiration for all the sculptures derives from Lord Edzell's travels in Germany. Fortitude is seen as a maiden in swirling robes whose physical strength is such that she has broken the top off a pillar of stone. Arithmetica is apparently baffled by a long division on her stone tablet.

Sadly for us today the mansion is in a ruinous state. Lord Edzell died in 1610. Some of the building was never completed and the rest of the dilapidation was a result of the combined ravages of Hanoverian troops and pressing creditors. The latter stripped the floor and roofing materials in 1746—the trees, a magnificent avenue of beeches, were also cut down. Today the castle is in the safe custody of the Department of the Environment, and the pleasance has been restored to its former elegant precision. But to match Lord Edzell's decorative taste in his garden we can only imagine a mansion resplendent with painted ceilings, moulded plasterwork and carved oak panelling, equal to the best examples that are still preserved today. 'Dum spiro, spero,' was his family motto—one of an optimist living in the hopeful interlude between bouts of debilitating war with England. But it was a bankrupt legacy he left. His mismanagement was such that with his death this delightful extravaganza, quite unlike anything in any other castle in Scotland, fell into ruin just as if its history had been one of storm and stress, and it would have particularly saddened Lord Edzell had he known that it would be demolished by—of all people—Hanoverian troops.

Just offshore, on a small rocky island at the end of Loch Duich, this 13th-century castle is one of the most spectacularly sited in Britain. It was rebuilt in the 1920s after virtual destruction by the English in 1719

Eilean Donan

ROSS AND CROMARTY

Visitors to the Isle of Skye in the 19th century who chose to approach it along the northern bank of Loch Duich would have been astonished and delighted to see ahead, at the junction of this loch with two others, the most exquisite of ruins, starting like a rough-cast gem from the blues and purples of the mirrored mountains. Whatever architectural features the island stronghold might once have had, all had by then merged into a picturesque grouping of high and low walls. And so it might have remained, but in 1912 Colonel John Macrae decided to rebuild the home of his ancestors. Over the next 20 years nearly a quarter of a million pounds was spent on the restoration of the ruins to the original plan of the early castle.

Long before the Macrae family became hereditary constables of the island on behalf of the earls of Seaforth, an early Pictish fort is thought to have occupied the site, and visitors today are shown a pile of vitrified rock as evidence of its earliest owners. More recently the island was fortified in 1220 by Alexander II as a precaution against Norse and Danish raiders. Fresh water was made available within the enclosure of the keep by sinking a shaft to a great depth through the rock, an essential safeguard in time of siege. The castle's history is more full of colourful local detail than great events—as when the Macraes succeed in displaying the heads of their foes on salient parts of the battlements, or else withstand an onslaught when outnumbered 400 to 1—but it was the family's loyalty to the Jacobite cause that spelt the castle's final doom in the early 18th century. In 1719 it was garrisoned in favour of the Old Pretender by Spanish troops, who were bombarded into submission by H.M.S. Worcester, an English man-of-war.

The modern castle is approached from the lochside across a stone-arched causeway. Inside, the courtyard is determinedly medieval with massive rough-surfaced stonework lodged in the hollows of the protruding rock. The rooms contain the usual collection of Highland relics, pistols and powder horns, with the addition of a set of teacups used by Dr Johnson and Boswell on their voyage to the Hebrides. Unfortunately these two 18th-century tourists chose the western approach to the Isle of Skye, and would not have seen the enchanting ruins of Eilean Donan, but the hospitality of the Macraes does not pass unrecorded, for Boswell gives a lively and somewhat amazed account of their reception in the glens: 'they brought us out two wooden dishes of milk, which we tasted. One of them was frothed like a syllabub . . . It was much the same as being with a tribe of Indians.'

Glamis ANGUS

Until Lady Elizabeth Bowes-Lyon became Duchess of York in 1923 and Queen Consort in 1936, it was for the castle's associations with Macbeth that her home at Glamis was best known. Duncan's grandfather, Malcolm II, is said to have been murdered in the castle, in a room still known today as King Malcolm's room. This is of course unhistorical, but the event may have happened in a building near the present one, though other sources say he died a peaceful death. It is known, however, that between the 11th and 14th centuries the building that existed here was used by the early Scottish kings as a hunting lodge. In the castle itself the most ancient stonework has been dated to the late 14th century: the Crypt, the Old Kitchen and Duncan's Hall are thought to have been built by the ancestor to whom the lands of Glamis were granted in 1372 by Robert II, when Sir John Lyon married the king's daughter, Joanna. Their grandson was created 1st Lord Glamis. Since then the family—now the earls of Strathmore and Kinghorne—have maintained possession of the estate, though at times in the face of extraordinary setbacks.

When Shakespeare wrote *Macbeth* at the beginning of the 17th century it must still have seemed recent history that 60 years earlier the Castle of Glamis had been associated with an appalling atrocity and miscarriage of justice. In 1540 Lady Janet Douglas, the widow of the Earl of Glamis, was seized by James V, imprisoned as a witch and finally burnt at the stake. Such was the power of the monarch that having thus expressed his long-standing hatred of the Douglases, he took over the castle with all the vast riches of this wealthy family, and lived there for four years. After his death Lady Glamis was proved innocent of witchcraft, and the impoverished and despoiled estate was restored to the Lyon family.

Reconciliation was of necessity quite swift in those days, (when dealing with royalty, anyway) and in 1562 King James V's daughter, Mary Queen of Scots, and a large retinue journeying northwards to

Originally a hunting lodge of the early Scottish kings,
the present building dates mostly from the beginning
of the 17th century with some later additions

The drawing-room with a fine plasterwork ceiling of 1621. Right, *the main entrance in the west front*

Huntly arrived at the castle and were apparently well received. Later James VI was to be a frequent visitor, and in the early 17th century a period of favour with the monarch ensured prosperity for the family and enabled the 9th Lord Glamis, afterwards 1st Earl of Kinghorne, to begin in about 1600 an entire remodelling of the castle. The central stone keep was preserved but enlarged, and into the angle formed by one of the wings he built a great spiral stair-case to replace the old castle's narrow winding steps leading to the crypt. Even so, Sir Walter Scott with his desperate thirst for the Romantic was able to find the earl's spacious and almost classical interior 'wild and straggling', though he may have been re-ferring only to the more pokey back rooms to which he was himself relegated. On the second floor the earl built a magnificent drawing-room. His son continued with the improvements and decorated the ceiling with splendid plaster work. The travelling Italian crafts-men he employed were also responsible for the superb decoration at Craigievar and Muchalls. Fortunately this part of the work had been completed before the 2nd earl's financially disastrous involvement with Montrose, on whose cause he lavished almost his entire fortune. Instead of inheriting one of the richest estates in Scotland, his son Patrick, later created Earl of Strathmore and Kinghorne, found himself burdened with a debt of £400,000. However, he managed his estates well and recovered his finances sufficiently to complete the reconstruction started by his grand-father. The central tower was raised, the west wing and chapel built, and the park formalized with trees, shrubs and a magnificent sundial. Earl Patrick's bust was set into the wall above the main entrance. This was the Glamis that Scott as a young man must have seen, and Defoe too, on his 'Tedious and very Ex-pensive five Years Travel, touring through Britain'. Defoe describes it as 'so full of Turrets and lofty Buildings, Spires and Towers, some plain, others shining with gilded Tops, that it looks not like a Town but a City; and the noble Appearance seen through the long Vistas of the Park are so differing, that it does not appear like the same Place any two Ways together.'

In the following century the castle's outer defen-sive wall was pulled down, leaving a vista of two appropriately ruined towers in an 18th-century landscape. In 1891, an east wing extension was added and further alterations made. But in spite of the castellated finish which it was given when the rage for medievalism was at its peak, Glamis still retains for the visitor today the character of its much older and more interesting origins.

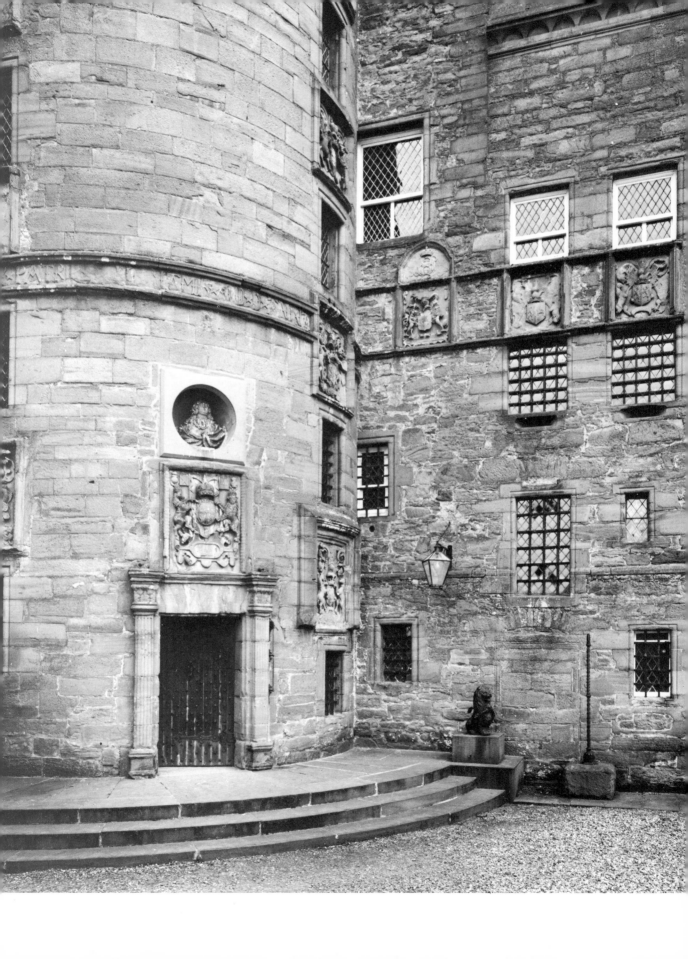

Hermitage ROXBURGHSHIRE

The brown sandstone walls of this powerful rectangular tower-house are broken by few openings, small and reluctant concessions to an unmilitary need, which do little to lessen the bleak visual impact of the heavy masonry. At the very top a row of doors once gave access from inside to a wooden gallery projecting out over the enemy. Brooding and oppressive within its earthworks and frequently hung with hill mist, this was the favourite castle of Sir Walter Scott, and the chosen background for his portrait painted by Raeburn which he gave to his friend Constable. For Scott, even more than its mournful aspect, it was the appeal of its troubled history and gruesome legends that set the emotional embers aglow. 'Its ruins', he commented 'are still regarded by the peasants with peculiar aversion and terror,' and it must have delighted him to discover a local tradition that the castle was supposed to have partly sunk beneath the ground 'unable to support the load of iniquity which had been long accumulating within its walls.'

The constant disputes and contentions between Scotland and England, which sometimes led to war and sometimes just to the brink of it, ensured that the Border Country was a place of unceasing turmoil and often the bridgehead for an English invasion. Hermitage as a result changed hands many times between the English and the Scots, but the ballads and legends associated with the castle are more to do with individual feuds and personalized villainy. The wicked Lord Soulis, one of the earliest owners, and one of the important hereditary King's Butlers of Scotland was believed to indulge in all manner of ignoble skulduggery including the drowning of a fellow knight by holding his head under the Hermitage Water, the river just below and to the south of the castle. However, after a life of triumphant misdeeds and communing with evil spirits he too met a terrible end by boiling in a brazen cauldron. A later owner in 1342, the famous Knight of Liddesdale, Sir William Douglas, disposed of his enemy, Sir Alexander Ramsay, in a comparatively ungallant way by leaving him to starve at the bottom of a frightful pit, no doubt similar to the festering dungeon of later date still visible in the north-east tower. Dire and inevitable retribution befell the great knight when he joined the English, and thereby forfeited his castle and also his life at the hands of the new owner, who

murdered him in Ettrick Forest. Perhaps most famous and romantic of all the castle's associations is that with Mary Queen of Scots, who in 1566 rode in a single day 50 miles from Jedburgh and back to visit her wounded lover, the 4th Earl of Bothwell.

Thus the castle passed from hand to hand. By the end of the 16th century it had reverted to the Crown, confiscated from the wild 5th Earl of Bothwell, and under subsequent ownerships its important military life came to an end. In 1820 the Duke of Buccleugh effected an extensive restoration of the by now totally ruined castle. Of the two great flying arches to east and west which connect the projecting towers just below the gallery, and which are perhaps the castle's most dramatic architectural feature, the one to the east is a reconstruction of this period. Otherwise the external appearance of Hermitage is today not unlike its 15th-century form, as left by the Douglas family who remained in possession until 1492. (Gunloops would have been introduced into the walls during the next century.)

The Douglases at the end of the 14th century had radically altered the existing building—which was more of a fortified manor house, dating from about 1360 and consisting of a rectangular courtyard enclosed by living quarters, English in concept and altogether unlike architecture found in Scotland at the time. What they made of it was a large tower incorporating the earlier work and resembling the other Scottish keeps of the day. Later small square towers were added to the corners and finally an oblong wing to the south-west.

Inside these powerful and well-preserved walls, however, it becomes harder to imagine the castle as it once was. Much is destroyed, but the early central courtyard is still enclosed by its original stonework, large squares of red freestone ashlar in pleasing contrast to the more sombre later walls.

Some 200 yards upstream from the castle there are the ruins of a small medieval hermitage, which though much more ruined than its distinguished neighbour, has nevertheless lived on by lending its name to one of Britain's most striking and romantic castles.

Perhaps the most dramatic of all the border castles, it was restored in 1820 to approximately its 15th-century form

Huntly ABERDEENSHIRE

King Robert the Bruce, falling sick in 1307 at Inverurie, was brought to convalesce in safety from his enemies at the Peel of Strathbogie. This was a 12th-century palisaded enclosure and would have consisted of timber buildings on the top of a mound surrounded by a large ditch—a typical fortified dwelling of the day, but one particularly well-sited on a small plain at the confluence of the River Deveron and its tributary the Bogie and surrounded on all sides by hills, thus forming an easily defensible point from which to control the route north to Inverness. The family at that time living in the castle was in origin Celtic, but by choice Norman—which it was possible to become simply by joining them and by conforming to the ways of the Norman barons. Duncan, the first of the family to naturalize as it were, adopted the territorial title 'de Strathbolgyn,' and his descendant David was no doubt delighted with the turn of fate which brought the sick king to his home. A later disaffection for the royal cause, however, turned out to be an unlucky misjudgment, for after Edward I's death in the same year Bruce's star was bright and rising and, with his final triumph in 1314 at Bannockburn, became firmly set in the heavens. The lands of Strathbogie were confiscated and given to Sir Adam Gordon of Huntly in Berwickshire. He and his descendants gradually moved up from the south and interested themselves in their new northern lands. By the early 15th century the former wooden structure had given way to stone and lime, though it probably continued to exist alongside the new tower-house until it was destroyed by fire half a century later during the battles between Stewarts and Douglases. The traditional name of Strathbogie survived on into the 16th century when in 1506 the Gordons received a charter confirming that the castle in future be known as Huntly, a recommendation that must have gone unheeded for it had to be repeated in 1544.

The Gordons, by now the earls of Huntly, continued to flourish and prosper, and the loss by fire of an old wooden peel could only in the long run be advantageous, for they set about building what must have seemed a splendid new castle, more of a palace than a primitive tower, and suitable for entertaining their numerous distinguished guests. In 1496 James IV was one of the many attending the wedding of the beautiful Lady Catherine Gordon, the 'White Rose of Scotland', and Perkin Warbeck, the English Pretender. Fashions, however, could change in the 16th century as quickly as in modern times; some 50 years later, when it must have seemed that the masons had hardly moved out, the young 4th Earl of Huntly decided to rebuild completely. Of his grandfather's palace only the vaults and dungeon were thought worth keeping as foundations for the new work, which was to rise up in its magnificence to receive those much sought-after distinguished visitors. But once again the arrival of a royal guest was the prelude to a disastrous and crippling episode in the family and castle's history. In 1556 Mary of Guise, the Queen Regent, arrived at this splendid new palace and was entertained most sumptuously by Lord Huntly. A mere six years later her daughter Mary Stuart fought and defeated him, executed one of his two sons and massively plundered the contents of the castle.

Meanwhile the Counter Reformation was gaining momentum, and Huntly became virtually the headquarters of this movement in Scotland. Yet James VI's attack on the castle in 1594 was more political than religious, aiming to quell a minor personal rebellion by the 5th earl. This time damage to the structure of the castle was considerable, but the earl made his peace and two years later was created a marquess. The main fabric of the 16th century had remained intact; the upper portions, however, were now completely rebuilt by the 1st marquess. Probably influenced by the architecture of the castle of Blois on the Loire, he installed beautiful oriel windows. Jutting out from the wall above richly moulded corbels, they are surrounded by an inscription in giant letters which, before the end section fell away, proclaimed the year of completion 1602—though the date of 1606 carved on one of the fireplaces may have been more precise. The magnificent entrance at the east corner is carved high with elaborate heraldic devices—an exuberant proclamation by the 1st marquess of his lineage and allegiance, the coat of arms of himself and his wife being surmounted by that of the king and queen.

After this final elegant flowering of the castle its history declines rapidly with the onset of the Civil War. The 2nd marquess was executed by Covenanters as a loyal supporter of the king. They also occupied the castle, but contented themselves with defacing any Popish emblems. The Huntly family lived there as and when they could until after the Civil War: they eventually moved to a house nearby. The castle once abandoned soon began to collapse into hopeless ruin, and now, today some 300 years since it was last lived in, all traces of roofing, floors and the painted decoration for which it was famous have inevitably vanished.

The main fabric of the castle dates from the mid-16th century with upper portions of the early 17th. The heraldic frontispiece on the entrance, is dated 1606

Inveraray ARGYLLSHIRE

The fortunes of the famous clan of Campbell were effectively established in 1296, when Sir Neil Campbell gave his support to Robert the Bruce, and their status was further enhanced when he later married Bruce's sister, Mary. Since then they have featured prominently in Scottish history, and consistently prospered. Inveraray, their headquarters, was created a royal burgh in 1648, but nothing remains today either of the original town or of the earlier castle of the Campbells, already the earls and soon to become the dukes of Argyll. In 1743 the 3rd duke engaged Roger Morris to build him a magnificent new castle, and, with that voracious rationalism characteristic of the 18th century, swept away the old town, and commissioned a modern one, orderly, spacious and at an elegant remove from his own residence. This was to be one of the earliest examples of a Gothic Revival building, evoking, with its lance-headed windows and arches, the architecture of the Gothic cathedrals, which was to be the dominant inspiration of the 19th century.

Both Roger Morris, however, and the 3rd duke died before the castle was complete. This task was to fall to John Adam and Robert Mylne, with the 5th duke as their patron. It was John Adam who built the fine Aray bridge, carrying the road between the shore of Loch Fyne and the castle.

In 1773, only some three years after the castle's completion, Dr Johnson—another intolerant progressive—journeyed through the Hebrides in his wet clothes and stayed in Inveraray's excellent new inn. He visited the castle and was obviously struck by this new architectural venture. Before meeting the duke, Johnson had maintained to Boswell that he must be 'a narrow man . . . narrow in his ordinary expenses, in his quotidian expenses'; but on becoming acquainted with the amiable aristocrat, whose princely seat impressed them so enormously with its grandeur and elegance, Johnson converted instantly and pronounced to Boswell: 'what I admire here, is the total defiance of expense'. And so indeed it was. The solid four-square façade of greyish chlorite slate resembles more the stately castles on the Loire than a functional Scottish stronghold. Its exterior is only moderately impressive, and gives no hint of the magnificently lavish décor, the painted rooms, richly ornamented ceilings, and other wealth of 18th-century architectural splendour that can be found within.

An early Gothic Revival castle built in the mid-18th century by Roger Morris. Seen here from the south with the fine Aray bridge by John Adam

Kisimul BARRA, HEBRIDES

This tiny three-storeyed castle of the Outer Hebrides was reconstructed and made habitable in 1938 by the Macneil clan chief. It is seen here from the rocks of the main island of Barra

At Eoligarry aircraft can land at low tide on the white shell sand of Traigh Mhor, or Great Cockle beach, doing their best to avoid the cattle which roam there; otherwise Barra is reached by ferry taking a full day or night from the mainland. This small island of the Outer Hebrides, where the inhabitants speak pure Gaelic, and, almost equally rare in Scotland, have remained through all the upheavals of history staunch Roman Catholics, is the remotest inhabited part of Western Scotland. Converted to Christianity from Iona after Columba's voyage there in 563, it was part of an area that suffered increasingly from Norse raids, until about 888 when the islands were annexed to the Kingdom of Norway. This Norwegian supremacy was challenged finally in the 13th century by Alexander II and his son, and although the first mention of the castle of Kisimul is in the early 15th century, and there is no account at all of its construction, it was probably during the course of these campaigns that the tiny sea-girt rock just off the shore was first fortified. It is possible that the castle had evolved independently of these wars and is indeed, as its Macneil owners maintain, an 11th-century building and thus the earliest existing stone castle in Scotland.

Seen from the rocks on the land, a viewpoint from which many generations must have contemplated with satisfaction its rough-harled walls, it stands solid and sheer against the enemy from the sea. The three-storeyed keep, with its one high window-recess looking out beyond the safety of the sheltered bay, projects like an ancient jewel from the setting of its strong curtain wall. The approach to the castle was a formidable one, reached between the twin perils of the keep and a reef of rocks, and protected by a wooden hoarding projecting out from the parapet of the curtain from which the defenders could assail the foe.

It is claimed by the Macneil clan that even before the castle emerged into the clear light of documented history it was their ancient home. It was continuously inhabited by their chiefs until after the Rising of '45, when—disappointed by the dwindling of Jacobite hopes—the then Macneil of Macneil joined the start of the great emigration to America. Several generations of his descendants remained there, and Kisimul castle stood for many years an uninhabited ruin. In 1938, however, the 45th clan chief, an American architect, bought the castle and with the co-operation of the Ministry of Works restored it into a habitable modern dwelling, complete with telephone and water piped from the main island, and it was here in 1960 that he rallied a great international gathering of the Macneils.

Quite unlike the ragged ruin seen in photographs of earlier in this century, the castle today has a spruce, purposeful appearance, and yet in spite of all these recent activities it has retained that haunting quality of remoteness and isolation which is the special attribute of these romantic islands.

Rothesay Castle BUTE

Protected at its northern end by the great encircling arms of the mainland—and surrounded in the larger context by the landmasses of Kintyre, the Isle of Arran and Ayrshire—the island of Bute is one of the most sheltered and populous in the Firth of Clyde, Rothesay, its largest town, has been a royal burgh since 1401, when Robert III made his son Duke of Rothesay. From then on the title was given to the heirs to the Scottish throne, and since the Act of Union in 1707 has also belonged to the heir to the English throne, second only among his titles to that of the Principality of Wales. The name Bute possibly derives from the Gaelic, meaning 'island of corn' in reference to its mild climate and fertile soil, so it is hardly surprising

that there were incursions here from an early date. The first recorded attack on the castle was in 1230 when it was besieged by Uspak and his Norsemen. The splendid 13th-century Saga of Hakon relates how the assailants protected themselves from the boiling pitch and molten lead, which the Scots inside the castle poured down on them, by constructing a wooden penthouse or shelter on wheels with a covering of wet hides to protect against fire. Under this they 'hewed into the wall, with axes because the stone was soft; and the wall fell down . . .' This was clearly a formidable undertaking. First, to cross the moat, a causeway would have to be made by hurling into it rubble and any other material available. Thereafter it was a matter of slowly effecting a breach of the wall with pick-axes and battering ram, which in the case of Rothesay took three days. The Norsemen were to attack again under King Hakon in 1263.

In neither of these sieges, however, was the castle demolished. It still stands most impressively on its deep-moated mound, a 30-foot high circular curtain wall with four round towers disposed evenly about the edge. This type of enclosed courtyard is to be found very rarely so far north in Britain, and only on the west coast; its particular circular shape, reminiscent of the Cornish castle of Restormel, is unique in Scotland.

Very few later modifications were made to the original plan. Its entrance was once a simple arched aperture in the wall, which in the 13th century was

A 13th-century castle still surrounded by its original wide moat, carefully restored by the Bute family in the 19th century

elaborated into a gate and portcullis. This was later turned by James IV, in 1512, into a great tower projecting into the moat, but the building of this was finished some 30 years afterwards by James V. Of unusual interest are the early 13th-century battlements which were used unaltered as a basis on which to add a higher section of wall and which thus remain still visible within it. Inside the courtyard the chapel, appropriately dedicated to St Michael the Archangel, patron saint of warriors, and dating probably from the 16th century, survives roofless but otherwise fairly complete. Two of the original four towers in the curtain wall are very ruined, but the north-west or Pigeon Tower is still remarkably preserved.

Thus in its early form the castle stood as a ready stronghold until the 17th century, when after being held for King Charles, then for Cromwell, it was much damaged by retreating Parliamentarians in 1659, and finally by Argyll's Highlanders in the rebellion of 1685. The state of ruin to which it deteriorated in the 18th century was set to rights at the beginning of the 19th by the Marquess of Bute, the hereditary keeper of this royal castle. His descendants continued with the repairing and restoration of the fabric until 1961, when it was placed in the care of the then Ministry of Works.

Stirling STIRLINGSHIRE

Traditionally the strongest and most strategic castle in Scotland, it nevertheless changed hands more than any other. Above, *the courtyard;* right, *a view showing its impregnable position*

When the power of the monarch depended not only on the army he could maintain but also on the forts and palaces he held, where he could live or take refuge and keep his munitions and prisoners, Stirling Castle, at the gateway to the Highlands and the main ford of the River Forth, was probably the most vital possession in Scotland. As at Edinburgh the strong grey ashlar walls of the castle, so eloquent of Scotland, dominate a narrow ridge of volcanic rock, which at one end rises sharply from the level meadows and at the other slopes eastward to the plain. Being further from England and nearer the Highlands it was considered by the Scots a stronghold of greater security.

No prehistoric fortifications have been traced, but this is hardly surprising since even at the time of Edward I's great siege in 1304 the castle was still mainly constructed of wood. Its period of greatest military importance was during the Wars of Independence when it represented the ultimate stronghold for both parties, for to hold it was the most telling factor in the fluctuating struggle. As a result it changed hands more frequently than any other Scottish castle, though not always after a siege. In his first invasion northwards Edward's reputation was already so

devastating that not an arm was raised: 'they that were in the castell ran away, and left non but the Porter, which did render the keyes.' Not typical of its later exchanges, however, for the great battles of Stirling Bridge and Bannockburn were soon to follow and decide its ownership.

The castle as it was even at the time of Bannockburn in 1314 has disappeared—the earliest parts now date from the 15th century. King Robert the Bruce promptly dismantled it after his triumph in that battle. It was subsequently repaired and refortified by the English who then once more relinquished it to the Scots. This constant to-and-fro was harsh on the early fabric, and only with the accession to the throne of the Stuarts did any significant building occur. It became a permanent royal residence, changing visibly from a fortress to a magnificent palace where tournaments were held and where one of Scotland's earliest ornamental gardens was created. The important buildings—the central turreted gatehouse with its flanking towers and curtain wall, the Great Hall, the Palace, the King's Old Buildings and the Chapel Royal—all date to a period of spectacular architectural achievement between the reigns of James III and James VI. James III was born there in 1451, and it became a dower-house for the various queens. £12,000 was spent on the castle and its celebrations for the baptism of James VI, and £100,000 in turn on that of his eldest son, Prince Frederick Henry. The boy was, however, the last Prince of Scotland to be brought up in the castle. With the Union of Crowns in 1603 and the sudden removal of the king and his court to England, the palace was virtually abandoned, and stood like an empty hive when the bees have swarmed, ready and perfectly appointed, but not quite suited to any other function. James VI paid it only two brief visits during the rest of his life. Subsequent monarchs stopped there for disappointingly short periods of one or two nights, but the palace was still maintained in readiness.

It was finally General Monck who arrived in 1651 to cause considerable damage with a bombardment that lasted three days. The garrison inside the castle mutinied and the King's Governor was obliged to surrender. Its last military involvement was during the Jacobite Rising when it was first held by King George's troops to prevent the Highlanders from crossing the Forth, and later in 1746 was besieged ineffectually by Prince Charles Edward.

Today the approach to the castle is guarded by a colossal statue of King Robert the Bruce, with a view of the two great battlefields associated with Scottish independence. Behind him appropriately are the Argyll and Sutherland Highlanders, who have their permanent regimental headquarters in the castle.

Tantallon EAST LOTHIAN

Two miles from the coast in the Firth of Forth there rises from the sea the huge and curious nugget of volcanic matter known as the Bass Rock. It is confronted on the mainland by a relatively recent arrival, the castle of Tantallon, whose red crumbling stones from the quarries of Canty Bay lasted a mere four centuries before falling into irreversible decay—a beautiful but fragile creature by comparison. Fragmentary though the remains of the castle are today, its original appearance and plan were obviously magnificent. A splendid natural promontory, its long seaward curve protected by high cliffs, afforded security on all sides but one, and that too could be easily defended by ditch and rampart outworks. There are in fact two of these great dry moats, extending across the promontory and sealing off the castle from cliff to cliff.

The approach road passes over a wooden bridge and enters the castle bailey or courtyard through its outer gate. Astride the promontory lies the great 12-foot thick curtain wall of dressed ashlar with its two powerful flanking towers and main entrance gateway leading through the close. This was where the lord of the castle could be accommodated in time of siege. The strengthening barbican has now almost completely disappeared. The tower is in a ruined state, as is the northern courtyard range which contained two great halls, a formal one for festive use above and a messroom for the garrison below. Although many additions and improvements were made in the 16th century, especially to strengthen the walls against advances made in heavy artillery, most of the buildings of the castle are originally of the 14th century; thus the keep-gatehouse is one of the earliest in Scotland.

Probably built by William, the 1st Earl of Douglas and slayer of the Knight of Liddesdale of Hermitage, the castle remained until 1699 one of the great Douglas strongholds, a centre from which this enormously powerful family advanced their influence on the Scottish political scene. The proximity to England was a source of constant distraction to those living near the border: the endless intrigue engaged in by the Scottish barons with the kings of England was both a matter of expediency should the English expand their territory northwards over the ever-fluctuating border, and also and more important a way of modifying the alarming powers of an often arbitrary and irascible monarch.

In their intrigues the Douglases were both more energetic and more successful than many of their contemporaries, though some were known popularly by modest and un-Machiavellian nicknames, such as 'the Good', the 'Long Leg' or 'the Dull'. Their coat of arms still bear today the emblem of a heart,

symbolizing the heart of Robert the Bruce which Sir James Douglas was to bear in a silver casket to the Holy Land in fulfilment of the Bruce's long-cherished wish to go there himself, but piety was not the family's most noted characteristic. The dreaded 'Black Douglas' was followed by his illegitimate son, Archibald 'the Grim', who in turn was father of James 'the Gross'; later came 'Bell-the-Cat', otherwise Archibald Douglas, 5th Earl of Angus, whose exploits were particularly provocative to James III: not only was he frequently engaged in intrigue with the English kings, a treasonable activity which broke out into open and successful rebellion in 1488, but in 1482 he seized and executed several of the king's favourites, among them Robert Cochrane. Further treasonable liaisons with England led James IV in 1491 to conduct a disciplinary siege of Bell-the-Cat in his castle at Tantallon, but as a measure of the king's inadequacy against this powerful baron, no punishment was

14th-century keep gatehouse on a promontory in the Firth of Forth, one of the earliest in Scotland. Later additions are 16th century

forthcoming, and the next year he created him Chancellor of Scotland.

Bell-the-Cat's grandson, also Archibald, prospered in a similarly ambiguous manner. He is celebrated as the man who never rode out except at the head of his private army of at least a thousand men, yet much of the time he had nowhere of his own to ride out of. His marriage to Margaret Tudor, widow of James IV of Scotland and sister of Henry VIII of England, gave him a foothold in both camps which did not always work to his advantage. His influence with his stepson, James V, looked slim when the young king burned at the stake his sister Janet and in 1529 seized Tantallon. Yet in exile at the English court, he was maintained in some style by his brother-in-law; and when James V died in 1542, Archibald recovered Tantallon only to find that in his absence it had been vastly strengthened and improved—by a king who clearly took the freehold for granted.

These long liaisons of the earls of Angus with the English, which were to continue into the reign of Elizabeth, resulted in the fact that Tantallon was, throughout its history until the arrival of Cromwell in Scotland, the target of attack by the Scots themselves. In 1651, however, after a 12-day bombardment with heavy cannon had resulted in a large breach, the castle surrendered to General Monk in the last siege it was ever to undergo. Thereafter the earls of Angus continued to live there, but with the dismantling of its fortifications the castle obviously lost its appeal as a residence, and in 1699 they sold it to Sir Hew Dalrymple whereafter it decayed into ruin.

Threave KIRKCUDBRIGHTSHIRE

Archibald Douglas, the 3rd earl, otherwise known to his contemporaries as 'the Grim', died in his castle of Threave on Christmas Eve 1400, like his father, known alternatively as the 'Black' or 'Good' Douglas, he was a figure dreaded by the English 'because of his terrible countenance in weirfair', and yet within his own extensive domains he seems to have been a benign and conciliatory patron, and a great benefactor of the Church.

'Dark and ugly . . . more like a cook-boy than a noble'—unprepossessing in appearance, illegitimate by birth, nothing seems to have held him back. He became Lord of Galloway and Warden of the Western March, and arranged brilliant marriages for his children: his daughter was given to King Robert III's son and heir, and his own illegitimate son to the daughter of Robert II.

The castle he built for himself was a tall, powerful tower, simple and sturdy. In this potentially unruly countryside it stood as an unmistakable statement of authority by a man whose other lasting contribution to the stability of the area was his codification of the Border Law. It is magnificently situated: the island of Threave on which it stands is a large, flat, grassy meadow of some 20 acres in the middle of the River Dee. Washed along its west side by the river and protected elsewhere by a ditch and mound, the castle could only be approached from the south where the waters were shallow enough to ford. Access was further restricted by a sweeping encroachment of the river, curving in to leave only the narrowest neck of land between the ford and the southern wall of the tower. The rest of this pleasant green island provided excellent pasture, to ensure a ready supply of food in time of trouble. Architecturally the castle was a straightforward building—the only surprising feature being a triple row of small holes running round beneath the roof line. Various explanations are offered for their presence, none of them conclusive. Possibly they were to support a hoarding or overhanging timber gallery for defence, but alternatively they could have been designed simply as nesting places for pigeons to supplement the diet of the garrison.

Under the gloved fist of Archibald Douglas the countryside remained relatively calm, and it was not until 1455 that the castle was to endure its first long and telling siege. His descendants had become increasingly powerful, and their defiance to the Crown was met by savage reprisals. In 1454 James Douglas, the 9th and last earl, openly accused King James II of his brother's murder and led 40,000 men against him. During this rebellion the king arrived in person on the banks of the Dee. With his famous great gun 'Mons Meg' (now in Edinburgh Castle) he bombarded this Douglas stronghold—the last to hold out against him—until finally it surrendered. With this episode the association of the family with the castle virtually ended.

During the first part of the 16th century it was declared a heritable possession in the Maxwell family, though by then the fabric was in such disrepair that it was only of doubtful value to its new owners as a stronghold. Lord Maxwell undertook to repair the castle, and it was probably under his supervision that the tower acquired a new outer defence—a surrounding wall built with drum towers at each corner and many gun-loops. The precise date of this new artillery fortification is hard to specify. Purely architectual evidence would place its construction during the Maxwell tenure in the first half of the 16th century, when the fashion for this kind of defence was well under way. But the Douglases were a bold and ingenious family, and could well have devised the outer wall as their own means of extra protection before the fatal siege. If so, an artillery defence of this sort in the year 1454 was unique in Scotland. Whatever its origins, the wall was of little avail to the Maxwells when they sided with Henry VIII and were consequently attacked by the Regent Arran in 1545, for the castle capitulated after a short siege of only two or three days. Some 40 years later the Maxwells, this time prominent in their support of the Catholic party, fared no better in their defence of Threave. James VI, hearing of their alleged conspiracy to open the nearby port of Kirkcudbright to the Spanish Armada, arrived in person to enforce the surrender of their castle. Thereafter it remained as a loyal stronghold of the Crown, and during the Civil War was garrisoned for King Charles by his devoted supporter, the Earl of Nithsdale. This was the castle's most heroic stand. At the end of 13 weeks the gallant and hard pressed soldiers received permission from the king to surrender their post, and Cromwell's troops allowed them to march out with all the honours of war. The castle itself was systematically dismantled, its fortifications and roofing all removed, and what was left of this once most convincing stronghold of the Douglases was then abandoned to further destruction by the wind and rain. The only later use to which it was ever put was during the Napoleonic Wars, when for a short while it served to accommodate French prisoners.

Inaccessibly situated on an island in the River Dee, Threave was the 14th-century tower house of Archibald 'the Grim', 3rd Earl of Douglas

◁ Newark Castle, Port Glasgow, Renfrewshire. 15th-century stronghold of the Maxwells.